The Hands-On Life

The Hands-On Life

How to Wake Yourself Up and Save the World

Amy E. Weldon

CASCADE *Books* · Eugene, Oregon

THE HANDS-ON LIFE
How to Wake Yourself Up and Save the World

Copyright © 2018 Amy E. Weldon. All rights reserved. Except for brief quotations in critical publications or reviews, no part of this book may be reproduced in any manner without prior written permission from the publisher. Write: Permissions, Wipf and Stock Publishers, 199 W. 8th Ave., Suite 3, Eugene, OR 97401.

Cascade Books
An Imprint of Wipf and Stock Publishers
199 W. 8th Ave., Suite 3
Eugene, OR 97401

www.wipfandstock.com

PAPERBACK ISBN: 978-1-5326-0666-3
HARDCOVER ISBN: 978-1-5326-0668-7
EBOOK ISBN: 978-1-5326-0667-0

Cataloguing-in-Publication data:

Names: Weldon, Amy.

Title: The hands-on life : how to wake yourself up and save the world / Amy Weldon.

Description: Eugene, OR: Cascade Books, 2018 Includes bibliographical references.

Identifiers: ISBN 978-1-5326-0666-3 (paperback) | ISBN 978-1-5326-0668-7 (hardcover) | ISBN 978-1-5326-0667-0 (ebook)

Subjects: LCSH: Information technology—Social aspects | Interpersonal Relations | Consciousness | Attention | Environmental Awareness / Ecology

Classification: HM851 .T90 2018 (print) | HM851 .T90 (ebook)

Manufactured in the USA   01/26/18

To Elizabeth and John

We must learn to reawaken and keep ourselves awake, not by mechanical aids, but by an infinite expectation of the dawn, which does not forsake us in our soundest sleep.

—HENRY DAVID THOREAU, *WALDEN*

Our own life is the instrument with which we experiment with the truth.

—THICH NHAT HANH

We are simply human beings, enfolded in weakness and in hope, called together to change our world one heart at a time.

—JEAN VANIER, *BECOMING HUMAN*

Contents

Acknowledgments

SOME OF THESE PASSAGES and ideas were developed in slightly different form elsewhere, including as postings on my personal blog, *The Cheapskate Intellectual* (http://cheapskateintellectual.wordpress.com). A version of my account of the 2008 flood appeared in a local arts magazine, *Inspire(d)*, in 2008. A version of the final pages of Chapter 6 appears as "Apple Eaters" in *Orion*, November/December 2016. A version of the opening pages of Chapter 5 was delivered in February 2006 as "One Teacher's Beginnings: Inside the *Nickel and Dimed* Controversy," a lecture in Luther College's Paideia Text and Issues Lecture Series, and reprinted in *Agora: Luther College in Conversation*. My visit to the Keats-Shelley House in Rome (Chapter 4) is also described in my essay "Keats-Shelley House, Rome, Italy" in *The Common* (https://www.thecommononline.org/keats-shelley-house-rome-italy/). A version of the passage in Chapter 4 about my pottery class and the learning process associated with it appears as "The Spinning Self: On Pottery and the Rest of My Life" in *Bloom* (https://bloom-site.com/2014/12/19/the-spinning-self-on-pottery-and-the-rest-of-my-life/).

The anecdotes about specific students in the Introduction and Chapter 5 appear with their permission, and with their names changed.

For support of my writing, friendship, fact- and translation-checking, and other intangibles, I offer my thanks to Jennifer Acker, Jutta Anderson, Patty Baum, Janine Brandt, Taylor Brorby, Carrie Burke, John Caldwell, Robert Christman, Victoria Christman, Sonya Chung, Marie Drews, Camille Dungy, Tim Dykstal, Alfredo Alonso Estenoz, Rachel Faldet, David Faldet, Erin Flater, Philip Freeman, Stephanie Fretham, Laura Fuller, Marybeth Gallant, Mike Garcia, Bryan Giemza, Kristi Giemza, Marianne Gingher, Elizabeth Golovatski, Kristy Gould, Chris Graffunder-Bartels, Linnea Graffunder-Bartels, Andrew Hageman, Patrick Hicks, Tom Horan, Steve Hornbacher, Kristine Jepsen, Martin Klammer, Kevin Kornegay, Erika Kraabel, Kristine Kraabel, Tom Kraabel, Kevin Kraus, Angela Kueny, Keith Lesmeister, Jon Lund, Patchen Markell, Steve McCargar, Douglas McLaughlin, Rebecca Morphis, T.C. Morphis, Jayme Nelson, Tessa Joseph Nicholas,

Aryn Henning Nichols, Jessica O'Hara, Jacob Otte, Todd Pedlar, Tara Powell, Kate Rattenborg, Britt Rhodes, Mark Rhodes, Liz Rog, Pete Russella, Steve Semken, Robert Shedinger, Lissa Skitolsky, Elizabeth Spencer, Amy Sweitzer, Heidi Swets, David Thompson, Kristin Torresdal, Jeff Wilkerson, and Joe Wilkins.

I deeply appreciated conversations with colleagues in the 2009 Lutheran Academy of Scholars Seminar at Harvard University, the Aspen Institute's 2012 Wye Faculty Seminar in 2012, and the 2009 Midwest Faculty Seminar on Arendt's *The Human Condition* at the University of Chicago. Anthony Doerr introduced me to Victor Shkolovsky in his lecture "On Defamiliarization" at the Tin House Summer Writers Workshop at Reed College in 2008; he also discusses Shkolovsky in his lovely book *Four Seasons in Rome* (New York: Simon & Schuster, 2007). Colleagues in the English Department and Paideia Program at Luther College have nudged my thinking along in numerous ways.

Very, very many thanks to my fellow writers at the Bread Loaf/Orion Environmental Writers' Conference, particularly my 2015 workshop group, led by Craig Childs and including Stephanie Camillo, William Cocke, Jenna Gersie, Sharon Harris, Rose Linke, Mila Plavsic, Jess Ryan, Christine Vatovec, and Isaac Yuen, whose feedback transformed this book. Thanks also to *Orion* Magazine editors, conference faculty, and friends: Rick Bass, Chip Blake, Belle Boggs, Noreen Cargill, Michael Collier, Allison Hawthorne Deming, Scott Gast, Ross Gay, Pam Houston, Jason Lamb, Scott Russell Sanders, Ginger Strand, Luis Urrea, and Matt Weiland.

Most of all, I appreciate my students, without whom this book wouldn't exist. Special shout-outs to the students of Paideia II 450 Capstone: "From the Cliché to the Critical: Religion, Writing, and Moral Inquiry" (Spring 2012), where I developed many of this book's ideas while teaching *1984* and *Eichmann in Jerusalem* together, the Paideia Section 21 (2014–2015) Alumni Book Club, particularly Elizabeth Budahn, Nathan Campbell (whose additional conversations with me about this book have been very valuable), Lucy Duan, Colin Landsteiner, Kjerstin Nelson, Taylor Romeo, Samuel Scheidt, Cory Wirth, and Spencer Young. Emma Cassabaum, Joel Denney, Lauren Nielsen, Allison Roe, and Marin Stellner read portions of this manuscript and provided great insights. I also thank the members of my community writing classes at ArtHaus in Decorah, Iowa.

Thanks for grants from the Luther College Doris and Ragnvald Ylvisaker Endowment for Faculty Growth and from the H. George and Jutta F. Anderson Faculty Development Fund and for additional support from the Office of the Dean.

And last but never least, thanks to my family.

Introduction

THE CLASSROOM'S DIM WHEN I walk in, because my students are already staring at something glowing on the overhead projection screen. Windows to the east frame the century-old cottonwood tree our college is famous for. Outside, raw March rattles its branches, but soon there'll be new leaves, fluttering with the music only Iowa cottonwoods can make: a liquid busyness like birdsong, urgent and lively and made to ride the air to any listening ear.

What are my students hearing here, right now? Pausing in the door, I look at them. They're shucking off jackets, un-mittening, and letting backpacks slump to the floor. Some are slipping earbuds out of their ears. Smartphones in bright plastic cases dot the desks. Sticker-plastered laptops hum. But all their eyes are rooted on that screen, their faces worshipful.

A familiar irritation flowers in my chest. For God's sake, this is a *creative writing* class. We've discussed how glowing screens like this one get between us and art. Each day we observe the living world in reality and memory, scribbling in notebooks by hand. My students and I develop real bonds with each other and with our art, even as they gently mock my flip-style Tracfone. "Dr. Weldon's got a burner!" they cackle. "Just like on 'The Wire.'" To be sure, they're ironic about screen addiction. They go mountain biking and string up hammocks in the trees on campus during finals week when the warm weather arrives, reading, rocking, and gazing at the sky. But maybe their cocoon of technology is thicker than even I can pierce. Glued to a screen on such a day, in such a world? I thought I'd taught them better what's at stake.

And then I turn to see what they're looking at.

Enormous on the screen, a pale eggshell quivers in a latticework of twigs. Cracks appear, a dimpling outward, then the egg-tooth ridge of a tiny beak. And then the head, slate-colored feathers plastered to its curve. Bright hooded eyes are already turning, taking in the light. The bony body wobbles forth from between two halves of shell—out of a space unknown until right now. A parent bird bends its head into the frame, wind parting its white feathers to the root. And the baby lifts its face to meet it.

Gasps and cheers erupt into the room. Overtaken by joy, my students and I grin at one other. A bald eagle chick is struggling forth aboard a wide, flat nest in a cottonwood tree three miles from this spot. And we are here to watch.

So is the world. Our Decorah Eagle Cam, live-streaming from that nest, is the most-viewed live stream of all time. It's all over Facebook, magazines, TV. A woman in Seattle's so obsessed with the Eagle Cam that she calls the school board to make sure everything's OK when she doesn't see the yellow bus rumbling past on the dirt road below the nest at its usual time. Even my parents, down in Alabama, get into it. "Have you biked out there and seen the nest this week?" they ask eagerly. More often than I want to admit, the answer is no.

Maybe this makes me just another hypocrite, nagging Kids Today about their zoned-out ways but telling myself I'm too busy, and too important, to be any different. Of course, I'm not. During my campus visit interview, an eagle flew right past the window, its white head stained gold in the morning light. "That happens all the time," my now-colleagues said. I marveled: how could *anyone* get used to *that?* Yet twelve years on, I'm in the habit too. Although my heart always lifts whenever I see an eagle, I'm caught in post-tenure breathlessness: six or seven courses every year, advisees on and off the books, and the bog of meetings and box-checking known as "service." Oh, yeah—and writing. Looking to the sky can be a luxury when we feel stuck in lives like the old joke about Midwestern extroverts: sometimes we're doing well just to be able to look at someone *else's* shoes.

Or maybe this state of life makes me normal. I've got a lot of thoughts about that. But they cluster around one conviction: we're in for some real trouble if we let ourselves get, and stay, this distracted. Technology's an obvious scapegoat, but not a simple one. Just consider the paradox of the Eagle Cam. Watching an eagle chick hatch in its nest is a greater lesson in wonder and particularity for my students than I could ever design. And it's made possible by a camera bolted to the cottonwood trunk above the nest, its gaze fixed downward to stream to the Internet, and thence to our devices, the daily lives of eagles: nesting, feeding, wobbling forth into the bright early-spring day. But technology's also one of several forces tuning us out of the living world that human and nonhuman beings can't afford. It's stealing from us a thing I can only call *plenitude of self*, an inner life that's echoed in and nurtured by the endangered plenitude of the natural world, a certain capacity to be alone but also to be meaningfully engaged with, even lost in wonder at—not just entertained by—all that isn't you.[1] Things with screens blind us to these losses even as they offer us illusions of pleasure, connection, and something called "efficiency," fostering an inattention that's fatal for ecosystems, societies, and selves. And young people, like the beloved students with whom I spend my days, will bear the weight of this inattention and come to grief if we can't act against it now.

I care about all this because I've watched screens crowd out of our days things that used to be normal—looking up and around at sidewalks and trees when you're walking, actually listening to the person in front of you, respecting the privacy of strangers—and replace them with habits that reroute the connection between *me* and *what's not me* down a corporation's greedy gullet: constant texting, constant browsing for something-else-than-what's-right-here, Twitter wars with people you'll never meet. At the same time, climate change has altered beloved places before my eyes, corporate money in politics has distorted our democracy, and even students who choose to come to college face new uncertainties about what *education* means and where it will lead. I don't think these things are unconnected from each other, or from our new screen-focused normal, which feels different in degree and kind from the distractions humans have historically sought. A life online streams your whole consciousness as bits and bytes and monetizable data, offering you up for sale while concealing that fact (and the profits) from you and presenting this state as *just the way things are*. And for digital natives, perhaps it is. But I learned to use email as a college sophomore (in 1994), so, for better and worse, I've got a built-in sense of the world before and after the Internet.

Sure, my screen brings me knowledge and fun: music on demand from Missy Elliott to Mozart's "Champagne Aria," former students' baby pictures, literary magazine editors Skyping in to my creative writing class, historical archives that peel the lid off the marvelous, strange past, and—yes—Netflix. Online, people can find community they need; for a young Egyptian in the Arab Spring or a queer person in deep-red America, Facebook can literally be a lifesaver. Twitter can alert us to political or social realities we can monitor, as citizens, in real time, enabling the engagement any functioning democracy needs. But our screen-focused mode of life is also stealing from us something we need to be real human beings, and, even more specifically, to be artists, thinkers, and doers—what my students and I want to be. Let's face it: adulthood is about doing the right thing as much as you can, often without rewards from anyone but yourself. So is life as an artist. Both rely

1. See Michael McCarthy's discussion of the natural world's endangered abundance in his wonderful book *The Moth Snowstorm: Nature and Joy* (New York: New York Review of Books, 2016).

on the capacity to be self-reliant, to live without that constant stream of glittering, artificial external reward that traps us in immaturity. And immaturity—based in the basic inability to be alone with ourselves—makes us prime targets for the feelings of discontentment and loss that enrich corporations, because those feelings make us want to buy something to feel less alone. Technology makes it easier to skip away from the present moment and to soothe our inevitable emotions with things, or entertainments that reduce people to things, or with simulacra of human interactions that become profitable for everyone but ourselves. But art, and making art, immerse us in encounters with the non-commercial and, ultimately, the non-controllable.[2] Art trains us for the long game rather than the quick payoff. It teaches care, rigor, heartbreak, uncertainty, and how to be surprised by joy. It teaches the value of sustained observation of and attention to the world beyond ourselves. It immerses us in our own humanity—including our kinship to other humans, past and present, and to nonhuman beings too—and in the emotions which, even when painful, lend depth, texture, and immediacy to our lives, the only lives on earth we'll ever have. And, crucially, art gives us an attitude of self-reliance with which we'll always be able to examine what we're doing, renovate our perspective, and rededicate ourselves to what really matters. It gives us back our lives. That's why, as I'll argue in this book, learning to pay attention and to practice life like an artist also means learning how to wake yourself up and save the world.

"To see what is in front of one's nose," George Orwell wrote in 1946, "needs a constant struggle."[3] This is the paradox by which we humans live, and which technology—claiming to help us see more and farther while really just training our eyes on itself—is always begging us not to investigate further, casting us into a weird bodilessness even as our Fitbits track numbers of steps and calories consumed. Paying attention is vital, but it takes work. Yet even as the preoccupied noise of *gotta do I forgot who just sent me a text what's going on on Facebook right now?* hums in our heads,

---

2. I think this is true of those practicing any craft, even something we might not define specifically as "art"—surgery, nursing, veterinary medicine, farming, engine repair, woodworking, masonry, fly–tying, and cooking (just to name a few)—call upon the same blend of intellectual and hands-on knowledge that art does. I'm indebted to philosopher and motorcycle mechanic Matthew Crawford's work, especially his first book *Shop Class as Soulcraft: An Inquiry into the Value of Work* (2009), for my thinking about this, and to its philosophical ancestors, Richard Sennett's *The Craftsman* (2008) and Hannah Arendt's *The Human Condition* (1958). (Sennett was Arendt's student.)

3. Orwell, "In Front of Your Nose," 1042.

Orwell's words bite deep. Tuning-out's destructive, but it's deeply human, and it's so hard to avoid.

Of course, paying attention to one thing at a time in the present moment has *always* been hard. Look at the centuries' worth of spiritual admonition against the distractible state that Buddhists call *monkey mind*. Look at the Roman philosopher Seneca, grousing in 49 AD that "You live as though you were going to live for ever, at no time taking thought for your weakness, and you fail to note how much time has already passed by; you waste hours as though you were drawing from a well that was full to overflowing, though all the while that very day you are giving to some person or thing is possibly your last. You fear everything as mortals but desire to have everything as gods."[4] Henry James's short story "In the Cage" describes a young telegraph operator whose job was "to mind the 'sounder,' which was always going, to dole out stamps and postal-orders, weigh letters, answer stupid questions, give difficult change and, more than anything else, count words as numberless as the sands of the sea, the words of the telegrams thrust, from morning to night, through the gap left in the high lattice, across the encumbered shelf that her forearm ached with rubbing." (As modern as this information overflow sounds, this story was published in 1908!)[5] Yet maybe we can't pay attention because there's so much to pay attention to—even, as Seneca writes, to fear. Disaster, flood, and drought sweep across our screens. Global weirding and political disingenuity accelerate, with each election bringing fresh reasons to weep for the planet and the republic. We bob in a stream of worries we feel implicated in yet powerless to stop: global poverty, refugees, near-constant war, terrorism, stranded polar bears, fat-silt in our blood. We go to school. We have jobs. We have responsibilities. Yet at the same time, something about our lives doesn't feel quite real. We post selfies, tweet our thoughts, and look to those electronic traces for proof of our own existence. But the thumbs-up "like" and dopamine hit of connection never quite lay our fears to rest: *If I don't take a picture of it, did it really happen? If nobody's watching me, am I real?*

Somehow, this state of blurry, jazzed-up anxiety has come to seem normal, so that we fear that quiet waiting on the other side. The Buddhist teacher Chögyam Trungpa has called this "putting makeup on space," or trying to dodge an emotion with some new distraction or habit.[6] Yet in that quiet, emotion does return. And when we feel its presence—which can seem threatening, in comparison to the habits of self-distraction that social

4. Seneca, "On the Shortness of Life," 142.

5. See Hankins, "Henry James on Twitter."

6. Chodron, *Living Beautifully,* 19.

media (in particular) can entrench—we break our self-imposed Facebook fasts. We reach for email, again. We tell ourselves we're too busy to settle down out of the torrent of daily "responsibilities" toward the softer, slower waters where reflection and real growth wait, especially if we're college students, told to *join in! Build your resume! Belong!* To soothe ourselves, we turn back to those very things with screens—the smartphone, laptop, or television—like Oblonsky in *Anna Karenin* "enjoy[ing] his newspaper, as he did his after-dinner cigar, for the slight haze it produced in his brain."[7] Some of that's necessary for work, connection, informed citizenship. But more of it's just a habit we tell ourselves we need.

Yet rocking along inside the norms our technology and media have created—and that corporations reinforce, for their own profit—blinds us to the fact that we're inside only one kind of paradigm, only one possible way of understanding the world. And that paradigm has costs. We get passive and listless, retreating to virtual worlds and online echo chambers and trivia. Reading difficult things gets harder, so we read fewer difficult things. We make ourselves "busier" than we actually are, with less time for the spouse, the resentful pet, or the pleading child who eventually just heads to her own room, to be alone with her own screen. We stay on the couch. We give the side-eye to the stranger. At the border of friction between us and what's not us, we falter, then turn back. *I'm just so tired,* we mutter. *I'll deal with this tomorrow.*

Unfortunately, this passivity is more dangerous right now than it's ever been. It keeps us consuming forms of food, energy, experience, and democracy produced by corporations for their own profit. It replaces the curious wisdom-seeker inside us with the anxious consumer.[8] It blinds us to the inequities that make safe places to bike or play the domain of those with money, and that make walkable communities an unrealistic dream for too many rural and urban people. And a passive world of commercial-tainment screens is really bad for kids. Sure, techno-fluency breeds dexterity with multitasking, which some call new intelligence. But from where I sit—in a college classroom, with students who've never not known the Internet—it looks more likely to feed the habits of mind that life on our resource-competitive planet can't afford: passivity; credulity; discomfort (even impatience) with difficulty and difference; self- and human-centered focus on present concerns and places; fear of the outdoors; helplessness to make things for ourselves; confusion about sources of experience and meaning; cynicism

---

7. Tolstoy, *Anna Karenin*, 19.

8. I'm indebted to Pema Chodron's discussion of this in Chapter 1 of *Living Beautifully*, "The Fundamental Ambiguity of Being Human."

disguised as sophistication; and the kind of entertainment addiction that kept Roman aristocrats lolling on their couches, vomiting up one course of whole roast pig and boiled-alive birds in order to stuff down the next one. People stuck in these habits of mind are prey for corporations and the politicians they've bought, and unable to see that state of dependence even as it depends on their exploitation. They're consumers, not citizens. And they're chained to ways of life that our planet can no longer support.

The real cost of all our screen-focused way of life is mass extinction: not only of the animal species dying out every minute, but of pre-Internet ecosystems of consciousness, varieties and plenitudes of self, kinds of human intelligence and languaging fed by contact with the external world and printed texts and the responsibility to cause-and-effect that real experiences in real life write onto our brains. I'm talking about a certain kind of interior depth and richness, a certain kind of soul I struggle to define and measure even as I believe passionately in its existence and even as I recognize in myself all the same bad screen-based habits I've just named. As a Romanticist, I think of William Wordsworth's sonnet: "The world is too much with us; late and soon, / Getting and spending, we lay waste our powers."[9] But maybe the world's actually not *enough*. Maybe we're ginning up such drama on our devices because our landscape of big-box stores and television and car-bound transit feels sensorily and spiritually impoverished. Indeed, despite constant Twitter and Instagram feeds, we seem to spend a lot of time both stressed and weirdly bored, our minds and bodies overstuffed yet nutrient-deprived, hungering for meaning and a voice in which to talk about it. "I'm from suburban Minneapolis," my students laugh. "Nothing's ever happened to me." Yet when we talk a little more, they point to moments of contact with something-not-themselves—a Boundary Waters canoe trip, the squeak of new snow underfoot on their familiar streets, helping to rescue a wounded loon—as shaping forces for their memories, inner sources of life that Wordsworth in *The Prelude* called "spots of time."[10] Observation, experience, and attention can be rich springs of meaning even if you don't think of yourself as a wilderness explorer, even if you don't live in a little town in Iowa, even if a farm is not your secret idea of normal, as it's mine. Wilderness can be anywhere because the living world is everywhere, and attention to it—nurtured, however counterculturally, within ourselves—can help us ask for something better in, and for, that world than what we've got.

9. Wordsworth, "The world is too much with us," 270.
10. Wordsworth, *The Prelude,* 428.

Let's go back to the classroom on another spring day, with me, my colleague Bob, and forty students, aged about twenty and a half. Outside, on the limestone bluff above the river, a brisk wind spins the college's new turbine, which will generate about a third of our electricity by this time next year. But today, our classroom's full of a different kind of energy. We're talking about the Internet.

The students are chatty and relaxed: they're digital natives, and this is ground they think they know. Fellow professor Bob and I see loss: electronic media can scatter attention, siphon away the deep focus possible with printed text, and make even our own scholarly minds as jittery and demanding as a six-year-old in an American Girl store. The students see opportunity: limitless reinvention of the selves they cling to and chafe against.

"Look," says a bright-eyed young man I'll call Darren. "Every single generation has its Big Scary Problems with the Young, right? First it was hippies, then it was drugs, then it was teen pregnancy. And somewhere in there was rap music. Now it's the Internet." All of us laugh. Darren, a spiritually aware computer science major, always has something interesting to say. He's taught me quite a bit about the Singularity and programming language; it's possible, he says, to think differently depending on which language you're writing in. In class, he sips from a pottery mug he's made. He's a thinker, and he's not the only one. And he reminds me: there's a fine line between just harrumphing over Kids These Days and speaking, out of concern, of what you fear is being stolen from them before they've ever had a chance to see it for themselves.

Of course, computers enable work and happiness that otherwise might never be, and I experience this every time I boot up and log in. I, too, found it hard to take middle-aged people seriously when I was twenty-one, overwhelmed by life's immediacy, slack-jawed with wonder. Like Isaac Newton, I wandered on the shore of a great ocean of truth all undiscovered before me. But when I was twenty-one, the ocean into which I waded was the sensory world, and the world of language that was rooted there, and the body of tactile knowledge it gave me. And increasingly, that's not a place my students seem to know. Otherwise bright first-years stop me, puzzled, as we read Shakespeare's *Much Ado About Nothing*: "Benedick says he will not bear the yoke . . . what's a yoke?" Reading Dante's lovely description of Paolo and Francesca in *Inferno* Canto V—"As cranes go over sounding their harsh cry, / leaving the long streak of their flight in air, / so come these spirits, wailing as they fly"—some students are at a loss, physically squinting their eyes as they try to focus a mental picture, until another classmate prompts:

"this sounds like the Canada geese that go overhead in fall."[11] Writer Jay Griffiths has remarked that language and metaphor are sourced in the natural world—"the human spirit needs language," she writes, "shimmering and liquid"—and so lacking a body of knowledge built around sensory experience can impoverish not only one's physical body but one's language and one's human emotional life, all of which are interconnected.[12] Similarly, philosopher Hannah Arendt (of whom more later) writes, "With the disappearance of the sensually given world, the transcendent world disappears as well, and with it the possibility of transcending the material world in concept and thought."[13] Losing our senses means losing our words and our minds, and losing access to the places only words and minds can go.

"But books were *your* escape from the real world," someone might riposte. True, yet books aren't really an escape. In its rich tapestry of ethics, psychology, and sensory brain-work, good writing creates a mental experience that calls us both out of and deeper into ourselves, just as analogies like the "yoke" net us deeper into a web of relationships between the world as summoned by language and the world as perceived by our senses. *Beloved, As I Lay Dying, Tess of the d'Urbervilles, The Shining, Catch-22,* and Ray Bradbury, to name just a few, put me inside experiences and lives I'd never known yet somehow recognized. (No junior high nerd *ever* forgets "All Summer in a Day.") By showing me what strange, bold wonders were possible with words, books made me bolder too.

So did my childhood on an Alabama farm. As Colette wrote in *My Mother's House* (1922), "To those who live in the country and use their eyes everything becomes alike miraculous and simple."[14] Like much of the rural South, mine was a landscape of wonder and sorrow present to the senses and the imagination: the dangers of a horse kick or limb-severing accident, the thrill of spotting crawfish sunning themselves in their mud-tower doors, the sweet tang of pecans fished from fallen leaves, the barn kitten broken in the dog's mouth, the half-felt presences and stories of all the others who had worked and died here, willingly or not. It was a place of risk that sharpened sight, as risk can indeed do in both writing and life. (Watch for the wrinkle of snake-back in the grass, the slippery patch of boot-sole–polished floorboard which could pitch you out our old barn's second-story door.) Animals were more real to me than people: the flock of miniature donkeys with the crosses on their backs (where baby Jesus, I

11. Alighieri, *Inferno*, 59.
12. Griffiths, "Artifice vs. Pastoral," 26.
13. Arendt, *The Human Condition*, 288.
14. Colette, 48.

understood, had blessed them for carrying his mama all that way), horses and cats and birddogs and Jack Russells and a rattlesnake-killing German Shorthair, soft-coated calves, slim green lizards doing pushups on the porch (even better were the grumpy rusty-judges, tiny stegosauruses in black and gray), swallows and hummingbirds and bobwhite quail and wild turkeys, thick-necked bulls slinging dirt over their shoulders and bellowing in testosterone-dazed loneliness. Emily Dickinson's self-description was also mine: "You ask of my Companions. Hills—Sir—and the Sundown—and a Dog—large as myself, that my Father bought me—They are better than Beings—because they know—but do not tell!"[15]

With so many creatures to respond to, chores to do, and books to read, I didn't think much about anything we'd call technology now, especially since, without the Internet, its presence was marginal and school-focused. Until I encountered my first computer—a boxy, square-moused Apple Macintosh, in eleventh grade—*typing* meant winding a sheet of paper around the sticky black platen of a heavy brown metal manual typewriter and practicing finger drills. By contrast, the avid, springy type on the Mac's bluish screen, its malleability (you can change the font!) and memory (the sonnet I wrote for English class is saved *forever*!) was weird and thrilling. "The phone" was a kitchen-based landline, like the heavy rotary-dialed box on my grandmother's wall, until, around 1991, a black-corded cellphone was bolted to the floor of our Suburban so my father, a doctor as well as a cattle farmer, could answer the beeper clipped to his belt. The first television I remember (around the Carter administration) had a heavy manual channel-changing dial that slid pictures into one another with a satisfying *thunk*. Cable didn't make it out to our house until I was almost in ninth grade, so other than Auburn-Alabama football and the news (Ronald Reagan jocularly urging Michael Jackson to "give some TLC to the PYTs," scary Russians, something called the Sandinistas, and a woman exotically named Fawn Hall), mine wasn't much of a TV world. When I rode in the car, I played alphabet games or mostly just gazed out the window at what was scrolling past: abandoned barns sieved by sweetgum seedlings, tire-flattened rattlesnakes, honeysuckle thronging up a telephone pole, pine forests stretching enticingly toward the dark, a wild-eyed dog trotting, teats dangling, in the ditch ("poor thing," my mother would say, "I wonder where her puppies are.") If I spotted a box turtle trundling across the asphalt, I could holler out and my mother might pull over to let me carry it safely to the other side or, even better, ride it home in the floorboard footwell, its blunt confused head bumping the carpet, to put it in our own pond. (What did we know of migration then, the cycles of

15. Sewall, *The Life of Emily Dickinson*, 542.

the small lives we were interrupting?) If I was bored in church, I wrote my sister notes in the bulletin until an adult leaned over and snatched the tiny collection envelope pencil from my hand and stuck it in its pew-back slot. All during the sermon, it sat there, just out of reach.

Basically, then, my options for tuning out were limited. Now, my students' smartphones seem always to be calling them away into some vague semi-social hinterland that doesn't touch their deep need, or the world's. On blazing blue sky winter days, they trudge between buildings, thumbing screens. They spring to text the instant class is over, as if the phones are little pets hungry for the touch they've been denied.[16] Some students have struggled or even dropped out of college because of video game addictions. Still more suffer from spiraling anxiety yet can't break the cycle of screen checking that, at least in my experience, only heightens it.[17] Reading aloud in class is sometimes difficult for students; so is reading silently, since, as you can see if you wander through the library on a school night, many students plug in headphones and start their music at the same time they open a book, blurring the particular music of the page with the generalized noise of the world. Given a diminished range of sensory contact with the world, they face an additional hurdle in accepting any writer's invitation on the page—*think with me in our common human language, the language of the senses*—since doing so requires a body of sensory knowledge to fit to those words. ("What's a yoke?")

Make no mistake: students are willing and able to learn otherwise. They hunger to be transformed, by their educations. But a small thing troubles me: many students struggle to write by hand or to read handwriting (especially cursive) at all.[18] That's neurologically significant, since writing by hand and the originality, complexity, and memory retention of what we

16. In this paragraph, I'm quoting Frederick Buechner's description of vocation—popular in Lutheran higher education—as "the place where your deep gladness and the world's deep hunger meet." Of course, the Internet is useful in the classroom. The virtual-reality version of the Sistine Chapel that lets you move your cursor up, down, or sideways or zoom in and out for a 360-degree view is priceless for studying Michelangelo in northeast Iowa. It can be nice when a student uses her device to look up a fact that's arisen in discussion. But if a student has his phone face up on his desk, even if she's outwardly attentive to the class, it's diverting a slice of her attention to itself from the beginning of class to the end. Therefore, some professors—even computer science professors—are challenging the use of laptops in the classroom. See Rockmore, "Case for Banning Laptops in the Classroom," and Curzan, "Why I'm Asking You Not To Use Laptops."

17. Kadison and DiGeronimo, *College of the Overwhelmed.*

18. See also Hensher, *The Missing Ink,* Trubek, *The History and Uncertain Future of Handwriting,* and Masson, "The Death of Cursive Writing."

write are connected.[19] (*Document* originally meant "that which teaches;" our bodies learn through writing, and vice versa.)[20] And despite the resurgence of Moleskine notebooks as delightful tactile object and worldwide creative brand, handwriting is endangered these days, even among writers like me, as typing, texting, and mousing stiffen our grips on pens and cursive, which I learned isn't taught much anymore in third grade.[21] Colleagues and I have observed an increasing number of students who don't take notes by hand (or at all) in class. Author Philip Hensher describes a creative writing student who "tells me that she is unable to carry a notebook around with her to make notes in with a pen . . . because she can't write with a pen and paper. Can't? 'It really hurts.' And, by the way, the student finds my handwriting really difficult to read, so could I give all feedback in typing? Including marginal comments?" When I read this, I nodded in dismayed recognition, because . . .[22]

Maybe so. Maybe I'm just an average forty-two-year-old. Or maybe not.

So, talking with my class about how technology might dim the brightness of our human lives in our human bodies on this earth, I find it hard to stay calm. I remember myself at that age, learning the world through each sense. I remember the intensity of that yearning, which already held in it the seeds of some art I dreamed of making. This memory presses against the back of my throat, rueful and immediate. "Yes," I answer Darren, "but this scary generational problem may be different in kind, not just degree. The threat's not the same, but there *is* a threat. Because if technology numbs us to the world, it numbs us from dealing with global warming. It numbs us and disables us as citizens. In our responses to art. As moral beings."

19. Konnikova, "What's Lost."
20. Smail, *On Deep History*, 5.
21. See Sax, *The Revenge of Analog*, 29–49.
22. Hensher, *The Missing Ink*, 39.

Of course, I'm being less than neutral. But that thickening in my chest, so close to love, feels like an urgent message from some lonely endangered thing pleading *save me. Speak of me to those who otherwise might never know.* The world pleads with teachers to help others see it, but also pleads with us not to become pedants. Teaching asks for a constant balance of this kind of personal passion with space for students to come forth and discover their own passions; after all, the *paedogogos* is the child leader, not the child haranguer. Inside, we're all selfishly insisting that other people ought to be versions of ourselves, and we've got to squash that ego where it lives. W. H. Auden's warning is useful: "When a man finds himself a social oddity, he is very apt to alternate between feelings of guilt—there must be something wrong with me—and megalomania—the fact that I am an oddity proves that I am superior to the average mass."[23]

The challenge lies in resisting this "megalomania" and being sure that your own reaction really is (as Immanuel Kant would say) pointing you toward something that represents a greater good for everyone. It's a thin line between *principled activist* and *crank*. And yet, convinced now that our survival depends on attention—which art can teach—and having seen the world changing in front of my eyes, I can't be neutral. Too much is at stake. Plenitude of humanity. Generosity. Self, spirit, soul. And all the billions of nonhuman beings who ride this spinning blue-and-green globe with us.

Sure, many of us Old People are every bit as wedded to our devices as The Young. But since I taught my first college class as a graduate student in 1998, I've seen some behavioral shifts that worry me *and* future employers, who plead with me (once they find out I'm a college professor), "Send us more curious thinkers—not people who expect us to hold their hands." Paradoxically, having the world in a box in your pocket can sap your ingenuity (if a Google search doesn't yield a result, what do I do now?) Being plugged in is sold to all of us as a way to be real grown-ups. But electronic multitasking isn't harmless, and a society now constantly preaching *convenience* to us as the greatest human good doesn't prepare us to evaluate that fact. You feel like you're on top of the world, switching from window to window as your data is fed back to you in a system others have designed, but you're actually accomplishing, and will actually remember, very little, and you'll be capable of even less as your brain becomes habituated to that fake productive dance. This is truer the younger your brain is. And the data you're feeding the Internet via your device is enriching others and impoverishing you in ways you can't see—ways that are, in fact, usually being hidden from you. As the futurist and musician Jaron Lanier writes, "This is one of the great illusions

23. Auden, "Lame Shadows."

of our times: that you can game without being gamed."[24] You have a right
to know that something important is being stolen from you, and to make
choices accordingly.

Of course, people have *always* sought what's easy and fun. (Remember
those Roman aristocrats, lolling on their couches, watching the fights?) But
intolerance for complexity, which technology can constantly reinforce in
ways different in kind and degree than humans have seen before, is a big
problem for a generation that will have to deal with a very difficult world—
the generation sitting in my college classroom right now. Facing global
warming, unequal economies, and student debt, and living in the shadow
of September 11, 2001, they're casting about for meaningful work, and for
meaning in general. But as a source of meaning and self-understanding,
many American teenagers are offered little else but media, and little critical
apparatus to help them interpret the way it's constantly fashioning them
into consumers of everything it presents as normal—including constant
connection to, and through, screens. One of the most important things
young adults learn is that their assumptions and "norms" *are* assumptions,
constructed by particular experiences and circumstances, that "natural" is
not the best word to apply to human behavior, and that the culture around
them is made, not born, not inevitable, and rooted in daily human choices
and habits.[25] I'm reminded of the story about the two young fish hanging
out in a stream, chatting, when an old fish swims by. "How's the water?" the
old fish asks. The two young fish wait till she passes, and then one asks the
other, "What's water?"

Here's the thing, though: even as they're bound up in Facebook and
Twitter and Instagram, many of my students also sense that they're being
cheated. They know there must be more to human experience than the
world (and the Internet) around them are offering. Some of them even
guess that the Internet may be a part of the problem. Alarmed, they tell
me that their twelve- and thirteen-year-old siblings use Twitter the way
they use Facebook—to broadcast even more personal "statuses" to an even
wider (and less controllable) audience without understanding the dangers.
They look at a small child absorbed in a smartphone and murmur, "That's
just sad." They laugh self-consciously about YikYak and other social media
rumor mills: "'yak karma?'" one student asked me, shaking his head. "How

24. Lanier, *Who Owns the Future?*, 114.

25. Anthropologist Wade Davis reminds us that knowledge of other cultures across
place and time helps us "draw inspiration and comfort from the fact that the path we
have taken is not the only one available, that our destiny therefore is not indelibly written in a set of choices that demonstrably and scientifically have proven not to be wise."
See *The Wayfinders*, 218.

have we even let that become a *thing*?" Having competed with smart-phones for their parents' attention, they're getting savvy about what device overuse does to relationships. They still enjoy books, not only particular authors but physical objects: the feel, the smell, the comforting presence of one's own small library on a dorm room shelf. They're looking for meaning, in and outside of a classroom. But school—particularly college—is the only place that many of them have a chance of encountering real analysis of why they find it hard to concentrate, what they can do about global warming, how to ride out the dizzying social shifts they're living through, where to look for meaning, and what all these things have to do with each other. Sports are one of the last sources of physical experience available to many kids, but even they may be disrupted by pushy adults.[26] Church is failing more young people than Christians like me prefer to admit, re-shaping itself too often around fire-and-brimstone exclusivities, self-help clichés, or disconnection from the problems they see around them every day: homeless women with shopping carts, summers that get hotter and hotter, wars that rumble on out of sight.

Even at my small Lutheran liberal arts college, among a mix of believers and doubters from traditions both Christian and non, I find this mix of hope, longing, and fear. In my English major seminar, reading Cormac McCarthy's post-apocalyptic novel *The Road* (2006), a joking discussion turned serious: if we were stranded in a burned-up world, could we survive?[27] None of us could start a fire from scratch or shoot deer with a bow and arrow. Only a few of us could identify edible plants. And who, besides me, had

26. The late Southern writer Harry Crews said of sports: "I think all of us are looking for that which does not admit of bullshit . . . . If you tell me you can bench press 450, hell, we'll load up the bar and put you under it. Either you can do it or you can't do it—you can't bullshit. Ultimately, sports are just about as close to what one would call the truth as it is possible to get in this world." See Michaels, "Harry Crews," 249. I think children seek this kind of truth, despite adults. I offer this moment from a parents' meeting for a six-year-old's Little League baseball team in the South, as it was described to me by one of the parents. "We practice seven days a week," the coach declared. A parent's plaintive voice rose from the group: "What about Sunday?" "Sunday practices are at 10:30," the coach said. "We go to church at 11!" the parent replied. "Not if he's on my team," the coach replied. Sometimes, of course, it's the parents applying the pressure. For a good discussion of "helicopter parenting," see *How to Raise An Adult* (2015) by Julie Lythcott-Haims, a former dean of freshmen and undergraduate advising at Stanford University.

27. Post-apocalypse seems to be the dominant genre for my students and their generation. See Miller, "Fresh Hell." See also Sobel, "Feed the Hunger": "[R]esilience and hope is what so many of these plucky characters exemplify, even when faced with the worst odds. If we want to avoid the environmental catastrophes and repressive central governments pictured in current dystopian fiction, we're going to need more adolescents willing to be heroic" (75).

homemade preserves in the basement? Yet, as writer and activist Naomi Klein reminds us, "the word 'apocalypse' derives from the Greek *apokalypsis*, which means 'something uncovered' or revealed.[28] With new eyes we turned to the subtle argument McCarthy puts forth: those who make and preserve things will keep humanity alive. But more than that, those who remember ideas, and ideals—or "carry the fire," as McCarthy writes—will preserve the best of us. What *is* the best of us? What *is* the fire? Students want the tools to ask those questions, and they want the answers. Because they want to carry that fire themselves.

When I talk to my students, including recent college graduates, I hear not just a hunger for new ways of being in the world but the humor and pragmatism to put them into action. Some are first-generation college students, some from families marked by joblessness or suicide or countries torn by poverty and war. Some have family members who came back to Iowa changed by military service, or who didn't come back at all. They're finding their places on any number of continuums from year to year: left to right, gay to straight, doubting to faithful, omnivore to vegan, naïve to wiser now. They join in to help work the college gardens. They tear up in wonder when they stand in front of Michelangelo's *David* in Florence and spot what you can only see in person—the facial expression that changes from defiance to doubt to fear and back again as you walk around him. They come from Wisconsin dairy farms and Lutheran parsonages and inner-city Chicago and Sudan and Afghanistan. It's difficult, thank God, to imagine these students ever hardening into young Silicon Valleyites who grudgingly yield their bus seats to old ladies while braying, "I don't know why old people ride MUNI. If I were old I'd just take Uber."[29] Nor can I see them ever falling prey to "the listless boredom" of the affluent young Californians in Sofia Coppola's 2013 film "The Bling Ring" (based on a true story), who broke into celebrities' houses to steal their clothes, "trying on another outfit, committed to the theater of meaning rather than the experience of it."[30] The millennials I know are funny, smart, and sincere, scornful of hipsterism and intent on pulling it away from the "authentic" ways and experiences (organic farming, handcrafts, music) onto which it's fastened itself. They're starting their own small farms and getting MFAs in writing and guiding troubled kids through the wilderness and helping build elementary schools in poor communities around the world and becoming teachers and nurses and doctors and writing dissertations on prairie insects and following their passion for social justice into the Peace Corps and the Lu-

28. Klein, *This Changes Everything*, 105.

29. Solnit, "Welcome to the (Don't Be) Evil Empire."

30. Dean, "The Listless Boredom of the Bling Ring."

theran Volunteer Corps and the ministry. They use their smartphones to run apps like Buycott, which allows them to scan a product's barcode in the store and trace its corporate heritage to decide whether it's an ethical use of their money. Their counterparts in Egypt and Iran moved the 2011 Arab Spring forward on Twitter, typing on Macbooks and wearing Johnny Cash T-shirts.[31] They made Macklemore and Ryan Lewis's anticonsumerist rap song "Thrift Shop" an international hit. They walked with Black Lives Matter[32] and helped prepare the anti-Dakota Access Pipeline protest camp at Standing Rock for winter. They're eager to stand up for the powerless, the ignored, the shoved-aside. They're idealists, and they are practical. They want to be moved and to make change. They can figure out how to do it themselves. But they also deserve elders, and teachers, who can help them.

Thinking of those students, and those who will come after them, and of the choppy waters of hope and fear in which we all bob every day, I'm convinced that the single survival skill most necessary in our post-peak oil world is the ability to wake yourself up and stay awake. It's the ability to be compassionate and curious, to go forward into the world with a spirit that is brave, generous, and reverent toward that which transcends this present moment in your own human life. We can't afford to trust anything—corporatization, technology, or "entertainment"—that erodes or commodifies this impulse. Not *anything*. Education and art, which, as my college's mission statement says, "lift us beyond our present concerns into a wider world," are what I place my faith in, since they lift us out of our own small selves toward generosity, even love. When you care about people, as I care about my students, you want to open opportunities for them to grow, and help them see ways to have hope. Our current state of passivity before technology and corporations—which make consumers, not citizens, and not mature, thoughtful human beings—is the last place to which you want to consign them.

So in this book, I'm trying to offer my students, and all of us, some ways to think about our world and where we are, right now. It's a big job. Sometimes as I write I feel like Mr. Causabon in *Middlemarch*, beavering away at his Key to All Mythologies, or like Walt Whitman's noiseless patient spider, flinging my threads out, hoping they latch on somewhere. Sometimes I just feel like I'm putting an octopus to bed. But I can't leave this project alone. Of course, I can't put myself in the prophet class (see *megalomania*, above), but I hope to be guided in this endeavor, as I'm guided in my life, by the words of the prophet Isaiah: "The Lord God has given me the tongue of a

31. See the photographs in the *New York Times* feature "Young Egyptians Spread Their Message."

32. Significantly for my subtitle, an admonition associated with Black Lives Matter is "stay woke."

teacher, that I may know how to sustain the weary with a word. Morning by morning he wakens—wakens my ear to listen as those who are taught."[33] My education has been the most precious thing in my life. And if it isn't turned to a greater good for the world, then I haven't used it well.

We've got to remember the words of Zen teacher and Nobel Peace Prize nominee Thich Nhat Hanh: "We are here to awaken from our illusion of separateness."[34] In doing so, we can see the local *and* look beyond it to the other creatures with whom we share what scholar Timothy Morton calls the "mesh" of being on this planet. "The ecological thought," he writes, "[is] a practice and a process of becoming fully aware of how human beings are connected with other beings—animal, vegetable, or mineral."[35] Since the interdependence and interconnectedness of people, objects, animals, political systems, and climate is inescapable now, ecological thought is the mind-set with which we need to approach reality. We can't let an idea of place delude us into thinking one place is separate from any other or resort to the various tricks of privilege or self-protection to exempt ourselves from ecological reality—like former city dwellers retreating to gated communities, or lobbyists buying their way around at-least-theoretically democratic processes of law, sequestering ourselves here from all the troubles over there. Because, as the old bumper sticker says, "Throw it away—where's 'away?'" We're all in this together. There is no *away*. Not anymore.

Sure, we can push naïveté to test itself a bit. But to reject sincerity is to reject the engine of everything that will sustain us in our global emergency. If we act to change what we can where we are, and to cultivate the small practices of attention to and conservation of a place we love, we can learn to see and to wonder at the larger web of life and consciousness that gets bigger, and stranger, and more absorbing as we keep looking. If we live deliberately in our own particular place, with one eye always on the big world, we can continually renew our perceptions and actions in humility and wonder, which ripple outward into art, communities, actions, and we can ride out even the difficult emotions, like grief, fear, or despair, as they come. "One can't love humanity," Graham Greene has written, "one can only love people."[36] Although we shouldn't *stop* with loving the individual, the local, or the person, that is how we learn to *start* loving, and how we learn to love and care for and protect by seeing. The single, local, small, particular thing always leads to more, and it leads you to a sort of love and courage and

33. Isaiah 50:4, NRS.
34. Palmer, "We Need To Find A Third Way."
35. Morton, *The Ecological Thought*, 7.
36. Greene, *The Ministry of Fear*, 223.

power that helps you go forward into the world, doing what you can to make it better. Even if—sometimes particularly if—you are doubting or afraid or just not sure what's next.

We are surrounded by uncertainty, and also opportunity. This is the reality for all of us as the twenty-first century rolls toward its third decade: if I don't do it, nobody else will. As Gandhi said, I have to be the change I want to see in the world. And I have to make that change happen for myself, even when it's hard. My world is full of political and economic systems that want to manipulate me. And they will, unless I wake up, stay awake, and make them work for me—or opt out of them altogether.

Why am I the one to say this? I'm not an expert in technology or politics. I'm an English professor, a writer, and a Southern Methodist farm girl. Steeped in the language of the Bible since my childhood, and brought as an adult every day up against my own failures, I know, in those resounding words, how often I have sinned and fallen short. I know how much I have yet to learn. But I can't look away from trouble in our world, and I know an awful lot of people who feel the same. My family's given our lives to teaching, farming, and healing (humans and animals) and see these vocations as service, even ministry, to the world. My own field's trained me to look for patterns, to be moved by beauty, and to reach for the intangible in words, and there's too much at stake not to try. So this book will be unapologetically romantic, wide-eyed, and wack-ass. As my late grandfather said, I'm going to put the hay down where the goats can get it.

The whole complex of screen-driven devices, processes, and habits that exists in our lives as something we call, however simplistically, "the Internet"[37] or "technology" isn't going anywhere, but we can choose how we live with it, and we can choose when—and how—to turn it off. We can draw on what's best about ourselves to live more thoughtfully with each other and to resist that which threatens to engineer our humanity out of existence. What follows is my best attempt—informed by stories from my own experience, activism, and teaching—to describe how a quiet yet titanic waking up in every heart and mind can come to be.

We are standing here, together, in a space of risk and hope. So much depends on how we look at it.

So I'm turning to my students, and anyone else who wants to listen. If you want to wake up, if you want to act on your sense that something's awry, if you want to take back your own mind and life and renew a sense of generosity and hope, here are some places to start. This book's for you. Welcome.

---

37. I'm persuaded by Evgeny Morozov's discussion of why "the Internet" may be too simplistic a label, since "perhaps there's nothing inevitable about how various parts of this giant 'Internet' work and fit together." See Morozov, *To Save Everything*, Chapter 2.

1

Consider what technology is doing to your life, without your consent.

> "The law of progress holds that everything now must be bet-
> ter than what was there before. Don't you see if you want
> something better, and better, and better, you lose the good.
> The good is no longer even being measured."
>
> —HANNAH ARENDT[1]

SEVERAL YEARS AGO, A strange video emerged on the Internet: a child at the zoo *not* getting eaten alive. On the screen, a baby has just been propped against the glass of a lioness's cage—presumably by his parents, who are also, presumably, the ones filming. Behind the glass, the lioness scratches and bites the barrier separating her from her prey. Her teeth scrape the invisible wall and her breath fogs it, right next to the child's face. She rears up to paw at the glass, then turns herself sideways, trying to get a grip. Incredibly, the man behind the camera giggles, "Say hi, kitty, kitty." A female voice directs the baby, "Look behind you." A second female voice, also giggling, volun-teers, "That's, like, almost . . . not cool."

It took me a while to get over my initial speechlessness at this. Thoughts of Jonathan Swift's "A Modest Proposal" battled with the usual self-admonition: *let's not overreact*. But I couldn't stop asking: *why are they laughing?* It's not funny for the lioness. It's not funny for the baby, innocent of danger, who turns his face backward into those open jaws. Online com-menters wrote things like "So much is wrong with this picture. Almost not cool is an understatement, those parents are lucky the glass didn't break," "What is wrong with you! That's a horrible thing to do to both the lion and the baby!" and "STUPID THICK PARENTS." Yet, this being YouTube, there are (pardon the pun) copycat videos all over the place: babies not being

---

1. Arendt, "Hannah Arendt: From An Interview."

eaten at zoos by cougars, tigers, and male lions even larger than the original frustrated lioness.

What makes this video so disturbing? What stirs up that sense in us, so easy to suppress as insufficiently ironic (it's, like, almost not cool!), that something here is wrong? Indeed, there's something eerie about the ease with which the whole world becomes fodder for our whims when we have smart-phones in our hands—particularly since, in that gap between the thing we're looking at and its image captured on our phones to replay for an audience, lies a swamp of moral and economic realities that the companies who make our devices find very profitable to hide. When parents play at child sacri-fice with lions, when giggling selfie-takers in the Accademia position their faces strategically next to David's junk, when a tweet ruins someone's life, we're driven to ask: what are these people *thinking*? They aren't. Yet exploring this thoughtlessness can be liberating: we can reclaim our right to say *this is wrong* and *don't take my picture, please* and *I don't do Twitter* by knowing what's at stake and understanding the way technology exploits us and our most thoughtless tendencies, without our knowledge or consent.

"Thoughtlessness" was an important word for the political philoso-pher Hannah Arendt (1906–1975), a German Jew who escaped from an internment camp at Gurs, France in the early years of World War II. Even-tually settling in America with her husband, Heinrich Blucher, Arendt turned her attention to defining what makes evil possible in the human heart, perhaps most famously in her book *Eichmann in Jerusalem: A Report on the Banality of Evil* (1963), an expansion of her article on the trial of Ad-olf Eichmann, Hitler's Minister of Jewish Affairs, for *The New Yorker*.[2] Her thesis is controversial (and historically complicated)[3] but useful to think with: what made the pencil-pushing Eichmann able to oversee the efficient transportation of Jews to their deaths was not active desire to do harm so much as it was a basic obliviousness to the fact that other people are as

2. Historian Deborah Lipstadt points out that although Arendt is sometimes de-scribed as "covering" the trial, she was not in attendance and watching it start to finish, as "covered" would imply. See Lipstadt, *The Eichmann Trial*, 178–179.

3. See Robin, "The Trials of Hannah Arendt," and Lipstadt, *The Eichmann Trial*. Lipstadt, reviewing trial transcripts and Eichmann's own "history of the Final Solution" recorded and transcribed before his capture, writes that he was not only a rule-follower but was also motivated by active anti-Semitism and a conscious desire to assist Nazi aims to rid the Reich of Jews. Following the war, "a number of Nuremberg defendants connected him to the Final Solution. They testified about his unrelenting quest to mur-der as many Jews as he could and his pivotal role in the annihilation process" (*The Eichmann Trial*, 4). Indeed, Lipstadt writes, "In every instance where his imprint was to be found—volunteering suggestions, giving orders, or interpreting policy—Eichmann always chose the most stringent option . . . . A portrait emerged of a man who was proactive, energetic, and a creative master of deception" (*The Eichmann Trial*, 65).

real as oneself, which let him carry right on with the comforting habit of his daily routine. In important ways, he was literally thoughtless. Such attention to moral responsibility, self-awareness, and action threads through Arendt's work; in a characteristic phrase, Arendt writes in *The Human Condition* (1958) that all of us must "think what we are doing," acknowledging our responsibilities to the real humans (and nonhumans) sharing a space with us at the present time and refusing to write them off as less important than ourselves, which makes them easy to exploit.[4] We'll return to Arendt later. But for now, hold this in mind: the way we all seek to slump back into habit, familiarity, the comfort of following someone else's orders, and the frictionless satisfaction of our own present desires may create a troubling thoughtlessness in any of us. We often prefer not to recognize that anyone or anything but ourselves is really real, and both our brains and our devices, in one big feedback loop, encourage this. Certainly, the Internet brings us images of suffering that can move us to act—think of the grieving outrage sparked by the photograph of the drowned body of a three-year-old Syrian refugee, Aylan Kurdi, washed up on a beach in September 2015.[5] But it can also anesthetize us, swaddling us inside echo chambers of like-minded media and entertainment, enabling disrespect or downright cruelty, and blinding us as we try to see the world beyond ourselves for what it *is*, not just what we need it to be for our own purposes, right now.

In the introduction, I described that dulled sense of ennui and distraction into which we may fall, and that we hope our electronic devices will alleviate—boredom with an edge of anxiety, a sort of worried, stoned half-seeking for something to wake us up in a life whose contents feel entirely familiar. Literary critic Victor Shklovsky (1893–1984), a survivor of World War I and the Russian Revolution, wrote about habit in his famous essay "Art as Technique" (1917). For him, the cure for that feeling of deadened, bored "habitualization" and pleasure-seeking that never quite brings pleasure was art, which "exists that one may recover the sensation of life; it exists to make one feel things, to make the stone *stony*."[6] Think about the sharpness of your first encounter with your favorite painting or the person

4. Arendt, *The Human Condition*, 5.

5. See Barnard and Shoumali, "Image of Drowned Syrian."

6. Shklovsky, "Art as Technique," 12, italics original. Paradoxically, this recovery of sensation can occur by recognizing something familiar in a work of art, which heightens both its familiarity and its strangeness. Southern novelist Walker Percy told the *Paris Review* that "The most commonplace example of the cognitive dimension in fiction is the reader's recognition—sometimes the shock of recognition—the 'verification' of a sector of reality that he had known but not known that he had known. I think of letters I get from readers, which may refer to a certain scene and say, in effect, yes! That's the way it is!" See Abadi-Nagy, "Walker Percy: The Art of Fiction No. 97."

you love—*never has there been that precise combination of colors, so arresting a smile!*—and you can feel what he means. Shklovsky's words are still justly famous—and useful—among writers:

> The purpose of art is to impart the sensation of things as they are perceived and not as they are known. The technique of art is to make objects "unfamiliar," to make forms difficult, to increase the difficulty and length of perception because the process of perception is an aesthetic end in itself and must be prolonged. . . . After we see an object several times, we begin to recognize it. The object is in front of us and we know about it, but we do not see it—hence we cannot say anything significant about it. Art removes objects from the automatism of percep-tion in several ways.[7]

Slow down and look at what's in front of you, Shklovsky says to us. No, really. *Look.* The artist has to do this all the time, paying attention to the object in front of her which is not herself and to the sensory world to which it refers. She has to short-circuit her own impulse to pass it off with a casual, clichéd glance: *oh, yeah, sure, that, I've seen that before. I know all about it.* She has to try for a particular combination of words or colors or notes to help what she sees be as present to others' imaginations as it is to her own. Thus she renovates her vision from the inside, and gets carried to some surprising places: how did this object come to be? How was it made? What kind of mind made this? And how is that mind connected to hers, in culture and time? What *is* it about *these* swipes of color on *this* canvas in *this* pattern that produces this feeling? Her questions may fall silent, too, before sudden and overwhelming emotions: *I am flooded with wonder or pity, and I don't know why.* Even challenging art can help you understand that discomfort or an encounter with something you don't immediately get can be normal too, and isn't always something to flee. Encounters with the natural world work this way too. And staying there at the friction point of difference between *me* and *not-me*, perhaps even venturing farther in—that's accepting maturity.

Yet technology and media are only one part of what makes that type of maturity difficult; achieving mindfulness can mean working against the structure of the brain itself, and the younger and/or the more technologi-cally immersed you are, the more difficult this may be. Since our brains develop from the bottom to the top and from the back to the front, among the most active portions of our brains when we're in our early twenties is the amygdala—the deeply rooted seat of "the emotional brain," which helps

7. Ibid., 13.

assimilate emotions and memories (particularly challenging or fearful ones) into long-term memory storage.[8] Since our twenties are full of experiences different from what came before, the amygdala can make us feel as if every emotion or event (particularly negative ones) is groundbreaking and crucial, while the prefrontal cortex of the frontal lobe—the last part of the brain to develop, in our mid-to-late twenties—hasn't yet assumed its full role as mediator, the site of reflecting, evaluating, putting life events into perspective, and calming oneself down. As college students, we may feel whipsawed by disappointments or uncertainties in work, school, or relationships that may seem minor even one year later, simply because, in neurological terms, that event is standing center stage in our brains, demanding what later comes to seem a disproportionate amount of energy but at the time feels simply like the way things are. New or uncomfortable things just get the brain's attention more, especially when we're young.[9]

To smooth those new experiences into the rest of our memories, our brains are always eager to do their own version of auto-complete, glossing over gaps or anomalies to harmonize incoming information in advance. We can recognize words just by seeing the top halves of letters—block out the bottom half of this phrase with a piece of paper and see what I mean. Similarly, we can unscramble letters on the fly, thanks to the parallel processors always humming behind our eyes: as lnog as the frist lteter and the lsat are the smae as teh rael wrod, and teh wrods hvae the smae genearl shpae, we cna raed this snetnece jsut fnie. (That was hard to type, ecspecailly snice Miscoroft Wrod ketp aucotorrcetnig it.)[10] This is why typos in your own work are hard to spot: since your brain knows what you meant to write, it's going to protect you, in its overachieving way, by spinning a web of order over the disorder right in front of it, creating meaning from chaos and, eventually, habit from what was once new and startling. As

8. See Jay, *The Defining Decade*. Thanks to my colleague Kristy Gould, Professor of Psychology at Luther, for offering feedback on this passage.

9. This is also why, to borrow the title of psychologist Douwe Draaisma's book, life seems to speed up as we get older: a new or startling event creates contrasts in memory with what's around it and marks a time period as distinct, while a string of days without much that's new, or to which the brain has become accustomed, tends to feel undifferentiated and therefore "faster" in our memories. Draaisma quotes philosopher Jean-Marie Guyau (1854–1888), early identifier of this phenomenon, who advised, "If you want to lengthen the perspective of time, then fill it, if you have the chance, with a thousand new things." See Draaisma, *Why Life Speeds Up*, 206–207.

10. I'm indebted to Anthony Doerr's lecture "On Defamiliarization" at the Tin House Summer Writers Workshop 2008 for introducing me to Shklovsky and for this information, which is also available from a variety of sources. See http://www.newscientist.com/article/mg16221887.600.

Shklovsky wrote, in what has to be the most quotable line in all of aesthetic philosophy, "Habitualization devours works, clothes, furniture, one's wife, and the fear of war."[11] And that's why writing teachers advise students to read their work aloud; since we read more by recognizing shapes of words than by actually interpreting combinations of letters, anything that jolts us out of that habit helps us see what we've actually done, not just what we *think* we have done, on the page.

Shklovsky describes the way our brains conspire with habit in dulling everyday life—a process against which artists must struggle:

> If we start to examine the general laws of perception, we see that as perception becomes habitual, it becomes automatic. Thus, for example, all of our habits retreat into the area of the unconsciously automatic; if one remembers the sensations of holding a pen or of speaking in a foreign language for the first time and compares that with his feeling at performing the action for the ten thousandth time, he will agree with us. Such habituation explains the principles by which, in ordinary speech, we leave phrases unfinished and words half expressed. In this process, ideally realized in algebra, things are replaced by symbols. Complete words are not expressed in rapid speech; their initial sounds are barely perceived.[12]

Shklovsky argues that just as our speech can be blurred by the carelessness of habit, so can our literal perception of objects. "By this 'algebraic' method of thought," he writes, "we apprehend objects only as shapes with imprecise extensions; we do not see them in their entirety but rather recognize them by their main characteristics. We see the object as though it were enveloped in a sack."[13] We pull into our usual parking spot at work with no memory of how we got there; we drop into our familiar chair without really seeing it. Our brains are always trying to auto-complete, to run our lives on habit. It's just easier that way.

Therefore, just as we can't afford to assume that our current techno-saturated lifestyles are inevitable, let's remember that what we experience as reality is being constructed by our malleable brains, which are always in flux and response to stimuli from within and beyond ourselves. We're always looking through a lens, and the brain itself is where the lens is built, with and without our conscious consent. In our own lives as thirty- and forty-somethings and beyond, we become able to calm ourselves even in difficulty

11. Shklovsky, "Art as Technique," 12.

12. Ibid., 11.

13. Ibid.

with memories of previous survival, experiences we can put next to new ones in our memories as we draw upon the reflective, judging, forecasting powers of the mature frontal lobe: *I went through this before*, we think, *and it didn't kill me; this feeling is painful, but pain* does *pass. Let's not take ourselves too seriously, okay? Okay.* By contrast, the active amygdala of a twentysomething and younger brain wants to be plugged in. It wants to be fed. It can't really help seeing itself as the most important thing in existence. And it *loves* the hit of dopamine, the brain's reward-and-desire chemical, it gets from every "like" or new message. This makes young brains especially susceptible to the roller coaster of anxiety and stimulus seeking that the Internet is designed to provide, and to the subsequent consumer anxiety that follows, while laboring under a relative inability to evaluate where those anxieties come from. Especially—it must be said—if your brain has never not known an Internet. "We start out with many more cells and connections than we need," a neuroscientist colleague has told me, "and as a result of experience (the right stimuli at the right time) those connections are pared down and optimized for our environment. What effect technology and our increasingly self-absorbed society has on that is yet to be seen."[14]

The networks of habit and reward our brains spin around our devices can mesh with neuroanatomy and psychology to deliver you up to a variety of states you might not choose if you had the chance. First, consider the obvious effects of dependence on things with screens: cramped mouse hands, stooped postures, burning eyes, obesity, bad backs, and high blood pressure. There's what former Microsoft senior executive Linda Stone calls "screen apnea"—our tendency to "hold our breath or breathe shallowly when we're working at our computers," which makes us "more agitated and impulsive than we'd ordinarily be."[15] There's the fact, according to a brochure from my eye doctor, that High Energy Visible Blue Light, emitted by computers, smartphones, and other electronic devices, can accelerate macular degeneration and damage to the retinal pigment epithelium layer of the eye. There's the increasing sense of scatteredness and distraction that comes from our attempts to multitask; we think we're processing much more information much more meaningfully than we actually are. There's the strange dull exhaustion of the offline brain, suddenly tasked with stimulating itself. There's the impatience with ideas that take more than three seconds to become clear, like anger at a slow-loading Internet page. There's the spike of excitement with an incoming message that becomes neurochemically addictive,

14. Thank you to my colleague Stephanie Fretham, Assistant Professor of Biology at Luther College, for this statement in an email to me.

15. Senior, *All Joy*, 37.

sending us down a Pavlovian spiral of rechecking in order to revive that euphoric mini-hit. Even a tech-company CEO has said, "I feel like we're in the early stages of a species-level change with devices."[16]

But most of all, and particularly alarming from a professor's point of view, is what omnipresent screen-driven technology has already done to our tolerance for difficulty, thought, and concentration, and how, therefore, it's eroding our deepest and most human selves. "For the last five centuries," writes technology analyst Nicholas Carr in *The Shallows: What The Internet Is Doing To Our Brains* (2010), "the linear, literary mind has been at the center of art, science, and society. As supple as it is subtle, it's been the imaginative mind of the Renaissance, the rational mind of the Enlightenment, the inventive mind of the Industrial Revolution, even the subversive mind of Modernism. It may soon be yesterday's mind."[17] For Carr, a print culture native like me, the Internet hasn't been neutral: "[W]hat the Net seems to be doing," he writes, "is chipping away my capacity for concentration and contemplation. My mind now expects to take in information the way the Net distributes it: in a swiftly moving stream of particles. Once I was a scuba diver in the sea of words. Now I zip along the surface like a guy on a Jet Ski."[18] A British study of library users concludes, "It is clear that users are not reading online in the traditional sense; indeed there are signs that new forms of "reading" are emerging as users 'power browse' horizontally through titles, contents pages and abstracts, going for quick wins. It almost seems that they go online to avoid reading in the traditional sense."[19] Playwright Richard Foreman is similarly suspicious of the Internet's effect on our brains:

> I come from a tradition of Western culture in which the ideal (my ideal) was the complex, dense and "cathedral-like" structure of the highly educated and articulate personality—a man or woman who carried inside themselves a personally constructed and unique version of the entire heritage of the West. . . . But today, I see within us all (myself included) the replacement of complex inner density with a new kind of self-evolving under the pressure of information overload and the technology of the "instantly available." A new self that needs to contain less and less of an inner repertory of dense cultural inheritance—as we all become "pancake people"—spread wide and thin as we

16. Widdicombe, "The Higher Life," 42.
17. Carr, *The Shallows*, 10.
18. Carr, "Is Google Making Us Stupid?"
19. Ibid.

connect with that vast network of information accessed by the mere touch of a button.[20]

Carr's and Foreman's concerns echo mine: something unique about human life, some inner plenitude and texture of self that is tied to a world of external reality and the history of imaginative and social encounters with that reality, is in danger of being lost if we don't pay attention.

You might be bracing yourself here for more English professor-ish complaining about the dumbing-down of media: listicles and clickbait and eyeball capturing (a chilling concept, if you really picture it) and the decline of long-form journalism and How The Internet Is No Place for Complex Thought and Long Sentences Like This One I Am Writing and No One Reads 800-Page Victorian Novels Anymore. It's true, of course. But you know that already. I'm going to argue that technology's reduction of our human complexity goes even deeper than a Top Ten List Of Things Wrong With Top Ten Lists. And—sorry—it's potentially even worse.

To go farther, I need to establish a basic reality here: just as any tool shapes its user (a shovel's handle gives you calluses, throwing pottery on a wheel strengthens your hands and arms), and language shapes our thoughts (metaphors of time as "spent" or "saved" connect our anxieties about time to our anxieties about money, and multiply both), software design shapes and reshapes what we look for, what we expect to find, what we prefer, and how we regard reality—online and off. Therefore, we're not as in control of our software and the devices that run it as we think; in fact, the reverse may be more true. The musician and virtual-reality pioneer Jaron Lanier argues in his book *You Are Not A Gadget* (2010) that "certain specific, popular internet designs of the moment—not the internet as a whole—tend to pull us into life patterns that gradually degrade the ways in which each of us exists as an individual," since "[t]hese unfortunate designs are more oriented toward treating people as relays in a global brain" and may therefore "[deemphasize] personhood, and the intrinsic value of an individual's unique internal experience and creativity."[21] Technology, Lanier writes, is always subject to a process called "lock-in," in which design decisions of any given moment (no matter what temporary needs, ideas, or errors created them) get enshrined in systems we use and then start shaping (or limiting) our experience and thinking—even our selves—through those systems. In a sense, we become prisoners of past human error that's replicated and magnified by computers, and we are guided down and eventually shaped by paths we didn't choose.

20. Ibid. Full text of Foreman's essay is at https://www.edge.org/3rd_culture/foreman05/foreman05_index.html, from which this portion is drawn.

21. Lanier, *You Are Not A Gadget*, ix–x.

Lock-in, Lanier writes, "removes design options based on what is easiest to program, what is politically feasible, what is fashionable, or what is created by chance."[22] Or, I'd add, what is profitable. These programs can, therefore, reduce people not only to things but to dollars—specifically, to the number of clicks that can raise or lower a website's advertising value—which is one of several ways they may undermine our autonomy and humanity by turning us into tools of themselves, for their own expansion and profit. Therefore, in engineering our behavior, these engineered devices may engineer our selves, in ways we might not see.

For example, think about files. I have always considered files on my Windows desktop to be basic to computers' natures, as paper files in cabinets are an ordinary part of work life. Yet early incarnations of the World Wide Web and even "the first iteration of the Macintosh, which never shipped, didn't have files," Lanier writes. "Instead, the whole of a user's productivity accumulated in one big structure, sort of like a singular personal web page."[23] You can see how this would be quite a change from files as we conceive of them, but it's also kind of hard to see that, since "the idea of the file has become so big that we are unable to conceive of a frame large enough to fit around it in order to assess it empirically."[24] (Remember, again, the young fish asking, "What's water?") The file is, Lanier writes, "a set of philosophical ideas made into eternal flesh," namely "the notion that human expression comes in severable chunks that can be organized as leaves on an abstract tree—and that the chunks have versions and need to be matched to compatible applications."[25]

Yet matching human experience to "compatible applications" risks shaping experience itself around software, even when the two would seem to be antithetical; our selves become modeled on our machines until it's hard to tell what's shaping who, and why. Consider the iPhone app Headspace, designed by Buddhist monk Andy Puddicombe, which guides users through meditation techniques and has been "downloaded by three million users" since its introduction in 2012.[26] Indeed, as *The New Yorker* reports, "a new class of app has emerged on iPhone screens, promising to relieve the mental afflictions—stress, distraction—that have been exacerbated by its neighbors."[27] Surely, anything that helps people become more mindful

22. Ibid., 10.
23. Ibid., 13.
24. Ibid.
25. Ibid., 13.
26. Widdicombe, "The Higher Life," 40.
27. Ibid., 42.

must be good, right? Yet as a longtime yoga practitioner, I can't help observing that what mindfulness traditions really ask is for people to inculcate a discipline within *themselves*, releasing their reliance on external systems of habit and reward over time. A smartphone app designed to calm a distracted, smartphone-centered life strengthens the very cycle of bondage it's supposed to break. And apps' commercial nature is another reason to be wary: if someone else is designing and selling your spiritual experience (and your personal data) for profit, how spiritual is it? One venture capitalist decided not to invest in Headspace because, although a real-live Buddhist monk at the helm is "authentic" and "true to brand," he says, "at the end of the day, we want to create the biggest company around this concept without being shackled by [Puddicombe's] Buddhist-monk tendencies."[28] In other words, too much Buddhism is bad for business—meaning that a Buddhist meditation app is an inherent contradiction in terms if business, not Buddhism, is doing the driving.

Similarly, as novelist Zadie Smith points out, Facebook shapes our social selves around an "interface with reality" that "was designed by a Harvard sophomore with a Harvard sophomore's preoccupations."[29] As it purports to connect us with friends, it also flattens those relationships into something somehow less significant than friendship, narrowing the emotional range of connection between users and shaping our interactions into predetermined categories in predetermined ways (like the drop-down menu for "relationship status.") Smith posits that the format of Facebook can subtly reduce a person to her string of posted photos, comments, and "likes," even in the minds of her "friends:"

> I have noticed—and been ashamed of noticing—that when a teenager is murdered, at least in Britain, her Facebook wall will fill with messages that seem to not quite comprehend the gravity of what has occurred. You know the type of thing: *Sorry babes! Missin' you! Hopin' u iz with the Angles. I remember the jokes we used to have LOL! PEACE XXXXX*
>
> When I read something like that, I have a little argument with myself: "It's only poor education. They feel the same way as anyone would, they just don't have the language to express it." But another part of me has a darker, more frightening thought. Do they genuinely believe, because the girl's wall is still up, that she is still, in some sense, alive? What's the difference, after all, if all your contact was virtual?[30]

28. Ibid., p. 47.

29. Smith, "Generation Why?"

30. Ibid.

The medium has degraded both the language and the relationship in which it's expressed, as media can do. "Lock-in removes ideas that do not fit into the winning digital representation scheme," Lanier writes, "but it also reduces or narrows the ideas it immortalizes, by cutting away the unfathomable penumbra of meaning that distinguishes a word in natural language from a command in a computer program."[31] *Penumbra of meaning* is an important phrase, signifying a cloud of personal and cultural association that arises within a human mind but can never be replicated by a computer, or, even, by another human. Reducing that "penumbra," its own type of inner plenitude, is a danger of Internet communication that goes beyond simplistic sentences or text language creeping into emails. Where language is compromised or limited by someone else's decisions about what and how we may speak, our thinking about personhood may be compromised too.

Let me return to Hannah Arendt to explain why stripping away meaning and complexity—especially in language—can reduce a human self. In *The Origins of Totalitarianism* (1951), Arendt wrote that totalitarian political states like Nazi Germany are based on the belief that "all is possible" or "everything is permitted," particularly when people who see themselves as the best and brightest use technology and engineering to overcome human limitation and approach the realm of pure logic and perfection. *Pure* is an important word here. For Arendt as for us, Nazi Germany was the model totalitarian state, engineering the deaths of more than six million members of its Jewish population in an effort it referred to as "the final solution." (Notice: *solution*. Which implies *problem*. Which implies a need for, and invites the creation of, a special class of engineers to process and solve that "problem:" if you have a hammer, the whole world looks like a nail.) "[Totalitarian leaders'] faith in human omnipotence," Arendt writes, "their conviction that everything can be done through organization, carries them into experiments which human imaginations may have outlined but human activity certainly never realized."[32]

The Nazis' most notorious such experiment, the concentration camps, "serve[d] as the laboratories in which the fundamental belief of totalitarianism that everything is possible is being verified."[33] The ultimate products of Nazi death camps were corpses, living and dead.[34] A category of prisoner called, by other prisoners (and survivors) *der muselmann*—the walking

31. Lanier, *You Are Not A Gadget*, 10.

32. Arendt, *The Origins of Totalitarianism*, 436.

33. Ibid., 437.

34. My knowledge of *der muselmann* and my initial contact with Arendt's work came to me from conversations and presentations by philosopher Lissa Skitolsky, to whom I'm grateful. See Skitolsky, "Tracing Theory."

dead—arose in the camps, recognizable by an utter lack of human affect. Other prisoners usually avoided them, meaning that they basically became human-shaped shells, maintained upright by the pressure of nothingness pressing out from within and a lack of community pressing upon them from outside. Nazis had demonstrated their total control by engineering a non-person which still retained at least something of the form of a person, amid the group of other people who feared slipping into such a state themselves. They sought to strip away every aspect of humanity other than the barest literal ones—breath, heartbeat, the ability to feel pain and to work—in order to demonstrate to others and themselves that their power to engineer toward perfection knew no limits, human or otherwise.

Therefore, the assault of the Nazi camps was not only against the body but against the essence of a unique, dignified human self that experiences itself *as* unique and dignified—the real object of attack in a totalitarian state. "Total domination," Arendt writes,

> which strives to organize the infinite plurality and differentiation of human beings as if all of humanity were just one individual, is possible only if each and every person can be reduced to a never-changing identity of reactions, so that each of these bundles of reactions can be exchanged at random for any other. The problem is to fabricate something that does not exist, namely, a kind of human species resembling other animal species whose only 'freedom' would consist in 'preserving the species.'[35]

Human emotion means uniqueness, variety, irreducible complexity and individuality, "penumbras of meaning" (as Jaron Lanier writes) and memory—everything that makes me *me* and no one else. All of these markers of a self are intolerable to the totalitarian state. Therefore, it seeks to engineer them out of existence so that it can experience itself as all-powerful and unthreatened by any resistance (internal or external) from its victims, who have lost all will of their own. These victims become hollow, interchangeable bundles of twitch reflexes, empty vessels stimulated to obey the will of the state by any message it chooses to broadcast. "The camps are meant not only to exterminate people and degrade human beings," Arendt continues,

> but also serve the ghastly experiment of eliminating, under scientifically controlled conditions, spontaneity itself as an expression of human behavior and of transforming the human personality into a mere thing, into something that even animals are not; for Pavlov's dog, which, as we know, was trained

35. Arendt, *The Origins of Totalitarianism*, 438.

to eat not when it was hungry but when a bell rang, was a per-verted animal.[36]

Of course, this "experiment" needs a controlled environment—the camps, which were sealed away as tightly as possible from anything that could remind guards or inmates of the outside world, or of any reality other than the one the Nazis sought to create. (One survivor referred at Eichmann's trial to "the planet of Auschwitz" for this reason.) [37] "Just as the stability of the totalitarian regime depends on the isolation of the fictitious world of the movement from the outside world," Arendt writes,

> so the experiment of total domination in the concentration camps depends on sealing off the latter against the world of all others, the world of the living in general, even against the outside world of a country under totalitarian rule. This isola-tion explains the peculiar unreality and lack of credibility that characterize all reports from the concentration camps and con-stitute one of the main difficulties for the true understanding of totalitarian domination, which stands or falls with the existence of these concentration and extermination camps: for, unlikely as it may sound, these camps are the true central institution of totalitarian organizational power.[38]

Therefore, we can see that an essential marker of totalitarianism, for Arendt, is not just denial of "freedom" but denial of some indefinable, fine-grained and uniquely textured thing called humanity. The totalitarian state tries to reduce humanity further by depriving its subjects of any other social reality with which to compare their current condition, sealing off its own territory in a bubble of ignorance, memory-less-ness, lack of connection to people and to a specific place, and fear. In the words of Arendt's student and biographer Elisabeth Young-Bruehl, the crimes of the Nazis

> involved denying human plurality, which in legal terms did not mean denying human beings any specific rights but denying them the right to have rights. From Arendt's point of view, a crime against humanity is one that assaults the right to belong to a human community: the right not to be reduced to a mass, not to be made superfluous, not to be stateless and rightless. It is the right to be remembered truthfully in stories told about human beings by plural human beings, not to be erased from history. 'Crimes against humanity' might be defined in Arendtian terms

36. Ibid.

37. Lipstadt, *The Eichmann Trial*, 160.

38. Arendt, *The Origins of Totalitarianism*, 438.

as crimes against human plurality, and to judge them as such
one needs to prove not a motive to genocide but only a motive to
deny plurality, for example, by making a group stateless.[39]

Reducing a group of people or an individual to something less than
human and entirely subordinate to the state itself—through removal of
lands, transgression of physical or psychological integrity (including memories and the artifacts that embody them) or the production of corpses in
death camps, in the name of some larger ideology—is the essential goal of
totalitarianism.[40] Fundamentally, its logic always focuses on the reduction
of the many to the one, and then on giving that one total control, with no
sense of moral obligation to anything but itself.

Like Arendt, the English writer George Orwell (1903–1950), born
Eric Blair, draws on his personal experiences of mid-twentieth-century
totalitarianism to describe how deeply it threatens humanity, in ways
which still speak to us now. Tall and gangly but scrappy, he went to fight
the Fascists in Spain after having been a colonial administrator in Burma,
a waiter in a grand Paris hotel, and a tramp back home in England (all of
which he wrote about.) His groundbreaking novel *Nineteen Eighty-Four*
(1949) describes life in a dystopian once-English state called Ingsoc, where
a shadowy government nicknamed "Big Brother" employs terror to keep
its population compliant, distort individual and collective memories, and
stigmatize "thoughtcrime" as the worst offense a citizen can commit. The
novel's protagonist, Winston Smith, works for the state propaganda apparatus (the "Ministry of Truth"), destroying or altering newspapers and
history books to reflect whatever version of the past suits the state's political purposes that day; any physical evidence to the contrary is dropped
down the "memory hole" into waiting furnaces.[41] Yet when Winston rebels,

39. Young-Bruehl, *Why Arendt Matters,* 59.

40. See the United Nations Universal Declaration of Human Rights: http://www.
un.org/en/documents/udhr/.

41. Almost twenty years after the publication of *Nineteen Eighty-Four,* Arendt engages the idea of the "memory hole," albeit without naming Orwell, in *Eichmann in Jerusalem:* "It is true that totalitarian domination tried to establish these holes of oblivion
into which all deeds, good and evil, would disappear, but just as the Nazis' feverish
attempts, from June, 1942, on, to erase all traces of the massacres—through cremation,
through burning in open pits, through the use of explosives and flame–throwers and
bone–crushing machinery— were doomed to failure, so all efforts to let their opponents 'disappear in silent anonymity' were in vain. The holes of oblivion do not exist.
Nothing human is that perfect, and there are simply too many people in the world to
make oblivion possible. One man will always be left alive to tell the story." Perhaps this
is a version of the subtle hope Orwell himself offers us: "The Principles of Newspeak,"
which ends *Nineteen Eighty-Four,* is a historical document, told in past tense, a device

first by keeping a diary (on paper, with pen), then by falling in love with a girl named Julia, the state acts quickly to torture him into submission, crushing not just his body but the independent self it contains. O'Brien, Winston's torturer, doesn't stop inflicting pain until Winston has reached a point where he's no longer able to assert any truth but the one Big Brother wants him to repeat, even if that "truth" is manipulated to contradict itself, and literal reality, from moment to moment. "The Party is not interested in the overt act," O'Brien says, "the thought is all we care about. We do not merely destroy our enemies; we change them . . . . It is intolerable that an erroneous thought should exist anywhere in the world, however secret and powerless it may be."[42] O'Brien promises Winston that, like *der muselmann*, "You will be hollow. We shall squeeze you empty, and then we shall fill you with ourselves."[43] To a totalitarian system, an individual's privacy—a space occupied by the self rather than the state—is antithetical, and intolerable.

Orwell anticipates Arendt in stating that to the true dictatorship, its own power is its whole reason for being, controlling the minds and perceptions of its citizens and viewing the individual self as—in O'Brien's words, "a flaw in the pattern . . . a stain that must be wiped out."[44] "The Party seeks power for its own sake," O'Brien tells Winston:

> We are different from all the oligarchies of the past in that we know what we are doing. All the others, even those who re-sembled ourselves, were cowards and hypocrites. The German Nazis and the Russian Communists came very close to us in their methods, but they never had the courage to recognize their own motives. They pretended, perhaps they even believed, that they had seized power unwillingly and for a limited time, and that just round the corner there lay a paradise where human beings would be free and equal. We are not like that. We know that no one ever seizes power with the intention of relinquishing it. Power is not a means; it is an end. One does not establish a dictatorship in order to safeguard a revolution; one makes the revolution in order to establish the dictatorship. The object of

---

echoed by Margaret Atwood (who has often acknowledged her fondness for *Nineteen Eighty-Four*) in her own groundbreaking dystopia *The Handmaid's Tale* (1985.) See Arendt, *Eichmann*, 232–233. And despite its very real potential for abuse and misin-formation, the inherent multiplicity and accessibility of the Internet (especially social media) does offer a vital counterweight to any Big Brother-ish governmental pressure toward oblivion and falsehood.

42. Orwell, *Nineteen Eighty-Four*, 261–263.

43. Ibid., 265.

44. Ibid., 263.

persecution is persecution. The object of torture is torture. The object of power is power. Now do you begin to understand me?[45]

The ultimate aim is not power for the sake of improving life in the state—it's power *itself*, total domination, the closed and unified circle of unchallenged, state-focused, state-controlled "perfection" as the state itself dreams of it. O'Brien promises Winston as the torture begins that "I shall save you, I shall make you perfect."[46] As Jaron Lanier writes, "No matter how petty a flaw might be in a utopia, that flaw is where the full fury of power seeking will be focused."[47] And that power is assisted by technology, which helps the state nose out any individualistic spark that threatens its domination: "With the development of television," says the imaginary history of Ingsoc within *Nineteen Eighty-Four*,

> and the technical advance which made it possible to receive and transmit simultaneously on the same instrument, private life came to an end. Every citizen, or at least every citizen important enough to be worth watching, could be kept for twenty-four hours a day under the eyes of the police and in the sound of official propaganda, with all other channels of communication closed. The possibility of enforcing not only complete obedience to the will of the State, but complete uniformity of opinion on all subjects, now existed for the first time.[48]

Although technology that enables constant surveillance—an uncomfortably live issue in our own age of NSA spying revelations and "big data"—is the tool of external domination, language is the internal one. Language is the thin edge of the wedge the Party inserts into the lives—and minds—of Ingsoc citizens to begin to achieve this goal of total power for its own sake, because language is the means by which we constantly create, reinforce, and live according to the collection of individualized perceptions of reality and memory we might call a self. If we can't call something by its proper name, can we know it? If we don't have the right word for a thing, might the thing itself someday disappear? In Ingsoc's nightmare world, language is willfully divorced from and used to distort people's ability to understand reality, thereby bringing their thoughts—which are both expressed in and shaped by language—under control as well. In Ingsoc's official language, Newspeak, multiple words are compressed into one, which eventually functions as verb

45. Ibid., 272.
46. Ibid., 251.
47. Lanier, *Who Owns the Future?*, 18.
48. Orwell, *Nineteen Eighty-Four*, 211.

and noun and is inflected in different ways by suffixes as needed—"good," "ungood," or "doubleplusgood." Newspeak always pressures language toward a simplistic uniformity that, because it can't express shades of meaning, helps to erase them and "to impose a desirable mental attitude upon the person using [the words.]" "[T]he special function of certain Newspeak words," Orwell writes in the fictional appendix to *Nineteen Eighty-Four*,

> [. . .] was not so much to express meanings as to destroy them. These words, necessarily few in number, had had their meanings extended until they contained themselves whole batteries of words which, as they were sufficiently covered by a single comprehensive term, could now be scrapped and forgotten. The greatest difficulty facing the compilers of the Newspeak dictionary was not to invent new words, but, having invented them, to make sure what they meant: to make sure, that is to say, what ranges of words they canceled by their existence.[49]

For the potential thought-criminal, "there would be many crimes and errors which it would be beyond his power to commit, simply because they were nameless and therefore unimaginable."[50] Therefore, totalitarianism attacks its ultimate adversary—the private, independent self—by chipping away at the "penumbras of meaning," in Lanier's term, it attaches to quintessentially human, unmonetizable, and irreducibly complex things like language, memory, and, yes, privacy. By attacking memory and language, it "locks in" the selves of future Ingsoc citizens to its own mold, making concepts like *freedom* impossible for those people to formulate because the culture has literally left them no words in which to do it.

Philosophy is made to think through our everyday lives with, to bear witness to outrage and injustice, to judge our own actions and motivations and to try to do better. And while historical Nazism, fueled by anti-Semitism, is a horror comparable only to itself, philosophical analysis of the logic of totalitarianism can help us identify threats to humanity we still face—particularly those threats that still arise in political and social systems because they arise first in human hearts. Restless, anxious times, as the twentieth and twenty-first centuries have certainly been, may exacerbate them: as Arendt said in a 1974 interview, "Totalitarianism appeals to the very dangerous emotional needs of people who live in complete isolation and in fear of one another."[51] To help name our fears, though, we must look to our own histories, to the art we've made, and to how the two reflect

49. Ibid., 315.
50. Ibid., 321.
51. Arendt, "Hannah Arendt: From An Interview."

each other. Look at what we're still afraid of—Big Brother, the overlord, the individuality crusher—even as, following Arendt's analysis, something in our anxious, fearful brains, huddled at home with our screens, might secretly long for it. (*Crush the dimly imagined enemy; remove my burden of self-awareness and choice; pass the popcorn!*) Look at our fascination with dystopia: over and over, novels and films summon the plots and visual styles of dictatorship and surveillance, as lived by real sufferers and imagined by Orwell, to strike in us a chord of anti-humanistic, technology-driven dread. Therefore, it's worth some effort to look more closely at what still gives that threat its force in our imaginations and in our lives.[52]

When I first used Arendt's and Orwell's visions of totalitarianism to scrutinize the world, past and present, I wondered if that sinister urge toward total domination and control might be one manifestation of a much wider and more insidious human tendency: the low voice always snarling inside our skulls, *I'll get what I want, regardless of you.* This is a view of existence that's black-or-white, winner-or-loser, based on dominance rather than accommodation and co-existence. *Greed* is one way of naming it; so is *ego*; so are *lack of humility* and *refusal to acknowledge limitation.* This paradigm is selfish rather than generous, reactive rather than reflective,

---

52. Think of—just for starters, and not already mentioned elsewhere in this book—Philip K. Dick's *The Man in the High Castle* (1962, which became a miniseries in 2015), "Minority Report" (1956, which became a film in 2002), and *Do Androids Dream of Electric Sheep?* (1968, which became the film *Blade Runner* in 1982); Suzanne Collins's *The Hunger Games* series (2008–2010); Veronica Roth's *Divergent* series (2011–2013); and the *Matrix* films (1999–2003). Dystopia also has a post-apocalyptic, ecologically oriented strain visible in Russell Hoban's *Riddley Walker* (1980), pretty much anything by J. G. Ballard (1930–2009), Sarah Hall's *Daughters of the North* (2007), Margaret Atwood's MaddAddam trilogy (2003–2013), Benjamin Percy's *Red Moon* (2013) and *The Dead Lands* (2015), Jeff Vandermeer's Southern Reach trilogy (2014), and the durable Mad Max (1979–2015) and Terminator (1984–2015) film franchises. "The Manchurian Candidate" (1962) extends dystopia toward fear of another human system—government. (Shades of that fear also flicker through 1957's *A Face In The Crowd* and the Netflix series *House of Cards*, 2013–present.) Capitalism and consumerism are objects of dystopian satire in the short stories of George Saunders, most recently in *Tenth of December* (2013), and in Kurt Vonnegut's first novel, *Player Piano* (1952). Two dystopic novels about American slavery—Colson Whitehead's National Book Award-winning *The Underground Railroad* (2016) and Ben Winters's *Underground Airlines* (2016)—arose amid fresh engagement with its legacies in the Black Lives Matter movement, amid multiple incidents of police violence against African Americans. Both were preceded by the groundbreaking African American science-fiction writer Octavia Butler's *Kindred* (1979), in which a modern black woman is transported back in time and forced into slavery. Like M. T. Anderson's *Feed* (2002), Gary Shteyngart's *Super Sad True Love Story* (2010), Ernest Cline's *Ready Player One* (2011), Marisha Pessl's *Night Film* (2013), and Benjamin Percy's *The Dark Net* (2017) engage the dystopian possibilities of virtual reality and the Internet.

and overtly aggressive rather than reasonably self-protective. It's blind to beauty and mystery: it shoots elephants to mount on its walls and hoards stolen Renaissance art in storage vaults.[53] It stalked the killing fields of Cambodia and Rwanda and Armenia and Bosnia. It may give lip service to charity, but the only real "value" it acknowledges is money and power. Its actions are sources of enduring shame for individuals and societies. It's all over human history up to this very moment as a kinship link among slavery, rape, genocide, war, religious terrorism and persecution, abuse, environmental plunder, narcissism, financial usury, dictatorships, or any other action or way of being that says in its heart *For my own ravenous self to flourish, yours must disappear.*

This is certainly where the problem begins, but not where it ends. I thought I'd identified the problem as basic human greed—maybe *original sin,* in certain old-school Christian circles—until I thought a little more. Now I think the real common thread in the totalitarian threats identified by Arendt and Orwell in the twentieth century and the interlinked problems we face right now—including war, poverty, political corruption, and climate change, all of which are exacerbated by the relentless profit motives of global capitalism and deepened by technology—is our human tendency to surrender control of and responsibility for our actions and environments to systems of our own making, while allowing ourselves to believe those systems are somehow inevitable, or operating according to laws as inviolate as those of nature itself. We build it and then act powerless before it, as if *it* made *us*—perhaps because, over time, it *can* remake us, as we've seen with Lanier's analysis of computer software. But humans do not behave well when we give our selves and our consciences over to social, political, technological, or economic structures we've made and, treating those systems and their consequences as "natural" or "inevitable," let them do our thinking for us, or, at worst, excuse our thoughtlessness and greed. ("It's just the price of progress." Define your terms: what's *progress,* and for whom?)

Human greed is the blood at this particular root, perhaps, but human *thoughtlessness,* as named by Arendt, makes it blossom.[54] Eichmann and his colleagues developed several ways—including linguistic ones, as we'll see in Chapter 3—to convince themselves and others they were only doing their jobs, following an apparently inevitable path toward their state's version of perfection. Their case studies can be a warning for the rest of us, and history can provide a corrective to the thoughtless temptations of the systems we de-

53. See Edsel, *Saving Italy.*

54. Yes, this is an echo of the anti-lynching song "Strange Fruit," first written by Lewis Allen (Abel Meeropol) in 1937 and memorably recorded by Billie Holiday, among others. See Blair, "The Strange Story of the Man Behind 'Strange Fruit.'"

sign to achieve our similar visions—our fantasies of all desires frictionlessly fulfilled, all unity achieved, a series of castles built on sinking sand. It may be true that, as James Joyce writes in *Ulysses* (1922), "history is a nightmare from which I am trying to awake,"[55] yet history also keeps awakening *us* to our own worst tendencies, and to the need to stay responsible for correcting them, chastening us by returning us to continual awareness of the worst of which we're capable. If we write off *you* as less than *me*, if we accelerate the pace of our invention and engineering and steamroll over whatever (or whoever) gets in our way, if we mock those who object to us as naïve tree-huggers and bleeding-hearts (or, ahem, Luddites, of whom more later), then we ignore the real costs of our endeavors and their dangerous spiral out of our conscious control by persuading ourselves their processes are normal, inevitable, with nothing, really, to do with *us*.

Its consistent presence in dystopic novels and films over the last seventy-five years, from *Soylent Green* (1973) to *Wall-E* (2008), is one of several clues that global capitalism, as assisted by the technological corporations which both belong to and drive it, is showing more than a few signs of being such a dominating force—sometimes with but sometimes without conscious human intent to do wrong. "This is the moral puzzle of Siren Servers," Jaron Lanier writes in *Who Owns the Future?* (2013). "In the network age there can be collusion without colluders, conspiracies without conspirators."[56] (As Arendt writes, thoughtlessness is not always a conscious state—especially when humans within an organization can tell themselves that they are not really responsible for what it does.)[57] The twenty-first century alone abounds in real-world examples: the financial-market, mortgage-bubble crises that evaporated ordinary people's home values,[58] Big Oil-driven catastrophes like the Deepwater Horizon spill, the industrial climate alteration on one side of the world that creates climate refugees on the other. And these large forces are driving other, destructive ones: a 2012 report from the World Economic Forum identified "severe income disparity," "rising greenhouse gas emissions," "water supply crises," and "unsustainable population growth" among

55. Joyce, *Ulysses,* 28.

56. Lanier, *Who Owns the Future?,* 72.

57. "I know many of the people who run the biggest, richest servers," Jaron Lanier writes, "where the money and power are being concentrated. They're remarkably decent, for the most part. You couldn't ask for nicer people. But that doesn't really help. Iconic online empires have been accepted as sacrosanct. It's okay to notice in the abstract that free online services aren't creating as many jobs as they destroy, but we still hold up these newfangled companies as examples of how innovation will drive the economy." See *Who Owns the Future?,* 60.

58. See the film *Inside Job* (dir. Charles Ferguson, 2010).

significant global risks in five categories.[59] According to a 2017 briefing paper from the international charity Oxfam, "[s]ince 2015, the richest one percent has owned more wealth than the rest of the planet" and "eight men now own the same amount of wealth as the poorest half of the world."[60] Such titanically concentrated amounts of money and power—which automation, as we'll see, is concentrating even further—can accelerate the effects of actions and reactions in our interdependent world.

But perhaps it's not our systems *alone* we fear—perhaps it's the way that unless we keep ourselves morally engaged and responsible, those systems can evade conscious control and take us farther than we ever meant to go. "We don't know the future," Arendt observed, "but everybody acts into the future."[61] Similarly, political scientist Patchen Markell describes "action's tendency to outrun or exceed the ends through which we attempt to govern it, whether those ends are grounded in identity, choice, or both. Tragedy teaches us that such impropriety is a constitutive feature of human action, not a contingent affliction: the very conditions that make us potent agents— our materiality, which ties us to the causal order of the world, our plurality, which makes it possible for our acts to be meaningful—also make us potent beyond our own control."[62] Just as a runner can't immediately switch from top speed to a halt but must "wind down," propelled by her own momentum past the finish line, human action can acquire a cumulative force of its own that carries it, and its results, beyond what individual humans may have intended. (Think of all those robots-take-over dystopias, of which more shortly.) Climate, again, provides a specific example. In 2008, NASA climate scientist James Hansen and his colleagues famously wrote that "If humanity wishes to preserve a planet similar to that on which civilization developed and to which life on Earth is adapted, paleoclimate evidence and ongoing climate change suggest that CO_2 will need to be reduced from its [then-]current 385 ppm to at most 350 ppm."[63] Yet even if we are to stop all emissions tomorrow, the momentum of the changes created by what we've *already* emitted would carry us past that stopping-point number. In 2016, we reached 400 parts per million and are still adding more, and climbing, which heightens the need for us to rein in the forces of human activity to shorten the horizon for the future long-term damage they will create. Yet the

59. World Economic Forum, "Insight Report," 4–5.

60. Oxfam America, "An Economy for the 99 Percent," 2.

61. Arendt, "Hannah Arendt: From An Interview."

62. Markell, "Tragic Recognition," 9.

63. Hansen et. al., "Target Atmospheric CO_2: Where should humanity aim?," 217. That preferred maximum number of 350 lent its name to the climate organization 350. org, founded in 2008.

size and power of some of those forces, such as global capitalism, heighten both the degree and extent of the damage they can cause.

As the writer, farmer, and activist Wendell Berry has written, complexes of big business feed on a moral fallacy—delusions of limitlessness—to devour everything in their path: "the commonly accepted basis of our economy," he writes, "is the supposed possibility of limitless growth, limitless wants, limitless wealth, limitless natural resources, limitless energy, and limitless debt," which "implies and requires a doctrine of general human limitlessness: *all* are entitled to pursue without limit whatever they conceive as desirable."[64] Any small business feeling the pinch from a nearby Walmart knows the reality I'm invoking here. In families, ecosystems, functioning governments and local economies, and relationships, we work together to help each other live and thrive, applying checks and balances to ensure the sustainability of the system as needed, because the health of the whole system, and therefore our own health, depends on it. But too many corporations refuse, in the name of wealth accumulation and value for shareholders, to accommodate themselves to anyone's needs but their own and insist, disingenuously, that the so-called laws of business, viewed as entirely separate from human choices and actions, demand it. Through their political and economic influence, they exert a disproportionate power to alter the world that all the rest of us have to live in—including long-term problems of environmental degradation, social inequality, and injustice. And in the face of climate change, too many of them just double down and keep right on going. Economist E. F. Schumacher observed as early as 1973 that "the modern industrial system, with all its intellectual sophistication, consumes the very basis on which it has been erected," since its overuse of the "irreplaceable capital which it cheerfully treats as income"—namely, "fossil fuels, the tolerance margins of nature, and the human substance"—will not prove sustainable.[65] "To define perpetual growth on a finite planet as the sole measure of economic well-being," anthropologist Wade Davis writes, "is to engage in a form of slow collective suicide."[66] Yet such "collective suicide" is still driven by what Naomi Klein describes as a "dominance-based worldview" that "provides" big business "with the intellectual tools to write off huge swaths of humanity, and indeed, to rationalize profiting from the meltdown."[67] And looking at increasing trends in automation provides a way to see this process at work.

64. Berry, "Faustian Economics," 36.

65. Schumacher, *Small Is Beautiful*, 21.

66. Davis, *The Wayfinders*, 217.

67. Klein, *This Changes Everything*, 48.

Most economists agree that in our society right now, we're seeing more and more small companies swallowed up by large ones and more and more wealth concentrated into fewer and fewer hands. This trend has particular relevance for technology companies, whose sphere of influence and control can swell while the number of humans on their payroll remains relatively small: "in 1964, the nation's most valuable company, AT&T, was worth $267 billion in today's dollars and employed 758,611 people," notes journalist Derek Thompson. "Today's telecommunications giant, Google, is worth $370 billion but has only about 55,000 employees—less than a tenth the size of AT&T's workforce in its heyday."[68] Large data-driven companies like online stores, mortgage finance companies, social networks, or anything that depends on aggregating and interpreting large amounts of data contributed by consumers (usually without their explicit knowledge, or any reimbursement) are particular offenders. Calling such companies "Siren Servers," Jaron Lanier writes that "the primary business of digital networking has come to be the creation of ultra-secret mega-dossiers about what others are doing, and using this information to concentrate money and power . . . . Whatever the intent may have been, the result is a wielding of digital technology against the future of the middle class."[69] In *Who Owns the Future?*, he describes this process:

> All Siren Servers deliver dual messages similar to the pair pioneered by Walmart. On the one hand, "Good news! Treats await! Information systems have made the world more efficient for you!"
> On the other hand, a little later: "It turns out you, your needs, and your expectations are not maximally efficient from the lofty point of view of our server. Therefore, we are reshaping the world so that in the long term, your prospects are being reduced."[70]

In short, he concludes, "the initial benefits don't remotely balance the long-term degradations," including (depending on the corporation you're looking at) degradations to the environment, to the rights of workers, to the economies of a town or a nation, or all three—or more. "Maybe you loved the supercheap prices at your favorite store," he writes, "but then noticed that the factory you might have worked for closed up for good."[71] While corporations (and the diminishing number of individuals they need to employ,

68. Thompson, "A World Without Work."
69. Lanier, *Who Owns the Future?*, 60.
70. Ibid., 73.
71. Ibid., 74.

and the even smaller number of super-rich individuals who run them) may be able to create what Lanier calls "persistent wealth" through the accumulation of capital and investments, the rest of us are living "real-time economic lives," paycheck to paycheck, if we have a paycheck at all—even though it's our labor, our taxes, and (in the case of tech corporations) our data, donated without pay as we use the Internet, that's making that wealth.[72] Therefore, the rich get richer as the poor get poorer—again. "In each case, someone is practically blackmailed by the distortions of playing the pawn in someone else's network," Lanier writes.

> It's a weird kind of stealth blackmail because if you look at what's in front of you, the deal looks sweet, but you don't see all that *should* be in front of you . . . . Great fortunes are being made on shrinking the economy instead of growing it. It's not a result of some evil scheme, but a side effect of an idiotic elevation of the fantasy that technology is getting smart and standing on its own, without people.[73]

And here's where theory meets the world, in a thought experiment it's urgent to conduct. The ultimate philosophical logic of computer and Internet technology—especially as it is disseminated and sold to us in the name of profit, and especially its claims that humanity can be "perfected" with just the right engineering tweaks—may have a quasi-totalitarian power to subject humanity to itself because it tempts us humans into thoughtlessness and holds us there in a variety of psychological and economic ways, despite the cost of our thoughtlessness to ourselves and the world. We must examine very, very closely technology's claims to improve the world by uniting all human thought and endeavor under its own banner, because that process concentrates all our human data, desires, entertainments, and job prospects into very few human hands. This opens up corresponding possibilities for dehumanization and abuse of power, usually without conscious evil intent but with considerable thoughtlessness. We can't fail to scrutinize what our drive toward engineering "progress" creates in our actual lives, or, as Hannah Arendt writes, we "will forever be unable to understand, that is, to think and speak about the things which nevertheless we are able to do."[74] And that would be disastrous, for our societies and our souls. Echoing this point, technology critic Siva Vaidhyanathan writes, "I hope we will all approach the future of human knowledge with wisdom and trepidation rather than

---

72. Ibid., 51.

73. Ibid., 61.

74. Arendt, *The Human Condition*, 3.

naïve, dazzled awe."[75] (If you've read *Nineteen Eighty-Four* or its cultural littermate, Aldous Huxley's 1932 novel *Brave New World,* you'll recognize "naïve, dazzled awe" as the condition to which the state tries to reduce its proletariat, and the condition to which any of us entering an Apple store might immediately fall prey.) To be clear: I don't have a problem with businesses turning a profit. But when they shift beyond providing reasonable services to us and a reasonable living for their employees into the sort of world-dominating drive that crushes everything in its path to achieve "market saturation"—and acknowledge no moral, financial, or ecological limits to their desires, even as their pursuit of their desires ruins others' opportunities to pursue their own—that's when they become a problem, because that's when they stop accommodating themselves to any reality other than that which they believe to be true, and to anyone's needs but their own. This is especially true when their highly engineered products and practices deepen our climate crisis and threaten the fragile human "penumbra of self," in Lanier's terms, which cannot and should not be monetized, collectivized, or fully known. We can't allow ourselves to forget that technology, engineering, and corporate capitalism are not forces of nature—they're human endeavors. And, as in any human endeavor, we humans must, in Arendt's landmark phrase, "think what we are doing" to keep ourselves and the institutions we run responsible to our own needs.[76]

Outsourcing our work to machines and the corporations that build and sell them may mean losing our own humanity, in more ways than one. At this moment, computers are replacing human workers in *every* field of work, not just in the assembly-line manufacturing trades on which it was once possible to build a middle-class American life. An increasingly automated world is pushing us now to ask what work is, why human beings need it, and who should get to decide, questions to which philosophers—not engineers or CEOs—must be our guides. No optimistic chirping about technology's "greater productivity" and "improved efficiency" can hide the fact that machines are making people vulnerable to a loss of employment, and therefore of personal meaning, as they unhook work from life. "What may be looming is something different," writes journalist Derek Thompson, "an era of technological unemployment, in which computer scientists and software engineers essentially invent us out of work, and the total number of jobs declines steadily and permanently."[77] As Martin Ford describes in *Rise of the Robots: Technology and the Threat of a Jobless Future* (2015), robots can

75. Vaidhyanathan, *The Googlization of Everything,* xiv.
76. Arendt, *The Human Condition,* 5.
77. Thompson, "A World Without Work."

not only flip and assemble hamburgers, or sort Amazon warehouse boxes for shipping—they can interpret radiology scans. A program named Quill can produce news stories in prose.[78] Researchers in the US and Japan are developing computerized camera systems that can track a chef's movements, analyze her tool use for "correctness," and even project a "virtual knife" onto a fish that can tell her where to cut.[79] Of course, the longtime vulnerability of so-called blue-collar jobs is only accelerating, if you'll pardon a grim pun; alongside Google's self-driving car, the Daimler Corporation has developed driverless semi trucks.[80] Who's the first person you think of as likely to be put out of work by self-driving semis? Probably working-class men, many of whom already experience a complex economic and social stagnation that a lack of opportunity will only deepen.[81] And they aren't alone. It's not only assembly-line workers and truck drivers who risk being stranded at the bottom of the economic ladder: it's all of us, in a world where, as Nobel Prize-winning economist Paul Krugman writes, "we could be looking at a society that grows ever richer, but in which all the gains in wealth accrue to whoever owns the robots."[82]

In the category of mechanized threats to real work, we can also put the labor markets sustained by the Internet, including peer-to-peer services like Airbnb, TaskRabbit, and Uber, flagships of the "sharing economy," which allow you to dial up an ostensibly independent peer to drive you somewhere in her own car, rent you a room in her own home, or perform a chore for which you don't have the inclination or time—cutting taxi drivers and hotel owners, just to name a couple, out of the picture. Such markets and applications, which skim off a fee for themselves with every chore, enshrine in the overall economy what writer Jacob Silverman calls "a kind of internalized

78. Ford, *Rise of the Robots*, 84–85.

79. Morozov, *To Save Everything, Click Here*, 11.

80. I heard this described on National Public Radio's news program "The Takeaway," June 25, 2015: http://www.thetakeaway.org/story/self-driving-trucks-are-real -and-theyre-road-now/.

81. See Hanna Rosin, "The End of Men"; Dionne Searcey, Eduardo Porter, and Robert Gebeloff, "Health Care Opens Stable Career Path, Taken Mainly by Women,"; and "Men Adrift" in *The Economist*. The *Economist's* unnamed writer observes, "The dead hand of male domination is a problem for women, for society as a whole—and for men like those of Tallulah [Louisiana, which is profiled as a test case.] Their ideas of the world and their place in it are shaped by old assumptions about the special role and status due to men in the workplace and in the family, but they live in circumstances where those assumptions no longer apply. And they lack the resources of training, of imagination and of opportunity to adapt to the new demands. As a result, they miss out on a lot, both in economic terms and in personal ones."

82. Carr, *The Glass Cage*, 33.

offshoring," in which "companies can focus on retaining and fairly compensating highly skilled (and highly sought after) employees, such as engineers, lawyers, programmers, doctors, and scientists" while less-skilled work can be "farmed out to low-wage freelance and temporary workers or subdivided into smaller and smaller units of work, which are then widely distributed through a cloud-based labor market."[83] Despite their cheerful, utopian rhetoric, these services not only create new kinds of labor inequalities but perpetuate social ones: Airbnb, for instance, has faced reports of discrimination against would-be guests, as collected by the Twitter hashtag #airbnbwhileblack.[84] And they also reinforce philosophically troubling divides between labor and leisure, skilled and unskilled work, and the people whose time is "worth" spending each way. (TaskRabbit's website promises, "We do chores. You live life.") In this, it's a new manifestation of a problem going back to ancient Greece: "Contempt for laboring," writes Hannah Arendt, "originally arising out of a passionate striving for freedom from necessity and a no less passionate impatience with every effort that left no trace, no monument, no great work worthy of remembrance, spread with the increasing demands of *polis* life upon the time of the citizens and its insistence on their abstention (*skholē*) from all but political activities, until it covered everything that demanded an effort."[85] It's also the thin edge of a troubling (and ironic) wedge: as automation threatens stable careers, too many people are driven into pieced-together, part-time lives of "work" at the will of the same corporations and cloud-based labor markets that profit from automation in multiple ways.

The digital equivalent of slaughterhouse kill-floor work has also persisted: being a content moderator for services like Google or Facebook. Often a low-wage worker in the developing world, the moderator sits in front of a screen to view and mark all content uploaded by users anywhere in the world, including every kind of grimly unseeable image you can imagine. One moderator told a journalist, "Think like that there is a sewer channel and all of the mess/dirt/waste/shit of the world flow towards you and you have to clean it."[86] The parallels with other flows of tech garbage between the First World and everyone else are too rich—and sad—to ignore. Consider the fate of the so-called obsolete smartphone or flat-screen TV, dumped on a trash barge and sent to a landfill overseas to be picked over by copper-seeking children, or the Chinese factory workers poisoned or driven to suicide by

83. Silverman, *Terms of Service,* 227–228.

84. See Penman, "#AirbnbWhileBlack."

85. Arendt, *The Human Condition,* 81.

86. Silverman, *Terms of Service,* 230.

their work assembling iPhones and iPads we discard as soon as the next one comes along. Consider the drowning Maldives, the scorching plains of Africa, the sufferers from our long years of First World energy consumption as climate change accelerates. Consider all the horrors that content moderator can never unsee. Let's not pretend our fun and convenience have no cost. Let's not pretend the "new tech economy" doesn't replicate—even exacerbate—the injustices of the old one. Because it does.

The rise of the robots, in Martin Ford's words, forces us all to ask: is an ostensibly human-controlled marketplace that values "efficiency" and "productivity" above every other human value still controlled by humans at all? When, exactly, did we humans agree to give up control of it? Even Adam Smith (1723–1790), the godfather of economics, was not so naïve as to pretend that the so-called laws of economics aren't created and driven by human choices and actions. (Look at his metaphors: even an "invisible hand" is still attached to a whole interdependent ecosystem of brain, body, and world.) Hannah Arendt, facing an increasingly automized mid-twentieth century, worried about what happens to modern people—encouraged by the market to define themselves *only* as workers and consumers, deprived of other sources of self-understanding—once work is gone. "What we are confronted with," she writes in *The Human Condition* (1958), "is the prospect of a society of laborers without labor, that is, without the only activity left to them. Surely, nothing could be worse."[87] How we can make the people developing and implementing technology that's edging human workers aside understand what human values are being lost when jobs are lost: the right to meaningful work, living wages, and feeling like a functioning contributor to society? And how can we hold *ourselves* to account, realizing that our peer-to-peer bookings on Airbnb and Uber, to name just one example, are among our tech-enabled consumer choices that put real people out of work?

As a society, we may think we can accommodate ourselves to the shuttering of hometown factories, the flood of anxious people into job-retraining programs and community colleges, or pieced-together lives of part-time gigs. Soon, we tell ourselves, everything will get resettled; everyone will be okay if we just work harder, like Boxer the Horse in Orwell's *Animal Farm* (1945). The almighty, all-seeing market will protect us! But in a robot-driven world that draws one hands-on task after another into the maw of automation, there is no safe place for these displaced humans—no matter how willing, diligent, and eager—to find work of dignity and meaning, much less reliable salaries and benefits. Nor is the forced leisure of unemployment an unmitigated boon to creativity, as some Silicon Valley entrepreneurs

87. Arendt, *The Human Condition*, 5.

have posited. Some such entrepreneurs have also proposed a guaranteed universal basic income to soothe technology-created joblessness, a paradox they face with no apparent irony (the government will pay for a problem that their own products help create and sustain, with the unemployed as the choice-deprived objects of both their "innovation" *and* their charity) and with what can at best be called naïveté: "I also think we cannot stop technological progress," one such entrepreneur has said, "and we should just figure out the way to include everybody in the benefits of it."[88] Others are hoping for a corresponding artisanal work resurgence with more time for one's craft, and lives pieced together from multiple small self-chosen jobs that aren't necessarily part of online peer-to-peer networks.[89] Yet in the face of loss of work on such a wide scale, these small-scale hopes feel a bit thin, and lonesome. As much as I believe in the value of such entrepreneurship, it grieves me to consider it as basically a last resort—a compensatory set of options if "efficiency"-seeking CEOs choose us out of real careers (with stable salaries and retirement plans) in advance, without our consent. And I worry about whether, in even twenty more years, those same corporations will have left us the literal *room* to work. Will we still have social, economic, and natural landscapes undistorted enough by pollution or financial chicanery to be still available for us to use? Obviously, I'm not opposed to a world of hands-on craftsmanship, small-business entrepreneurship, and creative piecing together of employment, vocation, and avocation. Far from it. But I *am* opposed to technology and corporate greed as the twin wheels that roll forward on a track called "progress," crushing our choices before we've even had a chance to understand the nature of the threat.

Economically and morally, that threat is deep. In an automated world, there is no work, in the deep sense of what we all need work to be: that thing that shapes our days, that trains our eyes and hands and brains, that makes us feel like actors in a larger network of social and economic relationships, that reassures us that we are contributing and we belong. As automation takes away available jobs and financial stability—and opportunities for them—it also takes the sense of our active, dignified human selves we acquire through work and agency in the world. Without a job, what are you? You're most likely depressed, thrust into a state of worried boredom, watching the good life spiraling out of reach as wealth is concentrated—with the help of the robots who now have your job and have released your CEO from even the minimal accountability he might have felt to you, a real person—into fewer and fewer hands. Economic terms will only get us so far: our real reasoning

88. Gardner, "How to Support Yourself."
89. Thompson, "A World Without Work."

must be a moral one, enabling us to say *enough*.[90] Pope Francis sees this, too: "these destructive realities are part of a system which has become global," he told an audience in Bolivia in July 2015. "Do we realize that that system has imposed the mentality of profit at any price, with no concern for social exclusion or the destruction of nature?"[91]

In this moral investigation, we can also be guided by artists—including the man who gave us the word "robot" in the first place. This was the Czech writer Karel Čapek (1890–1938), author of the play *R.U.R. (Rossum's Universal Robots)*, which premiered in Prague in 1921.[92] Čapek was also the first to introduce the word *robot* (from the Czech *robota*, or "labor," or *robotnik*, or "human laborer.") In *R.U.R.*, engineers grow human-looking robots from vats of organic materials[93] to free humans from the drudgery of labor and solve the "problem" of human workers' inefficiency: "the human machine," says one optimistic engineer, "was hopelessly imperfect. It needed to be done away with once and for all."[94] When the robots revolt after years of servitude, humans can't stop them because, enervated by their lives of leisure, they have lost the ability to reproduce—a plot twist echoed in later dystopias like P. D. James's *The Children of Men* (1992). The last human survivor, Alquist the craftsman, speaks eloquently of the value of work to humanity throughout the play: "You have no idea what good it does the hands to level bricks, to place them and to tamp them down . . . I think it's better to lay a single brick than to draw up plans that are too great."[95] Yet although he laughs at himself as "reactionary," only he retains enough intuition and dexterity to put his ideas into action. Left alone at the end of the world with two robots—male Primus and female Helena—and suspecting they have begun to evolve toward humanity, Alquist confirms his suspicions by offering to dissect Helena. Primus offers himself instead, demonstrating the robots have come to feel emotion and love. Echoing Luke 2:29 and Genesis, Alquist cries delightedly in the play's last lines, "O nature, nature, life will not perish! . . . It will begin anew with love; it will start out naked and tiny; it will take root in the wilderness, and to it all that

---

90. Thanks to Bill McKibben, who made this word a thought-provoking book title.

91. Francis, "Address."

92. Here I thank my colleague Andrew Hageman, Associate Professor of English at Luther, who introduced *R.U.R.* to our first-year Paideia course and has greatly assisted my thinking about dystopia, ecology, and technology.

93. This means that the robots look like the humans around them—and it also means that Čapek may have anticipated a form of "soft" robotics too. See Sklar, "Meet The World's First Completely Soft Robot."

94. Čapek, *R.U.R.*, 17.

95. Ibid., 34.

we did and built will mean nothing—our towns and factories, our art, our ideas will all mean nothing, and yet life will not perish!"[96]

Yet Čapek complicates this happy vision with the sinister robot Radius, leader of the antihuman insurrection. Programmed for maximum efficiency and constant work, just as the factory owners seeking savings on "imperfect" human labor intended, Radius is mortally offended by the frivolity and illogic of the humans he's sworn to exterminate, since in his world every activity and thought must bend to one great goal: "Work must not cease."[97] Even facing execution ("the stamping-mill"), Radius gives an uncomfortable and prescient warning about robot as master rather than servant: "I do not want a master, I know everything," he declares, "I want to be the master of people."[98]

Čapek had a particular way close at hand to think about the question of humanity and labor—a garden, which centers his warm, clear-sighted vision in the un-machinable mystery of biological life on earth. In his essay collection *The Gardener's Year* (1929), Čapek jokes about the way this simple hobby becomes a mania: "Let no one think that real gardening is a bucolic and meditative occupation," he declares. "It is an insatiable passion, like everything else to which a man gives his heart."[99] Yet gardening, which connects work, reward, and beauty, is also a way to think about the pleasure of labor and its results: "If one does a job," he writes, "one ought to do it because one likes it, or because one knows it, or finally because one has to live by it, but to sew boots on principle, work on principle, and for the virtue of it, means to do a job which is not worth much."[100] Close observation teaches good gardening, and good life: "You will know the soil as sour, tough, clayey, cold, stony, and rotten; you will recognize the mould puffy like pastry, warm, light, and good like bread, and you will say of this that it is beautiful, just as you say so of women or of clouds."[101] Ultimately, Čapek's garden widens his vision of life: "I tell you," he writes, "there is no death, not even sleep. We only pass from one season to another. We must be patient with life, for it is eternal."[102]

To read Čapek today is to be dazzled by his prescience. Six years before Fritz Lang's landmark film "Metropolis" (1927), with its beautiful, disturbing

96. Ibid., 84.

97. Ibid., 48.

98. Ibid., 37.

99. Čapek, "How A Man Becomes A Gardener," 7.

100. Čapek, "Holiday," 43.

101. Čapek, "The Soil," 87.

102. Čapek, "The Gardener's November," 104.

visions of cities in the sky and human becoming machine, and twenty to thirty years before Orwell and Arendt began to theorize the totalitarian state, this journalist and playwright with a front-row seat to two world wars was already thinking about how our drive toward "efficiency" and profit threatens our humanity.[103] "Perhaps the whole error of salvation," Čapek reflected in a 1922 essay, "lies in that we're used to saying 'to be saved' instead of 'to save ourselves.'"[104] We may be able to save ourselves, in the case of technology, by saying *enough*. And we can—even though the omnipresence and dominance of technology, from workplace email to the "fun" of apps and social media, may seem impossible to resist, or to say *enough* to.

What's the most ubiquitous technology corporation we might think of? Maybe it's Google, which runs my email, the banks of online documents I share with colleagues, my student-appointment scheduler, and an Internet search engine that tracks me and my potential consumer preferences, which flash up in ads alongside articles I read. Google has a map service. Google has "street view," which, depending how often its image feed is updated, can allow anyone to zoom in on a map of the earth and view what your house looks like right now. Google is developing a self-driving car. Google is trying to digitize every book ever published to make it available online. And on, and on. Eric Schmidt of Google shared its vision of the future as one "where you don't forget anything . . . . In this new future you're never lost . . . . We will know your position down to the foot and down to the inch over time . . . . Your car will drive itself, it's a bug that cars were invented before computers . . . . you're never lonely . . . you're never bored . . . you're never out of ideas."[105] What a great idea—we can all be passive, inert, and utterly controllable or findable, at any instant, by an invisible overlord, just like in *Nineteen Eighty-Four*! Maybe soon that overlord will even be able to re-engineer the flow of time, to fix the historical "bug" of its own late-in-the-game birth. (As Facebook once asked us to say, "sarcasm alert!")

We're used to thinking of corporations as making things, and technology as the secondary information service that assists them in that process, yet in the case of technology companies—or "Siren Servers"—information *itself* is the thing being made, controlled, and used to increase itself.[106] Cor-

---

103. Alongside *Metropolis*, we might put other beware-the-robots dystopic films like *2001: A Space Odyssey* (1968), *Blade Runner* (1982), and *Ex Machina* (2015), in which (spoiler alert!) robots are willing to kill humans to protect themselves. Perhaps they're cousins of the homicidal Plymouth Fury in Stephen King's horror novel *Christine* (1983).

104. Čapek, "Save Yourself If You Can," 256.

105. Silverman, *Terms of Service*, ix.

106. I'm indebted to *Who Owns the Future?* for this point.

porations get in between people in a relationship—that's their nature—and the layer of (often illusory and needless) complexity they add is what they point to (especially to shareholders) as "adding value," as giving themselves a reason to exist. Yet when technology companies insert themselves between us and the world, they capture information about us in the process and use it to make more money for themselves while slowly and steadily impoverishing us; as Jaron Lanier writes, if we were fairly paid for the use of our data and our other contributions to the "Siren Servers," we might not see the sort of economic inequality and withering away of "creative class" jobs that are accompanying the rise of technology now. "The Siren Servers," Lanier writes, "channel much of the productivity of ordinary people into an informal economy of barter and reputation, while concentrating the extracted old-fashioned wealth for themselves."[107] (Many writers, for instance, are asked to be content with "exposure" instead of payment for our work.) Ian Bogost, writer and game designer, has said, "We do tiny bits of work for Google, for Tumblr, for Twitter, all day and every day."[108] Google is one of many companies in which we can observe this process at work: its search rankings and the advertising dollars it gets from who clicks on what literally depend on us and our activities, after all. We create the value of the Internet by using it but don't get paid that money back.

Google's stated goal—"Don't be evil"—clashes with its goal of centering all the world's knowledge in Google itself, since engineering humans and our behavior toward a certain degree of "perfection" or "efficiency" as imagined by an overweening social entity does not respect human dignity. Although its mission statement contains optimistic "Ten Things We Know to Be True" statements—"Focus on the user and all else will follow," "Democracy on the web works," and "You can make money without doing evil"—its leaders, like other Silicon-Valley-ites, seem genuinely excited by the possibility of engineering away humanity itself.[109] Google cofounder Larry Page has said that "artificial intelligence would be the ultimate version of Google" and that "the ultimate search engine is something as smart as people—or smarter."[110] Cofounder Sergey Brin has remarked, "Certainly if you had all the world's information directly attached to your brain, or an artificial brain that was smarter than your brain, you'd be better off."[111] As Nicholas Carr writes, "their easy assumption that we'd all be

107. Ibid., 57.

108. Silverman, *Terms of Service*, 264.

109. http://www.google.com/about/company/philosophy/; accessed July 24, 2014.

110. Carr, *The Shallows*, 172.

111. Ibid.

'better off' if our brains were supplemented, or even replaced, by artificial intelligence is as unsettling as it is revealing," since "it underscores the firmness and the certainty with which Google holds to its Taylorist belief that intelligence is the output of a mechanical process, a series of discrete steps that can be isolated, measured, and optimized."[112] And Google's not alone. Another tech startup CEO has said, "I think we are going to see a new breed of intelligent life that looks not that much like the humans of 2016. That may be A.I., that may be cybernetically enhanced humans, that may be genome-edited humans that aren't humans at all."[113] Yet engineering humanity toward "perfection" means in many ways erasing it. "Imperfection, ambiguity, opacity, disorder, and the opportunity to err, to sin, to do the wrong thing," writes technology critic Evgeny Morozov, "all of these are constitutive of human freedom, and any concentrated attempt to root them out will root out that freedom as well."[114]

To Google, human intelligence is not only a series of discrete mechanizable particles but a flow of advertising dollars, since its mechanical processes aggregate and organize our behavior into a series of data points it can sell to corporations. "We are not Google's customers," Siva Vaidhyanathan writes, "we are its product. We—our fancies, fetishes, predilections, and preferences—are what Google sells to advertisers. When we use Google to find out things on the Web, Google uses our Web searches to find out things about us."[115] Yet Google is not only converting data from our searches to advertising dollars, it is flattening our responsiveness to search results and "locking in" our search behaviors to patterns that echo itself: "If Google is the dominant way we navigate the Internet, and thus the primary lens through which we experience both the local and the global, then it has remarkable power to set agendas and alter perceptions," Vaidhyanathan writes. "Its biases (valuing popularity over accuracy, established sites over new, and rough rankings over more fluid or multidimensional models of presentation) are built into its algorithms. And those biases affect how we value things, perceive things, and navigate the worlds of culture and ideas. In other words, we are folding the interface and structures of Google into our very perceptions."[116] A Google engineer who's developing the self-driving car in "Google X, the company's semi-secret lab for experimental technology," has said, "[Conventional automakers] want to make cars that

112. Ibid., 173.

113. Gardner, "How to Support Yourself."

114. Morozov, *To Save Everything*, xiv.

115. Vaidhyanathan, *Googlization*, 3.

116. Ibid., 7.

make drivers better. We want to make cars that are better than drivers."[117] Therefore, if Google, like any computer technology, can be seen as reshaping us in its own image—by redirecting our thoughts and assumptions and supplanting our attention to and control of daily processes (like driving) until capacities for that control atrophy without our noticing—it just may be accomplishing the Orwellian goal of inhabiting and hollowing us out, in ways that only seem small. Ultimately, such engineering seems on a path to replace what used to be us with what will be itself, leaving us as the upright human-shaped shell that, just like a smartphone, runs its software in order to function. And as the invention of robots and cool apps and "information systems" proceeds apace—diverting engineering attention from more enduring human problems—we need to ask whether our technology is really serving us or only serving corporations, and itself.[118]

Technology's efforts to bring all aspects of a user's experience under its own aegis, driven by an assumption that "efficiency" is the greatest possible good, is also distorting economic and social norms in the San Francisco Bay area, technology epicenter of the country. As early as 1995, British media scholars Richard Barbrook and Andy Cameron decried this solipsism in their stinging article "The Californian Ideology:" tech engineers, (or "disruptors," as they like to call themselves twenty years later) assume that "existing social, political, and legal power structures will wither away to be replaced by unfettered interactions between autonomous individuals and their software. These restyled McLuhanites vigorously argue that big government should stay off the backs of resourceful entrepreneurs who are the only people cool and courageous enough to take risks."[119] An increasing divide between tech workers and everyone else in the San Francisco Bay area has been much in the news in the current decade, with tech workers being perceived by many other citizens as arrogant, self-isolating, and entitled, driving up rents and driving out ordinary people.[120] "I have had

117. Bilger, "Auto Correct," 106.

118. This is perhaps the place to mention the meeting point of engineering and famine (especially in our climate-change-endangered world): GMOs, or genetically modified organisms, about which I, admittedly a First World resident and non-biologist, remain uncertain. First among my reasons to be cautious (as seen in the case of Monsanto, mentioned in Chapter 3) is that an engineered organism can become a proprietary one, protected by copyright and thus bound to the laws of corporate profit and political deal-making, not human betterment. Engineering is offering hope in other forms, though, such as "vertical farming" in cities. See Frazier, "High-Rise Greens."

119. Silverman, *Terms of Service*, 2–3.

120. A Facebook page, "Dispatches from Entitlementistan," keeps up a running commentary on the social absurdities and excesses of the young and, well, entitled in San Francisco.

more than one heated argument," Jaron Lanier writes, "with Silicon Valley libertarians who believe that streets should be privatized."[121] The "Google Buses," gleaming private buses with climate control, roaming Wi-Fi, and tinted windows to prevent outsiders seeing in, have become symbols of this divide: making regular rounds and stopping at municipal bus stops to pick up workers and ferry them to Silicon Valley, they have also become targets of protesters who block and even vomit on them. Yet as essayist Rebecca Solnit (a longtime San Francisco resident) writes, sealing themselves away in a bubble of privilege is an ironic move for tech workers: "All these young-ish people are on the Google Bus because they want to live in San Francisco, city of promenading and mingling," she writes, "but they seem as likely to rub these things out as to participate in them."[122] San Francisco resident Chris Tacy takes fellow tech entrepreneurs to task in a 2013 blog post titled "Douchebags Like You Are Ruining San Francisco:"

> Now it's worse than it was in 2000. Now it's only about the money. Now the only diversity we have left is ethnic diversity. Everyone is rich and privileged and entitled or hustling as hard as they can to become rich and privileged and entitled. A city once defined by people wanting to change the world is now de-fined by people who just want to be among the world's richest. A culture that once understood history and tried to create it now has a memory that's about two fiscal quarters long—and a vision that goes as far out as their funding allows.[123]

Young Silicon Valley entrepreneurs—despite their smiling faces and ostensible concern for "doing well by doing good"—often demonstrate considerable naïveté about the actual costs of the economic and tech-nological systems they view as "helping people:" "We now expect social entrepreneurs to solve problems that government used to solve," one San Francisco startup founder says.[124] The utopian "sharing economy" of Uber and Airbnb I discussed earlier attracts much unironic talk of "innovation" and "the will of the people" in the San Francisco area. "This cognitive dis-sonance might be cute," journalist Susie Cagle writes, "were it not backed by millions of dollars in capital investment and a steamroller approach to laws and regulations that protect workers and consumers."[125] An economy that connects like-minded (and privileged) people with one another and

121. Lanier, *Who Owns the Future?*, 80.

122. Solnit, "Diary."

123. Tacy, "Don't Be."

124. Heller, "Bay Watched," 79.

125. Cagle, "The Case Against Sharing."

encourages them to rent each other's couches and cars for "side jobs," Cagle argues, risks perpetuating economic inequalities and cutting professional innkeepers and taxi drivers (just to name a couple) right out of the economy altogether, not to mention exposing people to vandalism and assault. As Paul Dourish and Scott Mainwaring have written, "The overriding question, 'What might we build tomorrow?' blinds us to questions of our ongoing responsibilities for what we built yesterday."[126] Too much trust in privatization, in engineering "solutions" to social complexity, and in the power of money to build a bubble of privilege around yourself can lead to a thoughtlessness that has real consequences.

This blindness (pun intended) was exemplified around 2014 by Google Glass, a little voice-activated computer that attached to a pair of glasses. While technically allowing full vision, it also projected images and text onto the interior of the glasses, creating weird head-rolling motions, absent-mindedness, and headaches in its users as they tried to see what was in the Glass and what was in front of them at once. The computer's camera could be activated almost unnoticeably, capturing images and voices without the subjects' knowledge (and from there, of course, it was a short step to the Internet). As media law has established, private citizens have the right not to have their images and likenesses taken or reproduced without their consent—and as the scraps of common sense still clinging to our smartphone-addled brains can tell us, having your picture taken and put on the Internet by strangers is dangerous and creepy. That capability led to Glass users (whom some called "Glassholes," although they liked to call themselves "Explorers") being denied entrance to restaurants and other businesses unless they took their Glasses off. Yet some Glass users saw this request as a personal civil rights violation, ignoring the gap it indicated between their social reality and everyone else's.[127] "I'd be jealous too," snapped one Glass user at a bartender who was throwing him out, "if I couldn't afford one."[128] One San Francisco coffee shop owner said, "The Glass thing is a different beast [from cameras] in that when you ask [users] to take it off, they assume you're ignorant about the product and take it as an opportunity to

126. Morozov, *To Save Everything*, 1.

127. All these aspects and more were satirized on Comedy Central's *The Daily Show with Jon Stewart* (June 12, 2014). One website, glasshole-free.org, maintained a list of San Francisco bars where Google Glass was banned. The site's creator responded to objections that the ban is "unfair" thusly: "Is your Google Glass surgically attached, so it causes great pain to remove it? Is it dispensing life-saving fluids into your body, like insulin? Is it intimately connected with your racial, sexual, or religious identity? No? Then take it off in the bar." Since I recorded this text in an earlier version of this manuscript, the site (and text) seem to have become defunct. See also Honan, "I, Glasshole."

128. Cagle, "Through the Watching Glass."

'educate' you about Glass. They don't see it as an issue of etiquette."[129] One
Glass user, speaking on condition of anonymity, said, "In its obviousness,
[Glass] announces an entitlement. It doesn't have the decency to realize it's
being creepy. I had no bias against it when I got it. I just realized it's good for
basically nothing except being a jerk."[130]

So there they were, human beings volunteering themselves as wearers
of a device made by a giant tech company to capture and stream images
back to itself; as novelist Gary Shteyngart (author of the great 2010 dystopia
Super Sad True Love Story) wrote about his own experience with Glass, "I
cannot help but think of human and [alien], the latter's insect limbs wrapped
around the former's warm-blooded trunk, about to hatch something new."[131]
I can't stop being creeped out at the way we're offering ourselves as hosts
for our technologies, ready to be hollowed out. Reading news stories about
Google Glass and the social friction it created, you see that some Glass-
wearers didn't seem to understand why anyone would object to this cool
new face computer. Why *would* anyone object to being filmed by a stranger
without her knowledge and against her will? Why *would* people want to keep
their private lives private? "This is essentially the defense of the aggressive,
entitled Glass-wearer," Susie Cagle writes, "[w]e've already decided against
privacy, we've given it up, there's nothing left to preserve, and to wish or
work toward any other future is to be an enemy of technology's promise."[132]
(In fact, more than one tech company engineer has made public remarks to
the effect that if you are worried about preserving your privacy in our wired
world, you must have something nasty to hide, or otherwise you'd be willing
to let everything be—in that favorite computer engineer word—"open.") I
doubt that these people really mean to do harm. They just don't *get it*. And
that's why letting software engineers make all the decisions about privacy,
technology, and the dissemination of our information is a very worrisome
thing: fundamentally, their view of the private self resembles the Party's toward Winston Smith in *Nineteen Eighty-Four*. It's an obstacle to a certain
vision of technologically achieved perfection. It's inefficient. And it won't
make anybody rich. Again: *for my self to flourish, yours must disappear.*

Yet it's not only Google who's seeking to monetize and alienate our
self-images—we're doing it to ourselves, too. In the fall of 2014, a cute
teenage Target clerk named Alex Lee was photographed (surreptitiously,
I'm guessing, with a smartphone) bagging a customer's purchases. A

129. Ibid.
130. Ibid.
131. Shtenygart, "O.K., Glass," 37.
132. Cagle, "Through the Watching Glass."

teenage girl posted the photo on Twitter with the swooning caption, "YOOOOOOOOOOO." And just like that, "Alex from Target" became an Internet celebrity.[133] Even as he and his family tried to deal modestly with the unlooked-for attention (although they did appear on the *Ellen* TV show), strangers stole his and his family's bank account and Social Security numbers, posted them online, and, yes—this being the Internet—made death threats. "I've been in the house the entire time," Alex told the *New York Times*. "I'm kind of scared to go in public."

The case of Alex Lee is a study in Orwellian *ownlife* in the twenty-first century: what endangers it, what might preserve it, and how ubiquitous technology alienates self from image, to the cost of both. A stranger's Twitter-enabled whim shredded this young man's privacy. Indeed, the Internet can subject us, without our consent, to strangers' whims and bad decisions. When the link between thought and action, person and person-with-a-grudge, desire and "fame," can be so dramatically shortened by the medium, when your photograph can be snapped or your voice recorded in any situation by anyone with a smartphone, and when law and ethics (as is the case with any technology) lag so far behind in addressing and analyzing these connections, we should be concerned about how instant access to information turns into access to us.

In his "Principles of Newspeak" appendix to *Nineteen Eighty-Four*, Orwell links complexity of language, nuance of thought, privacy, and plenitude of the self. His hero Winston Smith notes that

> In principle a Party member had no spare time, and was never alone except in bed. It was assumed that when he was not working, eating or sleeping he would be taking part in some kind of communal recreations; to do anything that suggested a taste for solitude, even to go for a walk by yourself, was always slightly dangerous. There was a word for it in Newspeak: *ownlife*, it was called, meaning individualism and eccentricity.[134]

For Orwell, *ownlife* is the site of resistance to all that would colonize, commodify, or subject humanity. *Ownlife* is where reflection lives, and consideration for others as well as oneself, and the realization that you and your present concerns are not all there is to the world. It's a private space we inhabit when we experience an unmediated moment of joy, without a selfie to capture it, or freeze in wonder as a comet hurtles across the sky. It's where we don't have to explain ourselves to anyone, where our identity doesn't rest on anyone's opinions. It's where we are alone, whether we like it or not. It's what

---

133. Bilton, "Alex from Target."
134. Orwell, *Nineteen Eighty-Four*, 84, italics original.

we escape when we fill the minutes between things, thumbing our phones. It's not profitable. It's dignified and quiet, if we let it be. And it's what's endangered if someone photographs us and circulates that image without our consent. *Ownlife* and the privacy that enables it are worth protecting—legally as well as morally—in order to protect our own humanity.[135]

Like some pernicious version of secondhand smoke, smartphones and social media can bend your *ownlife* around themselves even when you aren't the one using them. Leading my study-abroad course on *Frankenstein* and the Keats-Shelley circle through Europe one recent January, I paused with my students in the Duomo, the great cathedral in the center of Florence. Despite signs pleading for silence and respect, the sanctuary hummed with voices, laughter, and flash after flash of smartphones and cameras. One of my students saw a boy posing in front of the crucifix at the altar in mimicry of the crucified Christ: extending his arms, selfie stick in one hand, letting his head loll against his chest, he took a photo, then snatched the phone, giggling, to see himself. Blue and white Facebook screens flickered in the crowd. For my students and me—people of faith, who'd been experiencing and discussing the atmosphere of these religious sites all along our trip's route—this was tech-heightened disrespect, filling us with a particular kind of incredulous disgust. Retreating to the side of the sanctuary, underneath the portrait of Dante on the wall (including Hell, Purgatory, and a Paradise that looks a lot like Florence), I lit a candle and closed my eyes. When I opened them, a man in a trench coat and bucket hat was pointing a big black camera straight at me. I could almost see the caption floating above his head: *Woman at Prayer*. Flooded by a rage I didn't try to control, I strode

---

135. Worries about privacy and written communication have always been present, of course. In her fascinating book *The Brontë Cabinet: Three Lives in Nine Objects* (2015), Deborah Lutz describes "anxiety about the privacy of letters" in Victorian England, in a time when the receiver, not the sender, paid postage (at least before the advent of the penny post in 1840) and enclosures, like the knitted baby socks or bits of lace Charlotte Brontë sent to her friends, could be stolen by postal clerks. "Yet a scandal of a larger order swept the post office not long after the institution of the penny post," Lutz writes. "The discovery that a 'Secret Office' of the London Post had been opening and examining mail to the Italian political agitator Guiseppe Mazzini, then living in London, led to a widely publicized backlash in 1844. Home Secretary Sir James Graham, the issuer of the warrant for the mail opening, was widely reviled, especially by the magazine *Punch*. An anti-Graham campaign sprouted up, which included the invention of metal seals, attached by metal 'claws,' that destroyed the envelope when opened, preventing letters from being clandestinely read and resealed. Anti-Graham slogan [sealing] wafers became the fashion, such as one with a picture of a fox and this message: 'You'll be run down if you break cover' ('cover' another word for 'envelope' and the whole a reference to aristocratic fox hunting.) A blunderbuss on full cock with the text 'I hope the content will reach you' expressed the violent feelings of some about their privacy. More simple ones stated, 'Not to be Grahamed.'" See Lutz, 140–141.

toward him. "Do not take my picture!" I demanded. Visibly blanching, he clutched his camera and scurried away. Absent some universal code of smartphone- and stranger-photographing etiquette, I dream of some kind of phone-jamming force field that stops all such lens-focused thoughtlessness in its tracks, leaving us—and our *ownlife*—in peace. That could be the biggest, and most necessary, "disruption" of all.

Philosopher Matthew Crawford, in his book *The World Beyond Your Head: On Becoming an Individual in an Age of Distraction* (2015), writes that protecting *ownlife* may be enabled by an interior privacy he calls "the condition of *not being addressed*."[136] He opens the book by observing that every small space over which our eyes might pass seems now to be monetized—in the seconds between card swipe and receipt at the grocery store, we may see ads on the touchscreen, and in the security line at the airport, we may see ads in the bottoms of the bins in which we place our watches and shoes. The proliferation of visual and auditory noise (and the sale of our attention for profit) erodes what he calls our "attentional commons" just as pollution erodes the quality of common resources like air and water.[137] "Just as clean air makes respiration possible," he writes, "silence, in this broader sense, is what makes it possible to think. We give it up willingly when we are in the company of other people with whom we have some relationship, and when we open ourselves to serendipitous encounters with strangers. To be addressed by mechanized means is an entirely different matter."[138] It sure is. If you've been in an airport, you know how insistent ads and TV voices are, everywhere, elbowing themselves into your consciousness like the man in the middle seat. By contrast, the delicate, ruminative space of privacy is where real ideas and selves are born and where we can choose what to attend to, what to nurture and let grow within our own minds. "A life spent entirely in public, in the presence of others," writes Hannah Arendt, "becomes, as we would say, shallow. While it retains its visibility, it loses the quality of rising into sight from some darker ground which must remain hidden if it is not to lose its depth in a very real, non-subjective sense."[139]

This self-protection is worth our effort in a world where anybody with a smartphone can snap a picture of us and circulate it without our knowledge or consent, perhaps altering it or placing it in a context that distorts our social or legal identities. As seen in my earlier discussion of climate and the way the consequences of our actions can spiral beyond our

---

136. Crawford, *The World Beyond Your Head*, 11, italics original.
137. Ibid.
138. Ibid.
139. Arendt, *The Human Condition*, 71.

control, technological development usually outruns law and ethics, leaving us struggling to define and understand our rights in the face of near-constant change. Private citizens can find themselves on the wrong end of Internet image alienation without quite knowing how, or what they can do about it. Media law may provide some redress for people seeking to retain control of their own "image and likeness," yet every day, a new conundrum—from the question of who owns the photos you post on Facebook to an old mistake following you around for years until you plead for "the right to be forgotten"[140]—shows how far behind reality the law actually is. Will it ever catch up with the way the Internet alienates image of person from person, likeness from reality, simulacrum from object, and then sends those unhooked images, thin as playing cards, around the world for years to serve the needs of (and make money for) people the original person will never meet, contributing "content" that swells the coffers of corporations who will never pay us for what is, technically, our own information? Will it ever define and prosecute the particular wounding and alienation that occurs when your face and voice are stolen, exposed to the public, and bent to uses to which you never consented? Or the hidden alienation of your online behavior from its immediate object, the reduction of your independent activity to a series of clicks and keystrokes tracked and stored in a company's database as monetizable information about what's "liked" and what's not? Can the law ever protect us against that particular icky feeling of having been exposed to public view without our consent? Until it does, we must do what we can to protect ourselves.

In his book *So You've Been Publicly Shamed* (2015), writer Jon Ronson explores what happens when your online reputation gets unhooked from your real self and both your real and virtual lives explode out of control, fanned by mob indignation like a wildfire in a California drought. Even the digitally nimble Ronson was flummoxed when strangers set up a Twitter account—run by a "spambot"—under a version of his real name and, shall we say, misrepresented him ("I'm dreaming something about #time and #cock" wrote the spambot our author refers to as "Fake Jon Ronson.")[141] When he tracked down the spambot's masters, they turned out to be a trio of professors and "creative technologists" who informed him that "the infomorph [wasn't] taking [his] identity. It [was] repurposing social media data

---

140. The Electronic Privacy Information Center reports that "In Google v. Spain," in 2015, "the European Court of Justice ruled that the European citizens have a right to request that commercial search firms, such as Google, that gather personal information for profit should remove links to private information when asked, provided the information is no longer relevant." See https://epic.org/privacy/right-to-be-forgotten/.

141. Ronson, *So You've Been*, 2.

into an informorphic esthetic."[142] When he protested, they scolded him for being so naively protective of his "brand." Reading Ronson's account of this reminded me of the slippery, dreamlike horror of George Kukor's classic film *Gaslight* (1944) or Franz Kafka's *The Trial* (1925)—or even *Nineteen Eighty-Four*—when your own identity begins to crumble under a stranger's serene certainty, and you flounder for grounds to insist on what you know is real. (Ronson was reduced to shouting that his name was not a brand, "It's just me tweeting!")[143] It's enough to make you as wary as the journalist friend of Ronson's who told him, "I suddenly feel with social media like I'm tiptoeing around an unpredictable, angry, unbalanced parent who might strike out at any moment."[144] These are the dangers we never see, because we and the other people sharing the Twitter- or Facebook-sphere with us can't see each other either, in the literal or moral sense of that word. At any second, it could all go really, really wrong.

Despite having grown up among omnipresent smartphones, many of my students haven't quite thought about how their online identities can become permanent distortions of their real ones. Many are sobered by the reality that photos uploaded to social media can be found by anyone who really wants to look. Some students ask, "If I'm not doing anything wrong, why should I worry? I don't have anything to hide." Yet this point of view ignores the reality of how a theft of image and likeness does echo a stereotypical reason to fear cameras: that box that captures your picture also steals your soul. And it *does* look very much like soul-stealing, once your image gets alienated from you and bent to other ends, in ways that can follow you around for the rest of your life. Especially when that endangers your Orwellian *ownlife*, in which the dignity of a private self is its own end and reward—not to mention when, as in the threats against Alex, the dangers are literal.

The dangers are moral, too, in ways that are hard for the girls sharing pictures of the cute Target clerk to see. The Internet has shortened the distance between impulse and fulfillment but widened the distance between us as people, reversing the mature moral order of being in the world, in which (ideally) action should follow reflection and we should take others as seriously as we take ourselves. Even as we succumb to the impulse to tweet the picture of the cute boy or snap a picture of a stranger, we're not really thinking about him as a person, as a human subjectivity who's as real to himself as we are. He's just a shadow, a simulacrum, an image, a ghost, drafted to

142. Ibid.
143. Ibid., 6.
144. Ibid., 282.

build our own image in others' eyes. On comment boards or Twitter, he's The Other, The Enemy, The Opponent, He Who Must Be Flamed/Smacked Down/Shamed. And if that isn't enough, pull out a threat of violence, or if "He" is a woman, rape.[145] He is so far away. And, after all, He is less real than you are, with your needs and your insecurities and your own desire to make an impression on the world that seems so close and yet so distant. He doesn't have a family or a job, doesn't feel pain or fear, has no life beyond the screen. He is there only for you, to inflate your own self-image on your own screen for your own shadowy, imagined audience, helping you dull the inherent uncertainty of *ownlife* in a world that posits celebrity as the greatest possible goal. He lets you be—in Hannah Arendt's word—thoughtless.

Maybe this is the paradox of the Internet: made up of millions of individuals and their actions, in the way a wave is made of water drops, it nevertheless achieves a destructive unanimity of force on its own, tending toward a monolith that can crash over anything—or any person—who steps into its path, willingly or otherwise. This trend works in step with the rise of literal corporate monopolies, large, financially powerful, nongovernmental institutions with no responsibility to the public good beyond what their founders have decided is profitable at any given time. "Digital network architectures naturally incubate monopolies," Jaron Lanier writes in *You Are Not A Gadget*. "That is precisely why the idea of the noosphere, or a collective brain formed by the sum of all the people connected on the internet, has to be resisted with more force than it is promoted . . . . Emphasizing the crowd means de-emphasizing individual humans in the design of society, and when you ask people not to be people, they revert to bad mob-like behaviors. This leads not only to empowered trolls, but to a generally unfriendly and unconstructive online world."[146] Democracy is structured on the principle of the many rather than the one; the multiple and complex rather than the singular and smoothly determined; the individual rather than the faceless and gleaming. It thrives on variety, plurality, and difference, even (or maybe especially) when conversations among those different parties are hard. Totalitarianism seeks the singular, the one, the smooth edifice with no windows and no way for ordinary people to see what goes on inside, because it seeks to subordinate others to itself at any cost. This is why our government was designed with checks and balances, and why our business laws (ostensibly) protect against corporate monopoly. In life and in politics, there's something healthy and human about the multiple, the

145. See Mead, "The Troll Slayer," and Taylor, *The People's Platform*.
146. Lanier, *You Are Not A Gadget,* 16, 19–20.

never-quite-explicable-or-reducible. There's something creepy and repressive about the one perfect silent thing.

Writer Dave Eggers developed this possibility in his dystopian novel *The Circle* (2013), in which a young woman named Mae joins the staff of an eerily friendly Google-like company where her social networking ties, customer interactions, and general corporate citizenship are bound tighter and tighter together, with an oppressiveness Mae's unable to recognize because she's so fully immersed in it. Describing for Mae the innocuous-sounding goal of reducing "secrets," Circle founder Bailey points to the "c" in his company's logo and says, "what's left to do here . . . is close it . . . . A circle is the strongest shape in the universe. Nothing can beat it, nothing can improve upon it, nothing can be more perfect. And that's what we want to be: perfect. So any information that eludes us, anything that's not accessible, prevents us from being perfect."[147] Eggers ends his novel with his heroine's chilling acceptance of the system that has overtaken her from within, just as Orwell devastates readers with Winston Smith's final degradation in the novel's last line: "He loved Big Brother." Mae's preoccupation is with the total transparency demanded by her employer: "They would find each other, soon enough, in a world where everyone could know each other truly and wholly, without secrets . . . . Completion was imminent, and it would bring peace, and it would bring unity, and all that messiness of humanity until now, all those uncertainties that accompanied the world before the Circle, would be only a memory."[148]

Indeed, we may conspire in our own takeover by the linked forces of big business and technology, not only because it feels good or convenient but because we vaguely think we should. Hannah Arendt writes that the apparent harmlessness of a totalitarian system can come not only from that system's careful propaganda but from our own "temptation to explain away the intrinsically incredible by means of liberal rationalizations. In each one of us, there lurks such a liberal, wheedling us with the voice of common sense."[149] *It can't really be that bad. Surely you're just overreacting/overthinking/overintellectualizing. Nobody will like you if you raise a fuss. And it all looks so nice and wholesome.* Yet Arendt reminds us that "Hitler circulated millions of copies of his book in which he stated that to be successful, a lie must be enormous."[150] *There is no privacy anymore, anyway, so what are you worried about? Information wants to be free—who are you to stand in its way?*

147. Eggers, *The Circle*, 287.

148. Ibid., 491.

149. Arendt, *The Origins of Totalitarianism*, 439–440.

150. Ibid., 439.

Isn't "convenience" worth giving up some of your old-fashioned scruples for? A smiling, pleasant façade surely helps hide the enormity of any lie—especially when it's backed by the old consumerist myth of satisfaction without effort or discomfort. We're always willing to believe that kind of lie, especially, perhaps, if we have never not known it. A fellow Generation X-er friend of mine, a professor at another college, told me that many of her first-year students, reading Eggers's *The Circle,* missed the dystopian creepiness entirely: "They just think it sounds like a great place to work," she said.

Unfortunately, we also seem willing to believe the dubious proposition that technology is good for children. More and more children are getting fluent with their parents' touchscreens, and more and more computers are appearing even in kindergarten and preschool classrooms (despite the cautionary example of the Los Angeles Unified School District, where an iPad-for-every-student initiative backfired spectacularly in 2014.) To be clear: I'm not a parent and so have never reached the state of total exhaustion parents reach, where your soul—let alone your iPad—seems like a reasonable price to pay for five minutes alone in the bathroom with a door that locks. But as educational psychologists, pediatricians, and many parents themselves have argued, interaction with other humans and with real objects in the real world are crucial for a child's development, not just psychologically but in the literal structure and growth of the brain—and it's more important the younger the child is.

As a college professor, I want to ask parents just one question about their child's use of computers and the Internet: are you *sure* you want to shape your child's developing brain and her means of self-understanding—her ideas of cause and effect, her sensory abilities, her ability to process words and other stimuli, her notions of what's interesting and what's boring and what's real and what's imaginary—around the paradigms created by screens and the so-called content they deliver? Are you *sure* you want to—literally—sell her out? I ask because too much (or perhaps any) use of computers (particularly touch-screen devices, which form swift sensory connections between action, device, and result) risks training up that small developing brain within the boundaries tech companies and advertisers have already drawn, like espaliering a young tree to a fence. In Jaron Lanier's words, a child who's too reliant on technology for her learning and entertainment will get "locked in," never having had the chance to know, choose, and develop for herself a different way of being in the world. Google's priorities will become hers, having slipped past the developmental equivalent of the blood-brain barrier to become part of the brain, perhaps even the self. Of course, we all grow up within paradigms that shape us in ways we can't see, and children routinely bend their toys, from computers to sticks and cardboard boxes, to their own imaginative ends. But plenty of parents who by college application time will be worried about "uniqueness" and "well-roundedness" (and believe me, I see a *lot* of that) may be training their children toward a docile corporate-technogical subjecthood almost from birth if they don't consider how computers construct our versions of reality in a way that may be particularly irresistible and problematic for digital natives.

Resisting that subjecthood means resisting much about the modern tech-centric landscape of childhood itself, from DVD players embedded in minivan seatbacks to keyboard-based writing instruction edging aside handwriting to a children's book called *Dot*—as in dot-com—by Randi Zuckerberg, sister of Facebook founder Mark. An "environmental awareness test" administered by computer to a first-grader in my own town's public school turned out (to the horror of her parents, who told me this story) not to be whether the bird in the picture was a blue jay or robin, but a series of corporate logos (Walmart, McDonald's, Chuck E. Cheese) the child was asked to identify.[151] Pokemon Go lures children outside to "find" imaginary creatures, implicating them further in electronic systems of reward, enriching the corporation that makes the app, and deepening a device-centered norm, while squirrels and snails go about their business unnoticed. Yet contrast these screen-focused children with a child who's been allowed more freedom of motion and more varieties of experience— particularly outdoors—and you see not only technology's will to power but its obliviousness in reducing the wondrous state of childhood to a passive, pseudo-adult one, where even "nature" is interpenetrated with technology. In her book *A Country Called Childhood: Children and the Exuberant World* (2014), Jay Griffiths writes, "To be born is, in Latin, *nasci,* and the world is related to *natura,* so birth, nature, the laws of nature, and the idea of an essence are related."[152] Into what type of world, then, and what type of internal "essence," is a child being born, if no nonhuman and nonhuman-created

151. This same child had read aloud to me—fluently and with understanding— from Laura Ingalls Wilder's classic novel *Little House on the Prairie* (first published in 1935). Yet, in her parents' account, she had some difficulty with the computerized "environmental awareness test" because her access to computers at home was purposefully limited, for all the reasons I've been describing, and because the school's desktop computer looked and felt quite different from her parents' laptops. Again, to return to Jaron Lanier's point, software (and hardware) designs are not cognitively neutral, or even universal. For teachers, this is yet another reason to be wary of the way computers and standardized testing—particularly when the two are linked—can "test" children with a series of social assumptions that can flatten variables of parental choice and home environments (not every family can afford, or wants to use, computers in the home). And we don't even have a Chuck E. Cheese in our town.

152. Griffiths, *A Country Called Childhood,* 5.

"nature" ever gets involved? Perhaps it's the world too many children inhabit right now—a world of obesity and other health problems, learning difficulties and attention issues, and social problems, all of which have been linked to too much screen time too early. Yet the need children are trying to meet with computers is the same one they (and all of us) are trying to meet: a richer understanding of the self through relationship with someone else. Nineteenth-century American novelist Nathaniel Hawthorne described this tendency in his five-year-old son: "The old boy is now riding on his rocking horse, and talking to me as fast as his tongue can go. Mercy on me, was ever a man before so be-pelted with a child's talk as I am! It is his great desire of sympathy that lies at the bottom of the great heap of his babblement. He wants to enrich all his enjoyments by steeping them in the heart of some friend."[153] A child's desire is all of ours, as articulated by E. M. Forster in *Howards End* (1910): *only connect.*[154]

Maybe the saddest and most infuriating thing is this: technology may be less about Orwellian power for its own sake than about selling us for advertising dollars. A few years ago, I learned about a free program called Ghostery, which identifies the names and functions of every application tracking you and lets you turn them off. When I installed Ghostery and went to the *New York Times* website, Ghostery tallied eleven trackers, of which four were ads and the rest were "analytics" and "beacons," which feed into advertising too. Among the tracker classifications Ghostery recognizes (and the numbers of them) are "Behavior Tracking" (forty-five trackers), "History Sniffing" (one tracker), "Affiliate Marketing" (forty-seven), "Social" (fifty-one), and something called "Pornvertising" (ten). We are being followed as we answer our email and surf around the web, doing our ordinary things. Our behavior is being tracked. Our history is being sniffed. And we are being converted into advertising dollars—consumer simulacra of ourselves.

For proof, consider an incident Jacob Silverman reports in his 2015 book *Terms of Service: Social Media and the Price of Constant Connection.* An Illinois man named Mike Seay received a junk mail solicitation from OfficeMax on which the words "Daughter Killed in a Car Crash" had been mistakenly printed below his name. While "OfficeMax blamed an unnamed third-party data broker for mistakenly printing the information on the envelope," Silverman writes, "[a] distraught Seay, speaking to a reporter, raised some important questions: 'Why would they have that type of information?

---

153. Mahoney, "The Hardest Art," 237.
154. Forster, *Howards End*, 147.

Why would they need that?"[155] Consider, also, the *New York Times* story "How Companies Learn Your Secrets," which described in 2012 how companies like Target deploy a complex blend of statistics, analytics, and feedback from customers' on- and offline behavior to refine the way they market products in general and the way they target (ha ha) particular products at particular consumers. One Target statistician developed a way to predict whether a customer was pregnant, based on her purchases, and send her coupons to entice her to buy more baby-related products, triggering a cycle of "cue-routine-reward calculators." Journalist Charles Duhigg narrates what happened next:

> About a year after [the statistician] created his pregnancy-pre-diction model, a man walked into a Target outside Minneapolis and demanded to see the manager. He was clutching coupons that had been sent to his daughter, and he was angry, according to an employee who participated in the conversation.
>
> "My daughter got this in the mail!" he said. "She's still in high school, and you're sending her coupons for baby clothes and cribs? Are you trying to encourage her to get pregnant?"
>
> The manager didn't have any idea what the man was talking about. He looked at the mailer. Sure enough, it was addressed to the man's daughter and contained advertisements for maternity clothing, nursery furniture and pictures of smiling infants. The manager apologized and then called a few days later to apolo-gize again.
>
> On the phone, though, the father was somewhat abashed. "I had a talk with my daughter," he said. "It turns out there's been some activities in my house I haven't been completely aware of. She's due in August. I owe you an apology."[156]

If Target knows you're pregnant before your own father does, and if OfficeMax knows your daughter was killed in a car crash, isn't that kind of scary? Um, yeah.

Yet when I talk to my students, I find that the fact that their online behavior is tracked and monetized is news to many of them, even though they are the first generation to come of age as consumers without ever having not known the Internet (and some are even fans of the tech-dystopian TV series "Black Mirror," a kind of "Twilight Zone" for the twenty-first century.) In one discussion with first-year students about technology, I told them about the "iPotty" (a toddler's toilet-training seat with an attached

---

155. Silverman, *Terms of Service*, 279.
156. Duhigg, "How Companies Learn Your Secrets."

iPad holder—"because of course," one student quipped, "no child must *ever* be bored!"), then asked them to do a little experiment: Google "iPotty," go to that page, then surf to other sites and see which ads follow them. Heads went down, keys clicked, and incredulous noises rose behind laptop lids. "You're getting baby product ads, aren't you?" I asked. Yes, they responded. How did you know? The shocked looks indicated they hadn't quite connected online behavior with ads that followed it, and were creeped out by the reality they are being watched. (Of course, those ad trackers already know they're of prime childbearing age.) This lack of awareness is what app makers are counting on—your toylike device will take and sell your data in exchange for "fun," counting on the veneer of sophistication and control you feel to keep you from being aware of it. "Do not flatter yourself in thinking you have much control over which temptations you click on," writes journalist Andrew Sullivan. "No information technology ever had this depth of knowledge of this consumers—or greater capacity to tweak their synapses to keep them engaged."[157] Yet we have to remember the warning of more than one tech writer: If the site or service is free, *you* (and your data) are the product. (One more time, Jaron Lanier: "This is one of the great illusions of our times: that you can game without being gamed."[158])

Significantly, in their private lives, the tech elites "gaming" us are swimming against the current in which their products immerse everyone else. Steve Jobs, the late presiding genius of Apple, told *New York Times* writer Nick Bilton, "We limit how much technology our kids use at home."[159] The Jobs household, Bilton writes, was one in which screens weren't allowed at the dinner table, but conversation about books and ideas was encouraged. Chris Anderson, the former editor of *Wired* magazine and CEO of drone maker 3D Robotics, father of five, "has instituted time limits and parental controls on every device in his home," because, as he told Bilton, "we have seen the dangers of technology firsthand. I've seen it in myself, I don't want to see that happen to my kids."[160] Other parents, among the inventors and tastemakers of the tech world, limit screen time for young children in particular and distinguish between using screens to "consume" (YouTube, video games) or to "create" (programming, creating computer art.)[161] The emphasis on screen-free, hands-on creative pursuits extends to the edu-

157. Sullivan, "I Used to Be A Human Being."

158. Lanier, *Who Owns the Future?*, 117.

159. Bilton, "Steve Jobs Was A Low-Tech Parent." Thanks to former student Allison Roe for sending me this article.

160. Ibid.

161. Ibid.

cation such "Silicon Valley giants" seek for their children, exemplified by the distinguished tradition of Waldorf private schools, where fractions are taught with cut-up pieces of fruit, focus and manual dexterity are honed by knitting, writing and language come with books, pencils, and paper, and tuition can be as much as $25,000 per year.[162] Yet these tech-company employees (including Google, Apple, Yahoo, and Hewlett-Packard) thereby endorse, with their practices and their funds, an approach to childhood development and education that's the opposite of the one their corporations' profit motives push on the rest of us each day. When you look at schools' computer-for-every-child deals—benefitting the bottom line of the corporations for which these Waldorf parents work—and the relentless, intertwined forces of marketing and entertainment streamed at children through an ever-wider range of devices every year, it's not hard to feel as if you are being sold a flippant, Marie Antoinette-ish dismissal of actions and consequences: let *them* eat (digital) cake. You don't have to be a Waldorf- or Montessori-trained teacher to see that hands-on, object- and sense-centered experience is a richer and more developmentally appropriate way for children to learn than screen-induced passivity. Yet the same tech giants shielding their own children from screens seem to miss the irony of saturating the market with ever-more–child-friendly and child-marketed devices for other people's—particularly poorer people's—kids. Sure, they seem to know something we don't. But that knowledge is something every one of us can apply in our own households too.

I'm not saying that using Gmail means inevitable submission to a totalitarian juggernaut, or that letting your child play with your phone means you are a bad parent, or that you can't be a computer programmer and still retain your humanity. Indeed, Jaron Lanier speaks eloquently of the humanistic possibilities of good design:

> It's fine for a person to love the medium they are given to work in. Love paint if you are a painter; love a clarinet if you are a musician. Love the English language (or hate it.) Love of these things is a love of mystery.
>
> But in the case of digital creative materials, like MIDI, UNIX, or even the World Wide Web, it's a good idea to be skeptical. These designs came together very recently, and there's a haphazard, accidental quality to them. Resist the easy grooves they guide you into. If you love a medium made of software,

162. Richtel, "A Silicon Valley School."

there's a danger that you will become entrapped in someone else's recent careless thoughts. Struggle against that![163]

Lanier's warning and the "lock-in" to which computer systems are subject (and to which they subject us) give new poignancy to the age-old lament of young people—"we're living in a world we didn't make." It's true— you didn't make the world, or the software and devices structuring your experience of it; you weren't present at their creation, and you may well be living under the tacit assumption they are "normal." That's why it's necessary, as in every generation, to "struggle against that" and become able to see the water you're swimming in so you can make choices about it. You can't afford to sign over your precious self and its powers of discernment to a corporate-technological entity whose logic, at heart, resembles Big Brother's: strengthening its own power and profit as its circular and sufficient goal and reaching into your self to sand away any resistance from the pesky, messy, above-all–unprofitable thing called *humanity*.

As a college professor, I see students "struggl[ing] against" or succumbing to prevailing tides of behavior-shaping technology every day as they text, tweet, tune out, or try to focus. "Convenience" or "keeping in touch" or "multitasking" is the reasonable-sounding excuse many are using, consciously or not, to shortchange their experience of their actual lives in the actual world, even when they're at a college costing (by my rough count) about $600 per hour of class[164] (see my calculations in Chapter 5). Let me repeat Jaron Lanier's remark again: "This is one of the great illusions of our times: that you can game without being gamed."[165] When technology critic Nicholas Carr, whose books have informed this one, came to lecture at our college in February 2014, I was stunned to see that even as he stood in front of us, describing the insidious nature of tech habit, students throughout the audience had their heads down, texting. A student journalist, in a college newspaper editorial entitled "@Luther College: pay attention," remarked on the irony: "I don't think Luther College hired a nationally known Pulitzer Prize finalist with an Ivy League education to deliver the Spring Opening Convocation address so that students could half-heartedly show up," she wrote the following week. "While many students seemed fully invested and engaged in the lecture, it was the disruptive and disrespectful behavior that

---

163. Lanier, *You Are Not A Gadget*, 21–22.

164. Of course, go to any academic conference (which can cost about this much depending on plane, hotel, registration fee, and preparation time) and you'll see their professors making the same mistakes.

165. Lanier, *Who Owns the Future?*, 117.

stood out."[166] And it stands out to me, too. At the end of one of my first-year common course lectures on Mary Shelley's *Frankenstein* (1818), during which I'd diagrammed the novel's onion-like layers of narrative on the board, a student who'd been less than engaged (yes, I *can* see you) approached the board, snapped a picture of the diagram with her smartphone, and left. She had come to the lecture (which supports students' work in their individual discussion sections) without pen or paper and had taken no notes, sitting passively during the entire hour. She wasn't the only one.[167] And there are students like her in every college and high school, everywhere.

I don't like resorting to money to measure an education's value, but like many professors I wonder, often, how to wake some students up from their electronic dreams. It's not enough to say, "They're adults—let them decide whether to pay attention," since laptops and smartphones distract everyone around the distracted user too, and roomfuls of distracted students devalue for everyone the quality of the educational experience—and, ultimately, the value of the degree—an institution grants.[168] Yes, students juggle many commitments, but shouldn't the educational experience that has brought you to college in the first place be the primary one? (In my experience, the students with the most serious reasons for continued access to smartphones—ailing relatives, unfolding job situations—are also the most responsible about notifying me of this and keeping phones from distracting others.) Some professors, even in computer science classes, ban laptops from the classroom, since studies show that handwriting increases memory, retention, and intellectual engagement (you are deciding what to write, and the motion of your hand spurs your thoughts), so laptops become transcription machines at best, distraction machines at worst.[169] Many teachers find that with the increased use of devices, students' ability to comprehend written and spoken language and shades of meaning goes down, but even more, their sense of initiative—"I can do this and find this out for myself! I am excited by this idea on its own terms!"—goes down. So does an amazingly wide range of what used to be known, optimistically, as general knowledge. In his 2015 book *The Glass Cage: Automation and Us,*

166. Jeide, "@ Luther College," 9.

167. I address this issue early in the semester now, talking with students about why, cognitively and intellectually, they need to write notes *as* I am writing on the board. I also include a detailed, research-driven technology policy on my syllabus (reproduced in Chapter 5), and students respond positively to the policy and the classroom climate it creates.

168. See Jacobs, "Even Just The Presence of A Smartphone."

169. See Rockmore, "The Case for Banning Laptops" and Curzan, "Why I'm Asking You Not To Use Laptops."

Carr describes the "generation effect," the means by which we retain information better if we struggle to learn it a little; by contrast, "by diminishing the intensity of their thinking," Carr writes of some tech study subjects, "the software retards their ability to encode information in memory, which makes them less likely to develop the rich tacit knowledge essential to true expertise."[170] As Evgeny Morozov writes, "Some geeks stubbornly refuse to recognize that challenges and obstacles . . . enhance rather than undermine the human condition."[171] As I said in the Introduction of this book, real life includes facing, even embracing, difficulty and difference. Work enriches brains and selves. The image of that student carelessly snapping a picture of my diagram as she left the lecture hall stays with me, in an uneasy pun: she's phoning in her own education, which represents one of the biggest investments many Americans ever make.

College can be where citizens and thinkers are made, but also where they have to make *themselves*, resisting the fundamental error technology can seduce us into: engineering can perfect humanity, relieving us of the need to confront difficulty, to make decisions, or to wake ourselves up and stay awake. I find persuasive sociologist danah boyd's findings that teenagers get so married to their electronic devices because overprotective parents and other things keep them out of the public sphere in which they would otherwise gather, and they want to find ways to be together.[172] I do think it's true that American culture and education ask children too much to be little adults—sit still, do "brain work" rather than tactile work, entertain themselves with devices and screens—rather than letting them play and take healthy risks outside in the world, and that these habits follow kids to college in unproductive ways.[173] But it's up to professors to foreground for students the reality that education requires contact with that friction of difference, discomfort, and novelty, and it's up to students to make themselves accountable for accepting that challenge and experiencing their own educations rather than hiding behind the comforts of digital "convenience." Brains are very plastic, and when combined with the

170. Carr, *The Glass Cage*, 77.

171. Morozov, *To Save Everything*, 12.

172. See boyd, *It's Complicated*. The lowercase spelling of her name is her personal preference.

173. This conversation looms large in recent parenting literature, including the debate over "free-range parenting" and concerns about overprotective parenting's short- and long-term effects. See, for starters, Hanna Rosin, "The Overprotected Kid" (*The Atlantic*, April 2014), Lenore Skenazy's *Free-Range Kids: Giving Our Children the Freedom We Had Without Going Nuts with Worry*, and Julie Lythcott-Haims's *How To Raise An Adult: Break Free of the Overparenting Trap and Prepare Your Kid for Success.*

training we get in a capitalist society to fulfill desires by buying, it means we're working against strong influences from within. As historian Daniel Smail reminds us, "cultural practices can have profound neurophysiological consequences;" indeed, the hits of dopamine and other kinds of good feelings we got from gossip, coffee, reading, and other consumer practices and goods around the end of the eighteenth century helped make those things even more widely available in the culture.[174] "The long eighteenth century, after all," Smail writes, "was the century of de-Christianization, of declining attendance at religious services and confession. It is reasonable to suggest that the two go hand in hand: where individuals once relied on religion and ritual as sources of dopamine and other chemical messengers, they turned increasingly to items of consumption, giving up God in favor of mammon."[175] A historical perspective—like an artistic one—is one of the ways we can get up above our current habits and desires for neurochemical fixes to see what's really going on in our minds and lives, and to try to determine whether we are shaping our culture or it's shaping us. We can also choose just to stop and consider what's really happening to us because of the habits we've let creep up.

The human-computer relationship gets even more poignant when considering handwriting, which is becoming another casualty of the way we falter at the border of complexity. Type—like televised pictures—slides easily into the eyes and the brain. But handwriting, like a thicket, slows down your passage through it, snagging you on the briars of an individual self. Why does she always make that giant loop at the base of the *y*? Why do his *H*s always look so angry? Why are these words and not these joined? On paper, the touch of the hand is clear across any distance you'd want to name, fragile but warm. Poet John Keats knew its power too: *This living hand, now warm and capable,* he wrote. *See, here it is—I hold it towards you.*[176] He died at twenty-five. And almost two hundred years after his death, his hand still touches me, not only in printed words but in his excited scrawl on a manuscript, which bears that elusive thing: the stamp of the living self, caught in hurtling forward motion, a snapshot of the mind in the act of making and writing down that which the moving hand, itself, is helping to create. Winston Smith's internal rebellion in *Nineteen Eighty-Four* begins with writing words on paper, with a pen. Deep in the Chauvet Cave in southern France, thirty thousand years ago, early humans sketched breathtaking drawings in charcoal on the walls: lions, horses, rhinoceri, and fighting bison whose

174. Smail, *Deep History,* 117.

175. Ibid., 184–5.

176. Keats, "This living hand," 384.

flailing legs may represent an early version of animation. Yet what stops my breath the most—folding time so that that barefoot artist is standing right next to me—is a handprint on the rock. Red and faintly smudgy, it is recognizable throughout the cave, because the artist's right little finger is crooked. Thirty thousand years ago. The print of a living human hand speaks to us across a nearly unimaginable expanse of time.[177] Yet how many of us—including me—have noticed a decline in our handwriting, simply because we just don't use it as much anymore? How many people under thirty have difficulty not only writing by hand but reading handwriting at all? What will survive of our human touch, thirty thousand years from now?

Perhaps technology feels so natural and insidious in binding us to itself because it plays so well to our essential human need for connection. (Screens and keyboards awaken when *we* touch *them,* after all.) For me, a big surprise of the 2013 Spike Jonze film *Her*—in which Scarlett Johanssen's voice "plays" Samantha, a computer operating system that enraptures Theodore Twombly (Joaquin Phoenix)—was that it really isn't about computers at all: it's about us. It's about our ever-present human need—which technology enters into and sharpens and shapes around itself—to *feel,* to experience something ecstatic and immediate humming in our brains and bodies. And it's about our equally present fear that we *can't* feel, that we are oh-so-civilized but empty bodies, aching with the memory of lost emotions, even lost souls. It's about humans drifting through a disenchanted world,[178] seeking the meaning we fear might not exist, seeking love even as we self-protectively intellectualize ourselves away from it. The sexy-voiced operating system is only a recent symptom of old human questions: who *is* this person I think I love? Am I really in love with this person or just with a projection of my own self? The muted colors, the stylish but barren cityscapes and indoor spaces, and Joaquin Phoenix's nuanced performance as a man conspiring in his own eunuch-dom (those high-waisted pants!) all suggest how we undermine our own desires every day, living in an emotional half-light. Among our human qualities is our longing for beauty, and our longing to feel ourselves reached for and touched *through* beauty. Michelangelo placed God—straining to

177. See Werner Herzog's documentary film *Cave of Forgotten Dreams* (2010).

178. The phrase "an enchanted/disenchanted world" has a long philosophical and sociological history. Appearing in Max Weber's *The Protestant Ethic and the Spirit of Capitalism* (1905) to describe the way that the decline of religion and folk tradition and the rise of rationalism helped to remove a sense of "enchantment" and invisible, omnipresent meaning from the world as average people experienced it, it has also been carried into discourse in books like Charles Taylor's *A Secular Age*, Jane Bennett's *The Enchantment of Modern Life: Attachments, Crossings, and Ethics* (cited elsewhere; Princeton University Press, 2001), and James William Gibson's *A Reenchanted World: The Quest for a New Kinship with Nature.*

touch Adam's hand—at the center of the Sistine Chapel ceiling. What wonder and beauty *are* always reaching for us from behind the visible faces of the world, in the voices of our family and friends, in what we see but never quite stir ourselves to fully acknowledge? And how do we, in the words of an old country song, look for love in all the wrong places, even as our desire to reach for and be touched by love would seem to be the one thing on which we could depend? As Orwell posits, might not love be the most anti-totalitarian, essentially human thing of all?

The obvious predecessor of *Her*'s Samantha is the famous ELIZA program, an early form of artificial intelligence developed at MIT in the 1970s. As Sherry Turkle writes in *Alone Together: Why We Expect More From Technology and Less From Each Other* (2011), ELIZA was programmed to respond to typed questions "in language that offered support or asked for clarification. To 'My mother is making me angry,' the program might respond, 'Tell me more about your mother,' or 'Why do you feel so negatively about your mother?'" Crucially, "ELIZA had no model of what a mother might be or any way to represent the feeling of anger. What it could do was take strings of words and turn them into questions or restate them as interpretations."[179] Yet even though they knew the program was not really "thinking" about their answers or responding as a friend might, users still displayed a significant (and increasing) desire to "chat with it. More than this, they wanted to be alone with it. They wanted to tell it their secrets." Within a very short time, ELIZA's users moved from a basic opening gambit like "Hello" to "I am worried that I might fail organic chemistry" or "My sister died." It's not that these MIT undergraduates (among the most tech-savvy people on the planet) really believed ELIZA was human. Rather, they were demonstrating what Turkle, who studies the psychology and sociology of computers and their use, has come to call "the ELIZA effect," or a type of "human complicity in a digital fantasy" that "does not depend on being deceived but on wanting to fill in the blanks."[180] Emotionally as with scrambled sentences, our brains want to complete. Or be completed by something on the other end of the line—no matter what.

Turkle describes the ELIZA effect at work in other forms of artificial intelligence and robotics: a baby seal named Paro, "a hit in Japan" which "now targets the American nursing home market" because, its inventors say, "the elderly need a companion robot because of a lack of human resources;" the famous Furby, a talking robotic toy that has been seen to prompt displays of deep empathy in children; even a talking sex doll. "For decades," she writes,

179. Turkle, *Alone Together,* 23.
180. Ibid., 24.

"computers have asked us to *think* with them; these days, computers and robots, deemed sociable, affective, and relational, ask us to *feel* for and with them."[181] And drawing on her studies of children with their Furbys and the elderly with their huggable, murmuring Paros, she asks, "If a robot makes you love it, is it alive?"[182] This may be a modern incarnation of the "Turing test," devised by the British mathematician and Enigma codebreaker Alan Turing (1912–1954): can a computer hidden from view and answering questions make you believe it's a person? If it can, then it has passed the test.

While a full examination of the philosophical question of robotic selfhood is beyond the scope of this book (although it *is* a philosophical question), I'd like to draw our attention to something that is important for my argument here: robots are meeting needs that other humans are not, both as repositories of emotion and expressors of what looks, particularly to vulnerable and disconnected people, like care. Marketers of a toy called CloudPets Teddy, which replays messages from parents' smartphones on a stuffed bear a child can hold, offer—heartbreakingly—free shipping to members of the military.[183] Yet some parental disconnection is the result of habit or choice, not duty. Ten-year-old Callie, interviewed by Turkle about her play with a robotic doll called My Real Baby, says that "taking care of My Real Baby makes her feel more cared for," since "her parents are very busy and don't have a lot of time to spend with her." Her father comes to her sessions with Turkle but "is visibly distracted," checking his email on his BlackBerry "every few minutes."[184] "Tellingly," Turkle writes, "Callie thinks that grown-ups would like My Real Baby as much as children do because, in its presence, adults would be 'reminded of being parents.'"[185] Callie's reaction is echoed by older children studied by Turkle and by danah boyd, many of whom, it emerges, crave the attention of perpetually distracted parents. "Longed for here [by children] is the pleasure of [a parent's] full attention, coveted and rare," Turkle writes.

> One high school senior recalls a time when his father used to sit next to him on the couch, reading. "He read for pleasure and didn't mind being interrupted." But when his father, a doctor, switched from books to his BlackBerry, things became less clear: "He could be playing a game or looking at a patient record,

181. Ibid., 39.

182. Ibid., 26.

183. See "Cloud Pets Teddy: Is it a scam or legit?" (www.highya.com/cloudpets -teddy-reviews). Thanks to my former student Joel Denney for sending me this link.

184. Turkle, *Alone Together,* 76.

185. Ibid., 77.

and you would never know . . . . He is in that same BlackBerry zone." It takes work to bring his father out of that zone. When he emerges, he needs time to refocus. "You might ask him a question and he'll say, 'Yeah, one second.' And then he'll finish typing his email or whatever, he'll log off or whatever, and he'll say, 'Yeah, I'm sorry, what did you say?'"[186]

Turkle's conversations with teenagers reveal that their own apparent obsession with devices may be in part a defense mechanism, a type of compensation for the real human attention and contact they seek but are not finding—and are perhaps, therefore, not being shown how to give and to receive. "When we talk to robots," Turkle writes, "our stories fall, literally, on deaf ears. If there is meaning, it is because the person with the robot has heard him- or herself talk aloud."[187] It's a sad image, an echo of the stereotypical lonely woman talking to her cat—except the talking is happening to and through devices rather than living creatures, bending into themselves the streams of human contact, emotion, and love we could be sharing with one another instead.

The good news is that many students are ready to reconsider the tech norms they've been living within, and to find other ways of making meaning, finding joy and beauty, and making things happen in the world. Some choose to quit Facebook for at least a little while to see what it's like. (One student—a Nobel Peace Prize scholar, dual religion and mathematics major, extremely thoughtful and ethical—described for me the pleadings of the site to get her to rejoin—including "Your mom misses you! Your friend [insert name] misses you!") Others develop practices of meditation, walking, working in the college gardens, or writing in journals, reaching through the body and the senses for something that feels individual and real. They fight the restless inertia of internet habit, as we all do (*I've been writing for ten minutes without interruption! Time to check email!*) but they're developing the survival skills of twenty-first-century life: mindfulness and self-control, discerning the truths that connect you to something larger than yourself, and learning how to keep yourself and your *ownlife* company.

Some students have described for me the attention-management practices they and their friends are trying to develop: for example, when eating together at the cafeteria or sitting and talking in one of our outdoor "council rings" or down by the Upper Iowa River (which runs right past campus), all cell phones get put away. In the age of much-discussed "helicopter parenting," this looks to me like a kind of self-parenting children need now more

186. Ibid., 268.
187. Ibid., 113.

than ever to do. Not all parents, wired into their own circuits of electronic contact, pleasure, and reward, spend much time actually *talking* with the children to whom they've been texting constantly or repeating for the past month, "I can't wait till you get home on break!"[188] Luther College's mission statement promises we are "committed to a way of learning that moves us beyond immediate interests and present knowledge into a larger world—an education that disciplines minds and develops whole persons equipped to understand and confront a changing society." This takes place one student and one conversation at a time.[189] It is highly inefficient, thank God. It has yielded moments of intellectual and emotional revelation and challenge and change that my students and I will remember all our lives. And it doesn't happen on a screen.

As impossible as it seems, we can ground our technology use in self-protection, self-organization, and choice. First, there's email management. We can change the relationship between email and our other work, delaying our first email check until after we've started on a more important task or "schedul[ing] email 'sprints' of 20–25 minutes . . . to focus on more compli-cated emails during morning times, when [we're] mentally clearest."[190] In my own email account, I keep multiple folders, labeled by project, course, or topic, in which I archive dealt-with email, so if it's still sitting in my inbox, I know it still requires some action from me. (This helps me get to "inbox zero" at least once a month, as do unsubscribing and deleting.) We can make lists of things to do online and do them all at once, rather than continually breaking away from offline tasks. We can keep social media in clearly limited boxes of time and place, saying no to that Facebook-checking habit in the same way we might also be trying to say no to the late-afternoon candy bar or taking the elevator instead of the stairs. Given that a person's "Internet trail" of identity is established ever-earlier and in ever-more detail, we can refuse to post pictures of or information about our children online, leaving the decision about how to establish their "trail" up to them.[191] We can shift the patterns of family life away from screens, establishing times and places where screens don't go: the dinner table, the bedroom, the family reading night. Do an Internet search for your own name, then your own name plus towns in which you've lived, so you can be aware of what comes up in search results and what information about

188. See Potter, "Bye Bye Birdies."

189. "You all are like fine craftspeople," said my late father on his first visit to Luther, "educating these kids one at a time, by hand." I am proud to say that I believe that's true.

190. Clark, "Actually, You Should Check Email in the Morning." See also Morgenstern, *Never Check Email in the Morning.*

191. See Webb, "We Post Nothing."

you may be available for others to view or purchase. Manage your online reputation and the release of your personal information. Install a program like Ghostery to detect and turn off Internet trackers and use a browser that doesn't track your search results. Monitor your credit reports and credit score to help guard against identity theft. If you're a creative professional or business owner, consider buying your domain name to safeguard it from others' use. Change your passwords, and choose good ones. Unsubscribe. Uncheck boxes. Read end-user-license agreements (those things we mostly just scroll through to click "I Agree.")

And reexamine your social media accounts with an eye to starving the Siren Servers. First, consider the basic ways we can return power to ourselves and one another on social media: update your privacy settings, don't "friend" people you don't actually know, don't photograph, post photographs of, or tag photographs of people in your account without their consent (especially given the persistent confusion about who actually *owns* the images we post). As Jacob Silverman suggests in *Terms of Service,* especially his chapter "Social-Media Rebellion," we can "consider what else we can do to make the networks worth less," essentially "devalu[ing] our data" whenever we can. Replace a profile picture of your face with something not your face: "Your Bigfoot avatar may appear in a Google+ or Facebook ad," Silverman writes, "but it will be worth less because your face won't be there to help sell the product. And perhaps more important, you're being a less valuable user by not providing a photo that the platform owner can use to improve its facial-recognition software."[192] We can also refuse to "structure our data:" "Don't append your location to tweets, don't check in anywhere, don't tag brands or businesses," Silverman writes. "Disable location services, disable notifications (you'll be more relaxed as a consequence.) Take a look at apps you've authorized and remove the ones you don't use or that look suspicious."[193] And really: think about it. Absent natural disaster or political calamity, why on earth *would* you "check in" anywhere electronically unless you're on parole? Is your data only worth a ten-percent-off coupon? Do you actually *want* all this noise in your head?

This brings me to my last point, a version of the earnest lessons we take in through "Sesame Street" and kindergarten training: don't be afraid to be different. And don't be afraid, as my students say, to call bullshit on what looks like bullshit to you. So much of what comes to us cloaked in professional-seeming, adult-seeming behaviors like "productivity" and "connectedness" is really intellectual and imaginative self-sabotage whose

---

192. Silverman, *Terms of Service,* 350–1.
193. Ibid.

results benefit Siren Servers and their corporate owners while impoverishing us. And so much of the consumertainment shrieking that surrounds us
in every waking hour can be resisted if you open yourself to other ways to fill
that space. People like me get mocked as "Luddites." But the original Luddites were actually early-nineteenth-century English rural laborers defending themselves against the machines that would take away their work—and
therefore, their humanity—by destroying those machines, the only means
of protest left to them.[194] They had their eye on the future—specifically, their
own future, and the economic and social health that made it worth living.
That active, skeptical impulse is fundamentally healthy, even wise. *Do I really need to stand in line to get this new phone that's a few millimeters wider
than the one I stood in line for* last *year? Do I really have anything to say on
Twitter? Do all these devices really enable human flourishing? What do they
cost the nonhuman world?* Don't let anyone scoff you out of asking those
questions, even if you're a teacher pressured by a school board eager to sign
that contract with a supplier for the latest iPad-for-every-student initiative,
or a professor surrounded by colleagues terrified of being thought—gasp—
insufficiently theoretical. Observe the spiking rates of anxiety and depres-
sion among people under thirty in our souring, warming world and ask:
how can I help them create a world that nourishes, not only entertains,
them, and in which they will have to live much longer than I will? Be countercultural, like science-fiction writer Bruce Sterling, who asked a crowd of
true-believer techies at the 2013 SXSW Interactive Festival, "A billion apps
have been sold. Where's the betterness?"[195]

And consider a point my students and I came to in our discussion
of Orwell's *Nineteen Eighty-Four*: Is there a power that an independent self
possesses, just by its very *existence as* an independent self? Can we model
alternative ways of being just by *living* them? Does our principled presence
provide a witness of its own? Given how hard Big Brother tries to erase the
individual self in its drive to total power for its own sake—"We shall empty
you, and fill you with ourselves"—we decided this might very well be true. By
insisting on protective boundaries around our own bodies, minds, and lives
("this is not you or yours, but mine"), turning off our phones, and focusing
on the real people and things in the present moment with us, we can assert
the value of selves and souls in a world that would reduce both these things
to data points or dollars. We become living beings with a plenitude of self
through our engagement with other living beings, and with the "media" of
the living world that are fitted to our means of cognition at its richest: music,

194. Byrne, "A Nod to Ned Ludd."
195. Silverman, *Terms of Service*, 3.

print, sunlight, dirt, the flutter of leaves against a blue September sky. Like Herman Melville's Bartleby the Scrivener, we can reclaim our power and our attention by saying *I prefer not to*. But unlike Bartleby, we can choose other activities with intention and joy: reading, walking, talking, or just lingering under a tree on a bright fall day, allowing ourselves to be quiet. And we can keep reminding ourselves: *we can choose*.

Ultimately I don't say *give up technology*; I say *be mindful of it and what it does, make your own choices about it, and don't take it as normal without asking what that term means*. I'm still pondering what *normal* will look like, especially as my students and their children grow. But there's one thing I do know: human beings need real and meaningful things to do, and a living world to do them in. And I'm really skeptical about whether either of these are ultimately improved by screens.

One afternoon, I sat on a couch with a dear eleven-year-old friend, playing with her mother's iPhone. This child, who is fluent with the phone but also loves books, turtles, cats, dogs, frogs, and her tire swing (and volunteered with the Tioman Turtle Project in Malaysia, using PowerPoint to educate her classmates and me about its work), had figured out how to use the phone's famous automatic voice guide Siri as a toy. She got it to address her as a string of nonsense syllables it thought was her name, adjusted the voice settings so Siri morphed from American to Australian to Chinese, and asked random questions to see what happened. "Tell me a story," she begged, and Siri—showing the hand of someone at Apple whose wit in these matters is far ahead of mine—spun a little charmingly self-referential tale about when she and "Eliza"—yes, *that* ELIZA—became friends. "Sing to me," the child commanded, and Siri, after demurring ("I don't think you'd like it"), began to recite, in a deadpan monotone that could have been the natural "voice" of a computer or could have been programmed to sound more ironically like a "computer" than it already would (so meta!): *I could while away the hours/ Conferring with the flowers* . . . . The girl, her mother, and I laughed, faintly chilled, and finished the lyric: *If I only had a brain.*

I took the phone and asked Siri a question myself: "What is the Turing test?"

Siri stalled, having registered my question as "touring:" *I don't understand you.*

"Where do you live?" I asked.

The data-loading wheel spun as Siri thought, then responded: *Right here.*

Like John in the Anne Sexton poem, I chose not to inquire further. But I'm still wondering—for myself, my students, my eleven-year-old friend, and our world—what *here*, in Siri's language and ours, meant for us, and what it will.

2

Pay attention—even when it hurts.

"The universe is full of magical things patiently waiting for
our wits to grow sharper."

—Eden Phillpotts, *A Shadow Passes* (1919)

"...among wonders we are born and placed and surrounded
on all sides, so that to whatever thing we first turn our eyes,
it is a wonder and full of wonders, if only we examine it for
a little."

—Giovanni Dondi, *De Fontibus Calidis Agre
Patavini Consideratio* (c. 1382)[1]

ONE BRIGHT, SOFT, RAINY June afternoon several years ago, I took a walk in
the woods. I was grieving, and I was confused, as a constellation of personal
doubts coalesced into a spiritual one. That morning I'd been to church and
seen some friends ordained as deacons. Four years earlier, I'd been in line
to be one of them. Not anymore. A spiritual pain had deepened to anger as
I sat on that wooden pew, my brain shuffling through its latest preoccupations and griefs from the news: black oil bubbling from the ocean floor BP
had punctured, Haitians waiting in line amid earthquake ruins with their
water cans, my own dear grandmother, gone. It had been explained to me
that bad things happened so people could learn to choose better ones, and
help each other along. *But why hurt people in the first place, God?* a caustic
inner voice jeered. *It doesn't make sense.* If I did not have God, did I have
love, from anywhere? Was I alone?

---

1. Bennett, *The Enchantment of Modern Life*, 33.

I fled to the woods that afternoon, trudging up my favorite path along the back side of a bluff. Maples and big oaks and walnut trees swayed and rustled overhead. The narrow track was almost covered by a carpet of wild-flowers whose leaves, glossy from a sudden rain, now reflected chips of blue sky. Roots stuck up like teeth through the soil. I wandered, gradually slowed by some need to linger, to wait. *Here am I.* This was the point where Moses turned and saw the burning bush, where Jacob spied the angel sitting by a stream, smiling, rolling up his sleeves for a wrestling match. Every angel is terrifying, Rilke wrote. So is time. So is love. Most of all, so is love.

Are you there?

A sudden coolness swirled around me. The shadows of the eagles and crows that live on that bluff flowed over the canopy of trees. Sun-cast shapes of wings crossed my face.

Are you there?

And I heard my grandmother, saw her, felt her: her soft, powdered cheek brushing mine, her small hands reaching, her voice speaking words she had said to me before she died: *Everybody loses faith sometimes, honey. It's not easy.*

Oh, Nana. I clapped my hands to my face and cried. *There's so much faith I've lost.* It was the sixth of June, three days before her birthday. She would have been ninety-one on that day, if she were living.

It's not easy. The voice spoke again, without sound. A warmth hummed in me around an image of her face that I had done nothing consciously to summon. Was she an angel? Was this how the whole afterlife thing worked: the dead and fiercely loved still subtly at work for us in Heaven, offering God coffee and cheese straws to ease Him into conversation on our behalf as smoothly as they would in life? This sudden quiet radiance in my own troubled, limited brain—was this the angel, here, inside me, who haunts wilderness, waiting to be found?

A few steps away, in the moss and ferns at the trail's edge, a big snail grazed, bending its neck slowly left and right. It was pale tan and cream and caramel all over, with a scuffed white patch on the raised central spiral of its shell. The fluted gray edge of its foot reached to touch a crumb of soil, testing it. The snail settled on the spot, and then its moist veined body gave one heave and hitched the whole shell forward. In its path lay a whole twig's worth of moist seedpods, and it stretched the front lip of its body over the tip of the twig and chewed. One by one the pods disappeared into some small mouth I couldn't see. The snail's long antennae bobbed. Its moist veined flesh pressed against the near-translucent wall of its shell, that house it dragged forward, and forward again.

Where else did that snail have to be? Absolutely nowhere. It was on forest time, creature time, snail time, unimaginably and wondrously strange.
And now I was too, outside my sadness in a place that was unhurried and
quiet, only itself.

How long did I hunker there, watching that creature hauling itself forward, in a frame of infinite patience, of a world of mute desire pressing on,
desiring—if anything—to become, only, more itself? Wanting, in Sappho's
verb τελέσσαι, *telessai*, to *happen?*[2] I don't know.

Was this my answer?

You are always already here, held and beheld, in this world of all things
homely, and lovely, and seen. Stop and look at this fellow creature. Just look.

A door in what I thought was reality swung open onto a vast place that
is always, already, waiting to be seen. And in those moments my grief and
anger and desire and wonder widened and blended into something I realized
was also love. Yet this love was bigger than any romantically derived notion
of that word I had ever had. It included my confusion and wonder and spread
them out at the edges until they blended with a larger unknowability I could
not define. If God is love, this is the love God is—mottled and dark as lichen
or marble, grown in the decaying or the broken or the deep-underground.
This love includes each of these emotions I have named and more I have not.
It forces you to look and see what is real, and to decide how you will respond.
It it is built on gazing carefully, and on remaining even in the midst of pain.
And it is always around us and waiting for us, everywhere.

Some things have changed since then. Some things have gotten clearer.
Fresh troubles and questions have arisen. Yet that desire to open my eyes on
this world every day is always here. It brings deep marvels, and deep pain.
I struggle to understand or to name it, especially since anger and grief are
always surging back and forth inside it, like the whole ocean's tides funneled
into the single narrow rock pool of my body and brain.

But now, when I say I love the world, this is the kind of love I mean.

And saving lives on Earth depends on our ability to welcome it into
our hearts, to see clearly in and through it, and to follow it, no matter where
it leads.

Our capacity for attention can bring us enchantment, delight, and renewed
acceptance of our place in the web of life that makes the world. It can also
bring us pain. So often an ache lies just on the other side of joy, sharpened

2. Thanks to my colleague Philip Freeman, Professor of Classics at Luther College, for this translation and for confirming my correct use of this verb.

by the inevitable progress of time: the child you're cradling will grow too big for your lap, the peonies in which you bury your face in June will be a memory in the January snow. Knowing we are human means knowing we are limited by time—but it also means confronting the fact that we make, and have made, some very big mistakes, and that we are summoned into the presence of suffering every day, whether we want to be or not. Wisconsin naturalist Aldo Leopold (1887–1948) wrote that "one of the penalties of an ecological education is that one lives alone in a world of wounds."[3] Let's face it: to be a sentient human being in the second decade of the twenty-first century is to live—even aside from personal circumstances, accidents, and losses—in a world of escalating and inescapable griefs.[4]

Perhaps it starts with honeybees. "Colony collapse disorder" (that alarming, matter-of-fact name) is killing them, and nobody seems to know why. Some keepers find hives full of dead bees, bodies tumbling out of the boxes like ash. Others find hives completely empty. Maybe chemicals have disoriented them, and they've gotten lost—a chilling idea for a creature so precise that it gets rattled by a hive moved more than two feet or less than two miles, so careful that it dances in patterns in the air to signal to other bees what kind of food it's found, and how much.[5] Rachel Carson's groundbreaking *Silent Spring* (1962) described the insecticide parathion's devastating effect on bees: "Honeybees become 'wildly agitated and bellicose' on contact with it, perform frantic cleaning movements, and are near death within half an hour."[6] Fifty-two years later, we're still catching up to her knowledge as we learn how pesticides and neonicotinoids poison and disrupt hives. Professional bee pollinators in California, who haul semi-trucks full of hives to orchards to pollinate crops like the handful of almonds I'm snacking on right now, are worried: without bees, much of human farming as we know it can't exist. Poet John Keats watched bees fumbling into the hearts of flowers, writing of their happiness in an autumn where good weather has *set budding more, / And still more, later flowers for the bees / until they think warm days will never cease.*[7] But they will. That's the hard knowledge in the heart

---

3. Leopold, "Round River," 183.

4. This seems to be one reason why, as writer Megan Mayhew Bergman observes, elegy is increasingly present in contemporary writing; see Bergman, "The Long and Pretty Good-bye." In her many books, philosopher Kathleen Dean Moore also engages with the necessity of confronting the griefs caused by climate change, most recently in *Great Tide Rising: Towards Clarity and Moral Courage in a Time of Planetary Change* (Berkeley, CA: Counterpoint, 2016).

5. See Wilson, *The Hive.*

6. Carson, *Silent Spring,* 29.

7. Keats, "To Autumn," 360. (Discussed further in Chapter 4.)

of Keats's wistfulness, and the ugly additional twist of our own knowledge today: the bees themselves will die massively and prematurely, their ancient patterns of being and making in their own dignified creature time shattered by us. They are innocent. We are not.

Or maybe it starts with any one of a hundred symptoms of life in our oceans, so fatally warmed and disrupted by human activity. Whales and dolphins driven mad by underwater sonar testing. Coral reefs bleached to barrenness.[8] Mercury poisoning accreting in the same top-of-the-food-chain fish that are now unsafe to eat in restaurants.[9] Jellyfish breeding like a science-fiction nightmare, overtaking all other life in our souring oceans.[10] Sea turtles choking on plastic bags, distracted from their homing paths to the ocean by beach condo lights. The infamous "five gyres" of plastic trash turning slowly in oceans worldwide.[11] And now, "sea star wasting syndrome," pictures of which are pathetic with an urgency that strikes something inside me absolutely cold. How mute and innocent the stumpy, deflating, afflicted stars look. How uncomfortably similar those stumps are to the hands of children amputated by warlords in Congo, or by white colonial overlords there a century earlier terrifying native populations into compliance.[12]

Or maybe it's fuzzy little baby chicks. In January 2014, as a brutally cold "polar vortex" sweeps across the country, we learn that Magellanic penguin chicks are dying in their home colony at Punta Tombo, Argentina, not only because of starvation (a longtime problem) but now because increased rainfall (a result of climate change) keeps their downy coats too wet for warmth. When it's dry, bird down is unbeatably warm. A Canada goose huddled chest-down on a frozen river eventually burns a goose-shaped hole right through the ice (I see this on our Upper Iowa River in January.) But

8. See McCalman, *The Reef*.

9. See the Monterey Bay Aquarium's "Seafood Watch List," online at https://www.seafoodwatch.org.

10. See Flannery, "They're Taking Over!"

11. According to the website 5gyres.org, which is dedicated to this problem, "Our oceans are dynamic systems, made up of complex networks of currents that circulate water around the world. Large systems of these currents, coupled with wind and the earth's rotation, create "gyres", massive, slow rotating whirlpools in which plastic trash can accumulate. The North Pacific Gyre, the most heavily researched for plastic pollution, spans an area roughly twice the size of the United States—though it is a fluid system, shifting seasonally in size and shape. Designed to last, plastic trash in the gyre will remain for decades or longer, being pushed gently in a slow, clockwise spiral towards the center. Most of the research on plastic trash circulating in oceanic gyres has focused on the North Pacific, but there are five major oceanic gyres worldwide, with several smaller gyres in Alaska and Antarctica."

12. See Adam Hochschild, *King Leopold's Ghost: A Story of Greed, Terror, and Heroism in Colonial Africa*.

when wet, it's very cold. "Imagine I put a wet down parka on you and throw you out in the snow," says a scientist on the radio, reporting from that Argentinian penguin colony. "How long do you think you'll last?"[13]

And this is only one sliver of only one type of suffering: wild creatures. I haven't even touched the human suffering that is taking place all over the world right now. (Pause to let the news headlines scroll through your mind. It may take a while.) I haven't touched the suffering in any one of our own lives. You already know this the hard way: staying alive to the world and accepting your own emotions without always trying to numb them out means welcoming into yourself an incredibly strong capacity for feeling, without always being able to control whether that feeling is pleasure or pain. "Break us open," my pastor prays, "so that we may share ourselves with others." Vulnerability is the basic requirement of art, and emotional connection and caring and service, yet anyone being even halfway attentive and vulnerable to the world could find ourselves flattened every day by the variety of suffering and wrongdoing that streams into our lives. We've already altered our world almost beyond the recognition of our great-great-grandparents and are witnessing its irreversible change as a result of that. We're living in the Anthropocene, the era of un-undoable human intervention in the climate, and of omnipresent information about the results of our actions. In her book *The Sixth Extinction* (2014), science writer Elizabeth Kolbert describes our current era of human-driven climate changes and species extinctions, writing that in addition to amphibians, which are "currently the world's most endangered class of animals," about "one-third of all reef-building corals, a third of all freshwater mollusks, a third of sharks and rays, a quarter of all mammals, a fifth of all reptiles, and a sixth of all birds are headed toward oblivion."[14] The same human drive for knowledge, communication, and awareness that fuels our discoveries, our attempts to help others, and our sense of compassion can also drive the problem, even as it drives our guilt about the problem: "as soon as humans started using signs and symbols to represent the natural world," Kolbert writes, "they pushed beyond the limits of that world."[15] In this and many other ways, the Internet—that tool for "clicktivism" that nevertheless can get some things done, driven by electrically powered servers humming away in rooms that must be artificially cooled for them to live—can also heighten our immersion in a hurting world, educating and implicating us in a perpetual loop of awareness and responsibility.

13. See Fountain, "For Already Vulnerable Penguins."

14. Kolbert, *The Sixth Extinction*, 17–18.

15. Ibid., 266.

Of course, you don't have to go far to witness the hurting world—which some just call *reality*—in big ways and small. One April afternoon, pulling out old tomato vines in my garden, I accidentally exposed a hollow in the dirt lidded with leaves and straw and fur, cradling a pulsing knot of velvet-skinned baby rabbits. Their eyes were sealed, their fingernail-sized ears laid tight against their skulls. In their sleep, they scrambled slowly over one another, taking turns in the nest's warm heart. Arguing with myself—did I really want to lose my peppers *again* this year?—I nevertheless relented and tried to hide the nest under a tomato cage. But as soon as my back was turned, a crow swooped down and flapped away, a small brown scrap of baby rabbit dangling from its beak. Again and again I shooed the crows. So did the mother rabbit, darting at them until they hopped away, which I'd never seen a rabbit do. But by the evening, the nest was empty.

The fact is that we are immersed in a hurting world, which these days always presents us an additional fact: climate change is here; the emergency is upon us; the science is in. In our interconnected world, consumer choices on one side of the globe shape lives on the other. First World affluence fuels the climate change that floods out island nations like the Maldives, whose prime minister has televised underwater cabinet meetings to dramatize that soon, if nothing changes, he and his constituents will be climate refugees, all their homes drowned like villages in the path of a great Chinese dam. Tracing familiar sled routes across what used to be ice, Inuit hunters are now greeted with open water. The accretion of our industrial and lifestyle choices has remade "Earth" into some planet not quite recognizable—perhaps, as Bill McKibben called it in a book title, "Eaarth."

Yet, as individuals and societies, we can be remade by attention, and by the discernment and appropriate action it can bring, which will provide the guidance we need to navigate our changing, omnipresent network of new relationships and realities. Therefore, we must cultivate our ability to keep ourselves from being numbed or distanced from the other beings sharing our world. We must think about how the culture in which we swim enables or disables attention, the impulse to feel the suffering of others in our own bodies, and the acceptance of that other's reality, since we need to keep our equilibrium in a social and ecological world that is constantly changing. "Change itself does not destroy a culture," anthropologist Wade Davis reminds us in *Light at the Edge of the World* (2009). "All societies are constantly evolving. Indeed a culture survives . . . when it has enough confidence in its past and enough say in its future to maintain its spirit and essence through all the changes it will inevitably undergo."[16] How might

16. See Davis, *Light at the Edge of the World*, 127. Jared Diamond's *Collapse: How*

technological, political, or artistic cliché, in particular, damage our culture's "spirit and essence," hastening the decline of attention that can turn us into oppressors, sometimes without our knowing it? And how can art, history, and spirit—among the most enduring features of our culture—keep us awake, compassionate, and able to act, even when it hurts?

Let's think about the positive effects of awareness—the moments of attention when we feel ourselves alert, alive, present, and joyful in body and mind. Stopping in front of Raphael's "School of Athens" in the Vatican to look at the notebook-scribbling boy with his sideways-streaming hair, fluid as weeds in river water. Swishing on skis across fresh snow crust. Drowsy with a baby asleep on my chest, his breaths quivering against my skin. On a bicycle, mind wiped clean by motion, pedaling forward. On my house's front steps, watching a thunderstorm come. Drawing up the spinning sides of a clay bowl, its inside and outside equally exposed, as clay-smeared hands have done for thousands of years: *oh jug of breath*, Mary Oliver writes, *in the garden of dust.*[17] Lying in the grass as bats flutter like blown cinders in the twilight sky. In such states we are present before and enmeshed in all that is larger than our own fragile selves. And somehow—even within the sadness this state can bring—we are not afraid. This kind of presence comes to us not just because of a single moment but because of the patterns of attention that moments like it have created over days and years. It's a feeling of plenitude, of being part of and surrounded by the richness of the world in a way that lends your own small self a sense of fullness, richness, and expansion too. It's like falling in love, being in love: this state of aliveness and attention that comes on you, that makes your art, that wakes you up.

Yet ours is a world that, more and more, makes it difficult to fall in love. Those difficulties start within ourselves and the textures of our everyday lives, including their lack of physicality and reports from the senses, which shrink that sense of plenitude to an airless chamber of smallness and boredom that only seems inevitable. We all fight what Walker Percy called "everydayness" and Cole Porter called "the old ennui," that feeling of having seen or done or felt everything in your social and emotional repertoire a million times, the dimming of perception, a tedium that carries a curious edge of stress, or vice versa. Yet we may also feel an urge to fight against this to live toward the best we're capable of, to not waste our lives or fail to perceive them as they pass. "The search is what anyone would undertake if he were not sunk in the everydayness of his own life," says Percy's protagonist

Societies Choose to Fail or Succeed studies several societies, such as Easter Island and the Greenland Norse, who may have ruined themselves by clinging to cultural practices inappropriate for their environments.

17. Oliver, "Where Does the Dance Begin, Where Does It End?," 381.

Binx Bolling in *The Moviegoer* (1961). "To become aware of the possibility of the search is to be onto something. Not to be onto something is to be in despair."[18] In *The Sources of the Self* (1989), philosopher Charles Taylor identified a similar need. "We are in conflict, even confusion, about what it means to affirm ordinary life," Taylor wrote. "We are as ambivalent about heroism as we are about the value of the workaday goals that it sacrifices. We struggle to hold on to a vision of the incomparably higher, while being true to the central modern insights about the value of the ordinary life. We sympathize with both the hero and the anti-hero; and we dream of a world in which one could be, in the same act, both."[19] It's a quintessential human problem: we're the only animal that can foresee its own death, and therefore the animal most susceptible to distracting itself from, rather than making life-enriching meaning from, that fact, since admitting our longing for meaning also admits the fact of finite life.

Yet the defamiliarizing effect of attention can widen this loop, even, perhaps, open a way out of it. As we've seen through the work of Victor Shklovsky in Chapter 1, we all let habit smooth out our sense of immediacy in encountering the world every day: we see an object in front of us, he wrote, "as though it were enveloped in a sack."[20] For Shklovsky, Leo Tolstoy is an outstanding example of a writer who "seems to present things as if he himself saw them, saw them in their entirety, and did not alter them" and "makes the familiar seem strange by not naming the familiar object."[21] As he emphasizes by quoting Tolstoy himself, artists keep their perceptions fresh through self-discipline, always making a conscious effort to keep habit from glazing over the surface of one's mind. Here's a passage from Tolstoy's diary (March 1, 1897) that Shklovsky quotes as proof of how the "over-automation of an object" dulls our awareness in daily life:

> I was cleaning a room [Tolstoy writes] and, meandering about, approached the divan and couldn't remember whether or not I had dusted it. Since these movements are habitual and unconscious, I could not remember and felt that it was impossible to remember—so that if I had dusted it and forgot—that is, had acted unconsciously, then it was the same as if I had not. If some conscious person had been watching, then the fact could be established. If, however, no one was looking, or looking on

18. Percy, *The Moviegoer*, 13.
19. Taylor, *Sources of the Self*, 24.
20. Shklovsky, "Art as Technique," 11.
21. Ibid., 13.

unconsciously, if the whole complex lives of many people go on unconsciously, then such lives are as if they had never been.[22]

For Tolstoy and for Shklovsky, allowing oneself to be habitualized or deadened to the world numbs us right out of existence, making our "whole complex lives . . . as if they had never been." It makes us live our lives on autopilot, or, more specifically, a sort of emotional version of auto-complete, which guesses as we type what word we mean to say. Within our brains, the world turns something like the texture British writer Iain Sinclair describes as created by security cameras: "These mean gray boxes were actually erasing truth, disqualifying natural color . . . . Their alien consciousness was a mortuary dream, the dream of someone left in a coma after a road accident. A dream with no rage, no anxiety, no phallic dew. A dream without symbols or archetypes."[23] On screen, everything eventually turns gray. Initial surges of interest dwindle to reflexive twitches of curiosity. Living in this colorless mental world sends us into the same familiar downward spiral as lapsed exercisers: you don't notice or seek or read more complex things, so you can't, so you don't, so you can't—only, ultimately, what we can't quite remember, or quite grasp, or quite get interested in is the daily texture of our own one wild and precious life.[24] Remember: "habitualization," Shklovsky declares, "devours work, clothes, furniture, one's wife, and the fear of war."[25] Habitualization leaves us feeling that we—and other people, and the world—are not quite real. And morally, philosophically, and economically, that is a dangerous feeling.

Yet habit is less painful for us than admitting pain itself. The challenge of continually renovating and renewing our perceptions isn't anything new; many spiritual practices remind us to be fully present and to perceive each moment, person, or thing as it is—only as it is. Buddhist nun and teacher Pema Chodron describes it as "being fully present, feeling your heart, and greeting the next moment with an open mind."[26] Accepting what is actually happening in a moment is hard for human beings to do—we prefer to distract ourselves from it or tell ourselves stories about it: *I must be hungry, that's why I'm tired. [Insert name here] always makes me so mad—this is all her fault! Let me just finish my imaginary conversation in which I tell [name] exactly what I think of him!* Moment to moment, Chodron writes, "we are constantly projecting our preferences onto whatever is manifesting. Every-

22. Ibid., 12.

23. Sinclair, "Bulls & Bears," 106.

24. Mary Oliver's phrase. See Oliver, "The Summer Day," 386.

25. Shklovsky, "Art as Technique," 12.

26. Chodron, *Living Beautifully*, 41.

thing comes with our mixed feelings."[27] However, "[t]he path to unshakable well-being lies in being completely present and open to all sights, all sounds, all thoughts—never withdrawing, never hiding, never needing to jazz them up or tone them down."[28] Pay attention. Because what you are paying attention to is your own life as it passes by.

Paying attention, in body and mind, means letting reality nudge your internal clamorings and agendas aside so that you can hear it, feel it, and see it speak. It means letting the physical world, in the words of French poet Francis Ponge, "disarrange" you, and doing your best to view that world as it is, not as you might use it or interpret it to your own advantage. "Ponge advocated a manner of regarding the world's constituents," says writer Trebbe Johnson, "not as inferiors that we must somehow corral for our use and understanding, but as equals capable of startling us with the marvel of their particular selfhood."[29] This is the simple truth on which you can build a life of spirit, social curiosity, and art that all feed one another: so much of the suffering we cause ourselves and others—anxiety, jealousy, anger, which harden into rigid internal molds we try to press experience into—can be eased by accepting the truth that the world is not built to serve us, that we are here to learn, again and again, *it's not about me.* The world is conversation that happens through doing and seeing and understanding and thinking as well as through speech, always remaking and revising us. It's as small as the quiet exchange of smiles and nods with a passing stranger, the zoom and chitter of hummingbirds in your backyard on an August evening. It is conversation that happens in a world of material experience and contact, not primarily through the mediation of a glowing screen.

Such encounters and the wonder they bring can also help us recognize our interdependence with beings who share the Earth. To illustrate this, Timothy Morton borrows "Indra's net," an image of interdependence from Buddhist scripture: "At every connection in this infinite net hangs a magnificently polished and infinitely faceted jewel, which reflects in each of its facets all the facets of every other jewel in the net. Since the net itself, the number of jewels, and the facets of every jewel are infinite, the number of reflections is infinite as well."[30] Reality, seen through the lens of truly ecological thought, looks like Indra's net; everything reflects, affects, and is reflected and affected by everything else, as biology, quantum mechanics, philosophy, economics, and other fields have their own ways of explaining.

27. Ibid., 105.
28. Ibid., 106.
29. Johnson, "Gaze Even Here," 67.
30. Morton, *The Ecological Thought*, 39–40.

Ecology itself provides continual models of its own interconnectedness. In a prairie ecosystem, for instance, the roots of plants form a thick net that protects soil, a mesh of vegetation which the manure and hoof of the bison—native prairie beast—is uniquely suited to delve and "cultivate" and fertilize as it grazes. Even in heavy snow, a prairie can shelter pheasants and mice, who pick up fallen seeds in the air pockets formed by drooping stems and burrow from chamber to chamber underneath an apparently solid white roof. (Life goes on underfoot, even in the cold.) To describe the mutual gravitational forces of objects, a physicist colleague of mine quoted Paul Dirac: "When you bend down to pick a flower, you are moving the farthest star."[31] (You actually are, since you are adjusting that network of gravitational forces between flower and star.) You can see at least the top layers of this interrelationship in your own life: the city installs a sidewalk in your neighborhood, so you walk more and lose weight. Agricultural subsidies inflate the price of corn so farmers plant every square inch of field, erasing the hedgerows that had been habitat for the few pheasants left, making rare the sight of a brilliant ringneck rooster picking in roadside gravel. You discard your cellphone and it goes to a landfill in some place where economic injustice makes protesting First World trash unprofitable, there to be picked over by locals (including children) whose bodies absorb the mercury and other toxins from what was once your brand-new toy.[32] Mercury also makes its way into seawater, absorbed in higher and higher doses in fish as they ascend the food chain, and in the bodies of humans who eat that fish. I could go on. So could you.

Because our actions always ultimately trickle down and pool in the bodies of other beings—usually those we mistakenly think of as "below" us—and then reverberate back, we must *see* the other. The encounter with that other being makes us fully aware that the world is not a story about us, jolting us off the pedestal at the center of things on which we like to place ourselves and back into the net of ecological connections of which we are one part. It makes us stop and look again, picking up that single fallen blue jay feather from the sidewalk. It prompts wonder, gratitude, mercy. Several philosophers and critics have called this sensation *enchantment*, positioning

31. Physicists have little trouble understanding the ecological thought, since that's already always their own universe; the "strangeness of the other" can be seen in the same colleague's description of quantum mechanics processes: "you may put something into a black-box system and get results at the other end—like Schroedinger's cat—but what's in the middle is opaque to you." An eternally, irreducibly strange space—which, as the Heisenberg uncertainty principle reminds us, may never be fully measurable at all. I like that. Thanks to Elizabeth Golovatski for this reference.

32. Grossman, "High-Tech Wasteland."

it as a way to renew our generous, curious spirits. "To be enchanted," writes philosopher Jane Bennett,

> is to be struck and shaken by the extraordinary that lives amid the familiar and the everyday . . . . If popular psychological wisdom has it that you have to love yourself before you can love another, [I suggest] that you have to love life before you can care about anything. The wager is that, to some small but irreducible extent, one must be enamored with existence and occasionally even enchanted in the face of it in order to be capable of donating some of one's scarce mortal resources to the service of others . . . . This life provokes moments of joy, and that joy can propel ethics.[33]

Bennett emphasizes that enchantment begins with "a moment of pure presence," no matter how small, that makes us pause and focus, physically and mentally, on something that is not ourselves: "To be simultaneously transfixed in wonder and transported by sense," she writes, "to be both caught up and carried away—enchantment is marked by this odd combination of somatic effects."[34] While enchantment may share a border with the famous Romantic "sublime," an aesthetic state in which one is held rapt before an experience or object (particularly a large or overpowering one, like a mountain or thundering waterfall) with a combination of wonder and fear, the "overall effect of enchantment," Bennett writes, "is a mood of fullness, plenitude, or liveliness, a sense of having had one's nerves or circulation or concentration powers tuned up or recharged—a shot in the arm, a fleeting return to childlike excitement about life."[35] Indeed, as historians Lorraine Daston and Katherine Park have written, "in early modern Europe, the terms for wonder and wonders—*admiratio, mirabilia, miracula*—'seem to have had their roots in an Indo-European word for 'smile.'"[36] This fascinating linguistic fact captures, like a fly in amber, a human experience we can still recognize: arrested by delight, we smile. Aroused to awareness of that other thing, we are then primed to care for it, even to love it, and to be reminded—as humans always *do* need to be reminded—that our own preoccupations aren't all there is to the world. Sometimes these moments, as the poet Rainer Maria Rilke writes in his *Duino Elegies* (1923), echoing Wordsworth's idea of the sublime, overwhelm us with a mixture of beauty and terror: "For beauty is nothing / but the beginning of terror," he writes,

33. Bennett, *The Enchantment of Modern Life*, 4.
34. Ibid., 5.
35. Ibid.
36. Ibid.

"which we still are just able to endure, / and we are so awed because it serene-
ly disdains / to annihilate us."[37] At such moments, we are also reminded, as
political philosopher (and motorcycle mechanic) Matthew Crawford writes,
that "the quality of being wide-awake, of being a clear-sighted person who
looks around and sees the whole situation, isn't something I can take for
granted in myself. It is something that needs to be achieved on a moment-
to-moment basis. The presence of others in a shared world makes this both
possible and necessary."[38]

Encountering the stranger has profound ecological and spiritual consequences. "One of the things that make me love writing or looking at pictures is that you become unconscious of yourself," wrote the English author
Diana Athill. "Anything absorbing makes you become not 'I' but 'eye'—you
escape the ego."[39] Like the Romantic poets, we cross those friction lines
where internal and external reality come together. In "Lines Written A Few
Miles Above Tintern Abbey," (1798), William Wordsworth famously described the effect of walking in and gazing on the natural world: "with an
eye made quiet by the power / Of harmony," he wrote, "and the deep power
of joy, / We see into the life of things."[40] Like Wordsworth, we can look at
and into the painting, the sound, the flicker of leaf-light, the dusk-blurred
border of forest and field until we feel that instant of time is not centered
only on ourselves anymore. French philosopher Maurice Merleau-Ponty
described this state as "chiasm," a crossing and catching that echoes Walt
Whitman's image of the "noiseless patient spider" spinning its web and of
the intersecting mesh of Indra's net. (Philosopher Kimberly Curtis wonderfully describes this as "philosophy at the joints where sensed and sens-
ing crossed over, encroached, reciprocated.")[41] Merleau-Ponty writes, "As
many painters have said, I feel myself looked at by things . . . so that the
seer and the visible reciprocate one another and we no longer know which
sees and which is seen."[42]

The narrator of that most mind-blowing of American novels, Herman
Melville's *Moby-Dick* (1851), goes to this place of crossing over and over
again, and takes us with him. In one chapter, he finds himself in a tiny boat
in the center of a pod of whales swirling around their calves, some of which

37. Rilke, "The First Elegy," 151.

38. Crawford, *Shop Class as Soulcraft*, 125.

39. This quote comes from an interview Athill gave to the magazine *Intelligent Life*
(now *1843*) in 2008. See also Weldon, "Diana Athill: The Sufficient Self" and "In Her
Own Words: Diana Athill."

40. Wordsworth, "Lines Written A Few Miles Above Tintern Abbey," 132–133.

41. Curtis, *Our Sense of the Real*, 28.

42. Ibid.

are still attached to their mothers by umbilical cords. "The lake, as I have hinted, was to a considerable depth exceedingly transparent," he says,

> and as human infants while suckling will calmly and fixedly gaze away from the breast, as if leading two different lives at the time; and while yet drawing mortal nourishment, be still spiritually feasting upon some unearthly reminiscence;—even so did the young of these whales seem looking up towards us, but not at us, as if we were but a bit of Gulf-weed in their new-born sight . . . . One of these little infants, that from certain queer tokens seemed hardly a day old, might have measured some fourteen feet in length, and some six feet in girth. He was a little frisky; though as yet his body seemed scarce recovered from that irksome position it had so lately occupied in the maternal reticule; where, tail to head, and all ready for the final spring, the unborn whale lies bent like a Tartar's bow. The delicate side-fins, and the palms of his flukes, still freshly retained the plaited crumpled appearance of a baby's ears newly arrived from foreign parts.[43]

Calling himself only "Ishmael"—a Biblical model of the outcast in this novel haunted by Milton and the Bible and God—the narrator scrambles for similes as Homer and Shakespeare and Faulkner and Woolf scramble, as any human scrambles, to render into two-dimensional words the fathomless mystery of what we are looking at: this thing that is always looking *towards us, but not at us*, at something we are straining to see, some invisible thing beyond the visible world, *some unearthly reminiscence*. And as we try to speak of it, the struggle to render that thing into language helps us share the world with it, even if—as is also the case with Ishmael—we are actively helping to destroy it. The slipping and climbing-towards in words, like a novice mountaineer, can help us see the thing as clearly as Ishmael in his boat, our brains temporarily wiped clean by wonder. The whale is right here. We look into its eyes. The whale looks back, from a realm and a type of consciousness we will never fully explore or understand.

As Hannah Arendt wrote, people become aware that they are real because of their contact with others, including nonhuman others like animals, objects, works of art, and ideas, and this contact creates an inward space for dialogue and conversation that ultimately keeps the self honest. Everyday encounters with the reality and variety of the world expand the self just like the potter's fingers expand a hollow vessel from the inside, gently moving it up, out, and sideways, all the time. In this inherently honest inner space, conscience also lives, because for Arendt, "conscience" is not a matter of

---

43. Melville, *Moby-Dick*, 325 (Ch. 87, "The Grand Armada").

obeying whatever changeable social code might be in place at that time but of obeying the need to remain in conversation with this inner self, and to be answerable to it. "Its criteria for action," Arendt wrote, "will not be the usual rules, recognized by multitudes and agreed upon by society, but whether I shall be able to live with myself in peace when the time has come to think about my deeds and words. Conscience is the anticipation of the fellow who awaits you if and when you come home."[44] Therefore, Arendt says, those who hid Jews from the Nazis did so because they could not stand to live in the same "house"—the same mind, body, and consciousness—with a murderer. This is one definition of that abstract, often-sought thing, "plenitude of self," and a reason to have it.

Despite its potential for abuse by tech-centrists and politicians, science opens a space for wonder in the self by giving us ways to describe and observe reality. In his landmark *On the Origin of Species* (1859), the great evolutionary biologist Charles Darwin (1809–1882) leaves much more room for encounters with mystery—and expresses much more humility and wonder—than modern anti-evolutionists acknowledge. To read *On the Origin of Species* is to follow a curious, humble, scientific mind led by its own discoveries into enthusiasms that unspool in rapturous sentences: "It is a truly wonderful fact—the wonder of which we are apt to overlook from familiarity—that all animals and plants throughout all time and space should be related to each other in group subordinate to group, in the manner which we everywhere behold—namely, varieties of the same species most closely related together, species of the same genus less closely and unequally related together, forming sections and sub-genera, species of distinct genera much less closely related, and genera related in different degrees, forming sub-families, families, orders, and classes."[45] While a non-scientist might be considerably less carried away than Darwin by what looks like the specialist minutiae of classification systems, we can still hail and honor the presence of a fellow geeker-outer, reveling in the "wonder" (that carefully chosen, unexpected word) of natural systems. This is a man who as an insect-collecting Cambridge student put a beetle in his mouth to hold onto it because both his hands were full of other beetles.[46] When students read excerpts from

44. Arendt, *The Life of the Mind: Thinking*, 191.

45. Darwin, *On the Origin of Species*, 122–123. (This passage and the "Tree of Life" analogy come near the end of Chapter 4.)

46. I learned this from my colleague Todd Pedlar, Professor of Physics at Luther, in his lecture on Darwin for our first-year common course, Paideia, which quotes this passage from Darwin's autobiography: "But no pursuit at Cambridge was followed with nearly so much eagerness or gave me so much pleasure as collecting beetles. It was the mere passion for collecting, for I did not dissect them, and rarely compared their

Darwin's *On The Origin of Species* in our first-year common course, they realize that the text doesn't support the arrogant, hostile-to-religion cliché of Darwin still in circulation. "It's not that he doesn't think there couldn't be more to the physical world than we understand," one student said. "It's just that, because he's a scientist, and a humble man, he's not going to *say* that there is, because the evidence doesn't show it. He just can't *know*." Right. And neither can we. But we keep looking anyway.

Darwin has a lot to teach—especially because *wonder* is such an important word to him. A onetime-potential clergyman, Darwin can perhaps best be described as agnostic, although even that label's a bit messy. Referring to "the stamp of far higher workmanship" apparent in nature and the "primordial form, into which life was first breathed"—a very significant use of the passive voice—Darwin asks, "It is scarcely possible to avoid comparing the eye to a telescope . . . . But may not this inference be presumptuous? Have we any right to assume that the Creator works by intellectual powers like those of man?"[47] He never closes the door to beauty, mystery and the need for humans to open ourselves to the ineffable and challenge ourselves to see how—in the words of Shakespeare's Hamlet—"there are more things in heaven and earth . . . than are dreamt of in [our] philosophy."[48] Darwin's not blind to suffering. In sobering terms, he describes the "struggle" for life between plants and animals competing for existence, even within "a plant which annually produces a thousand seeds, of which on an average only one comes to maturity," and contrasts it with "the face of nature bright with gladness" we may apprehend if we aren't really looking: "we do not see, or we forget, that the birds which are idly singing round us mostly live on insects or seeds, and are thus constantly destroying life; or we forget how these songsters, or their eggs, or their nestlings, are destroyed by birds and beasts of prey; we do not always bear in mind, that though food may be now superabundant, it is not so at all seasons of each recurring year."[49] Yet his vision always returns to "the beautiful and harmonious diversity of nature," rising to the symphonic analogy of life as a giant tree with which he ends chapter 4

external characters with published descriptions, but got them named anyhow. I will give a proof of my zeal: one day, on tearing off some old bark, I saw two rare beetles, and seized one in each hand; then I saw a third and new kind, which I could not bear to lose, so that I popped the one which I held in my right hand into my mouth. Alas! it ejected some intensely acrid fluid, which burnt my tongue so that I was forced to spit the beetle out, which was lost, as was the third one." See Darwin, ed., *Charles Darwin: his life told in an autobiographical chapter, and in a selected series of his published letters,* 20. See also Weldon, "Darwin's Beetle: On Geeking Out."

47. Ibid., 83, 422, 173.

48. Shakespeare, *Hamlet* (Act I, Scene V), 942.

49. Ibid., 65.

of *On the Origin of Species*. To appreciate its slow build and its deep, radiant attentiveness, let's read it in full:

> The affinities of all the beings of the same class have sometimes been represented by a great tree. I believe this simile largely speaks the truth. The green and budding twigs may represent existing species; and those produced during each former year may represent the long succession of extinct species. At each period of growth all the growing twigs have tried to branch out on all sides, and to overtop and kill the surrounding twigs and branches, in the same manner as species and groups of species have tried to overmaster other species in the great battle for life. The limbs divided into great branches, and these into lesser and lesser branches, were themselves once, when the tree was small, budding twigs; and this connexion of the former and present buds by ramifying branches may well represent the classification of all extinct and living species in groups subordinate to groups. Of the many twigs which flourished when the tree was a mere bush, only two or three, now grown into great branches, yet survive and bear all the other branches; so with the species which lived during long-past geological periods, very few now have living and modified descendants. From the first growth of the tree, many a limb and branch has decayed and dropped off; and these lost branches of various sizes may represent those whole orders, families, and genera which have now no living representatives, and which are known to us only from having been found in a fossil state. As we here and there see a thin straggling branch springing from a fork low down in a tree, and which by some chance has been favoured and is still alive on its summit, so we occasionally see an animal like the Ornithorhynchus or Lepidosiren, which in some small degree connects by its affinities two large branches of life, and which has apparently been saved by fatal competition by having inhabited a protected station. As buds give rise by growth to fresh buds, and these, if vigorous, branch out and overtop on all sides many a feebler branch, so by generation I believe it has been with the great Tree of Life, which fills with its dead and broken branches the crust of the earth, and covers the surface with its ever branching and beautiful ramifications.[50]

Wonder and humility shimmer around Darwin's descriptions of the living world he so closely observed and so well loved that he calls it "beautiful," and they shape his diligent investigations toward the form "into which

50. Ibid., 123–124.

life was first breathed." As a mature thinker, Darwin learned to live with uncertainty—"the origin of species," he wrote in his introduction to the book, "that mystery of mysteries"—and even to thrive on it, since it propelled him forward into all he had yet to discover and into the living world that brought him such joy.[51] This spoke powerfully to my students and to me. How can this openness shape our own educations and personal quests? How can we discern meaning, even beauty, amid the confusion of our changing ideas and changing lives, and how we can remain open to, accepting of, and curious about that change?

At our best, we humans keep trying to coexist with that greater mystery, to stay in a space of uncertainty even when intensity of feeling, and grief, threaten to undo us. Writer Trebbe Johnson visited the site of a clear-cut, old-growth Canadian forest to confront the inner suffering that a suffering landscape prompts in us when we look at it. In photographs of her visit, she sits on a stump the size of a tabletop. Even thinking about touching such a giant wound makes me cringe, because, as she writes, "aversion is a natural response to bearing witness to something tragic." Yet Johnson argues for the importance of "gaz[ing] even here,"[52] despite the shock and grief that a clear view of ecological destruction can bring. This type of grief has been named by philosopher and professor of sustainability Glenn Albrecht as "solastalgia" (from Latin *solacium*, "comfort," and Greek *algia*, "pain"), meaning "the pain experienced when there is recognition that the place where one resides and that one loves is under immediate assault."[53] The echo of "nostalgia" in the term is deliberate, for, as Johnson writes, "the dark side of nature seeps into your memory and imagination, reminding you not just of what the place used to be, but what you, too, used to be when it was part of you."[54] Then we have to confront the multifaceted reality that the place we loved—that we still love—is gone, and that that very love—*not enough to save*—is itself a source of pain.[55] Action can combat solastalgia in advance, but only if we recognize that correcting the decline of our beloved places requires more difficult and longer-term work than

51. Ibid., 11.

52. Johnson, "Gaze Even Here," 67–71.

53. Ibid., 69.

54. Ibid. I hear an echo of this passage from Colette's *My Mother's House* (1922), 4: "Both house and garden are living still, I know; but what of that, if the magic has deserted them? If the secret is lost that opened to me a whole world—light, scents, birds and trees in perfect harmony, the murmur of human voices now silent for ever—a world of which I have ceased to be worthy?"

55. Also the title of a book by Melissa Holbrook Pearson, describing the experience of *solastalgia* for her childhood landscape in Akron, Ohio.

the mere romance of grief or the obliviousness of consumerism demand. Essayist Hal Crowther has astutely observed that "Americans never turn sentimental about something of real value—wilderness, wild animals, small towns, baseball, mountain music, our privacy—until the way we live and do business has pressed it to the edge of extinction. Then we administer affectionate last rites to everything we failed to love enough."[56] Solastalgia may be important after the fact, as a sign we *did* love a place, but its presence is even more useful as a wake-up call.

And it's not only Americans, of course, who feel it. When Italian writer Eduardo Nesi sold his family's textile mill in Prato to stop the long, globalization-induced hemorrhage of profits to "cheaper" materials and labor from other countries, he felt buffeted by a pain not only personal but cultural. In his 2010 book *Story of My People,* Nesi mourns what felt to him like the loss not just of a particular craft tradition but of a whole way of being in the world, orderly, prideful, responsible, and built on the right of people in a particular place to do meaningful work and make something that will reflect that place, and their values. Solastalgia, in his case, is not just emotional but cultural and economic. Globalization, he writes, has falsely promised to bring an increased respect for the sort of high-quality Italian craft signaled by names like Ferragamo, Ferrari, or Armani, and instead, has destroyed the economy that nurtured those firms under very particular (and highly local) circumstances. "[These companies] liked to call themselves industrialists," he writes, "but they weren't industrialists and never had been:"

> They were artisans, extraordinary and fragile artisans, the distant great-grandsons of the masters of medieval workshops, and in spite of that they represented the structural framework of an economic system that, incredibly, rested on their shoulders . . . that chaotic and deeply vital economic system of ours, created by unlettered artisans, was the single most important factor in the transformation of a mediocre, snarling, frightened, Fascist Italy into a modern nation.[57]

Nesi's view here is Darwinian, but not in the clichéd sense of the word. Like Darwin's "tree of life"—and like the great state university systems now under attack all over the United States—the Italian craft economy is the result of long, patient accumulation of growth tempered by accident, chance, and luck over time. While it took centuries to grow, it can take a decade, or less, to destroy. With the loss of the unique products of particular places and their traditions, against which worldwide movements like Slow

56. Crowther, *Gather at the River,* 27.
57. Nesi, *Story of My People,* 137–138.

Food are attempting to protect, a larger cultural identity rooted in a beloved place is also lost. It's not only about keeping Parmigiano-Reggiano cheese or sparkling wine from Champagne "authentic"—it's about acknowledging and preserving the particular relationships of people, workers, land, and animals in a place that weaves cultures, and ways of life, over time. Such relationships are what "the economy," "globalization," or any other such glib shibboleth is really stealing from us. The problem is, once they are gone, their complexity and the layers of meaning and knowledge they accrete over time are difficult, if not impossible, to resurrect. Solastalgia can alert us to their loss by signaling, with its particular sharp, twisting, longing pain, all we stand to lose if we let them pass away for good.

In one recent October I stood at the well on my grandparents' farm in Alabama, a wide concrete pipe surrounded by a cedar-post scaffold and roofed with tin. The well is dry; the hill is bare. Yet in my childhood, everything was different. Behind a twelve-foot, deer-repelling wire fence, with aluminum pie tins swinging and flashing in the sun, was a garden of collards and tomatoes and melons, ripening, swelling, mute and intent. Right next to the well was a giant fig tree, "the Biblical fruit," my father never failed to remark. And covering the whole hilltop was an orchard with peach and plum trees and a cedar-post scuppernong arbor, all fed by that cool living water, deep underground, reflecting my own face back to me against a floating blue circle of sky. Like any little Methodist girl, I'd learned in church about the Israelites who wandered in the desert, hoping for a lasting and bountiful home—a home that, when they found it, would be marked by water. Water was the way God spoke to his people, after all: in the angry rising flood, in the apology of the rainbow; in the spring that gushed out when Moses struck that rock and those wanderers stumbled forward to sluice their faces and their hands and drink and drink and drink. Jesus spoke of water too, of repleteness and rest, of seeds that fell on barren ground and seeds that sprang forth from good soil to bring forth fruit. Like any great teacher—or artist—he spoke to his listeners in the language of the body, and in the language the body learns from its life in the living world: thirst, hunger, quenched, satisfied, root and branch, green sprout and rough bark jacketing the life within the tree that pushes itself up and up. Even as a child I knew in some space below knowing that this life must be God, that God was in the land as surely as soil or mineral or rock, that the vibrant and unpredictable flow of water signaled the presence of the invisible forces moving the whole world for which God was only one name. It ran together in my imagination with the buckets and baskets overflowing with fruit, in the voices of my little sister and my baby brother and my mother and my grandparents and my father, in the gnarled shapes of plum-tree branches and the summer sun flickering through the leaves, with the faith I had then that this world as I knew it would never die.

Now the well stands alone. The orchard and the fig tree and the scuppernong arbor and the garden are gone. So is the silver-burnished tin dipper from which we drank that well water on every single trip to the orchard. So are my grandparents. So is my father, who loved this land the way I love it still. On that October day, warm even for Alabama, my mother lifted the well cover and he dropped a stone inside. From twenty feet away I heard the thunk—not a splash—where it hit. "Dry," he said. I wanted to look inside. I didn't want to look inside. That lost orchard painted itself across my mind so vividly it threatened to eclipse the actual sight of the remaining trees in that spot. Alone at my desk, eleven hundred miles and five years away, it's with me now.

Solastalgia. The place you loved is gone, or dying. *The Book of Common Prayer* gives us words to plea for it: *For the good earth which God has given us, and for the wisdom and will to conserve it, let us pray to the Lord.*[58] It gives us also that terrible and accurate reproach, that plea for forgiveness we fear we can never deserve: *in your compassion forgive us our sins, known and unknown, things done and left undone.*[59]

What are all the things we have left undone to save a place, or its creatures, knowing full well what we should do?

What indeed.

When I let the weight of grief and responsibility settle on me—*really* settle in, including grief for all the things I have done and left undone and how I have contributed to the threatened world—I realize that grief, *solastalgia,* terror, and loss as I am invoking them here do not let me resort to cliché. They do not fit into small, neat shapes. They don't trim down. They haunt, and they don't go away. Therefore I am driven to keep hammering at them, to try to get the thing into words, to write the things I mourn and sense and feel. Jaron Lanier usefully writes that in the twenty-first century, we can't let ourselves be drawn into too-simple "Rousseau-ist" fantasies of a lost, "authentic" world. But neither can we ignore our haunting connection with those vanishing things. "[T]he cost if I let go might be great," he writes, "even if the resulting amnesia would hide the loss from me."[60]

If we really see that fact, and if we see—really see—the magnitude of what we are always casually ignoring and squandering, that vision can strike us to the heart, intense and often literally unbearable, both in its wonder and

58. From *The Prayers of the People,* Form I, *Book of Common Prayer,* 384.

59. From *The Prayers of the People,* Form VI, *Book of Common Prayer,* 393.

60. Lanier, *Who Owns the Future?,* 132.

in its corresponding pain. We can't kid ourselves; awareness is also dark and troubling, just as full humanity is not always "happy." Seeing too much can kill. Compassion can become compassion fatigue. George Eliot acknowledged this possibility in her great novel *Middlemarch* (1871–2): "If we had a keen vision and feeling of all ordinary human life," she wrote, "it would be like hearing the grass grow and the squirrel's heart beat, and we should die of that roar which lies on the other side of silence. As it is, the quickest of us walk about well wadded with stupidity."[61]

Yet avoiding any discomfort of spiritual or material kinds—as much as our culture urges us to—reduces our capacity for not only imagination and empathy but for human existence. It makes us less than adult, and it discombobulates even more than the inevitable troubles, anxieties, and difficulties inside and outside our own heads that come with life in this world already would. "To be fully alive, fully human, and completely *awake*," says Pema Chodron, "is to be continually thrown out of the nest."[62] *Thrown out of the nest*—it's a metaphor of disarrangement, of being nudged aside to make room for what else there is on the earth with us, which we are continually invited to see and to see again. Any amount of awareness can help us renovate our perceptions from within, which will lead to actions. "Since death is certain but the time of death is uncertain," Chodron often teaches, "what is the most important thing?"[63] How rich our lives can be if we really consider this. And how different the art we make, and our treatment of everything else in creation, can look.

The American patron saint of attention turned to spiritual and political action is Henry David Thoreau (1817–1862), son of a Concord, Massachusetts pencil-maker and famous not-quite-hermit who build himself a cabin on the shores of a pond. "I went to the woods because I wished to live deliberately," he writes in *Walden, or Life in the Woods* (1854), "to front only the essential facts of life, and see if I could not learn what it had to teach, and not, when I came to die, discover that I had not lived . . . . Our life is frittered away by detail . . . . Simplify, simplify."[64] His detailed observations of the natural world were part of his larger project: disentangling the self from political and corporate structures that would co-opt it, and trying to establish some ground for what is true and good and worth trusting and what is not in this, the one life we will ever have. His famous efforts to "simplify," so easily adaptable to bumper stickers, are really about stripping away illusions

---

61. Eliot, *Middlemarch*, 194.
62. Chodron, *When Things Fall Apart*, 71.
63. Chodron, *Getting Unstuck*.
64. Thoreau, *Walden*, 86–87.

to find a bedrock of what is real, deeply informed by the Eastern philosophy he was one of the first intellectuals in America to read. Despite his more-than-occasional crankiness, he struggled, like Martin Luther, to see with the eyes of conscience and something like transcendence, and to cast away what does not serve human relationships with the intangible, even divine, forces larger than ourselves. Lots of people know about the ten-by-fifteen–foot cabin he built himself in the woods at Walden Pond (with timbers he cut and boards repurposed from an Irish railroad shanty he bought from its owners for $4.25) and began to occupy on July 4, 1845, but fewer know this passage, from the "Where I Lived, and What I Lived For" chapter:

> Let us spend one day as deliberately as Nature, and not be thrown off the track by every nutshell and mosquito's wing that falls on the rails. Let us rise early and fast, or break fast, gently and without perturbation; let company come and company go, let the bells ring and the children cry,—determined to make a day of it. Why should we knock under and go with the stream? Let us not be upset and overwhelmed in that terrible rapid and whirlpool called a dinner, situated in the meridian shallows. Weather this danger and you are safe, for the rest of the way is down hill. With unrelaxed nerves, with morning vigor, sail by it, looking another way, tied to the mast like Ulysses. If the engine whistles, let it whistle till it is hoarse for its pains. If the bell rings, why should we run? We will consider what kind of music they are like. Let us settle ourselves, and work and wedge our feet downward through the mud and slush of opinion, and prejudice, and tradition, and delusion, and appearance, that alluvion which covers the globe, through Paris and London, through New York and Boston and Concord, through church and state, through poetry and philosophy and religion, till we come to a hard bottom and rocks in place, which we can call *reality*, and say, This is, and no mistake; and then begin, having a *point d'appui*, below freshet and frost and fire, a place where you might found a wall or a state, or set a lamp-post safely, or perhaps a gauge, not a Nilometer, but a Realometer, that future ages might know how deep a freshet of shams and appearances had gathered from time to time. If you stand right fronting and face to face to a fact, you will see the sun glimmer on both its surfaces, as if it were a cimeter, and feel its sweet edge dividing you through the heart and marrow, and so you will happily conclude your mortal career. Be it life or death, we crave only reality. If we are really dying, let us hear the rattle in our throats

and feel cold in the extremities; if we are alive, let us go about our business.[65]

The marvelous layering of thinking here about the way we buy into social illusions—where Plato, the Bhagavad Gita, and New England common sense meet—can perhaps be summed up in this way: "You say 'I have to?' Why?" Think about the Hydra-headed consumer world we live in, where necessity shades into whim with frightening ease. (Thoreau gets irritated elsewhere in *Walden* when a tailor tells him "they aren't making jackets like this anymore," asking, "who's 'they?'"[66]) He's not saying *don't ever have anything*—he's saying *provide for your needs, but be sure they really are* your *needs, and* your *decision about* how *to provide for them. And don't let some slick-talking salesman get in between you and what's real.*

Thoreau's project took him into socially uncomfortable places (he famously spent a night in jail in 1846 for refusing to pay taxes that he saw as supporting national reliance on slavery), and it can take us there, too. "Our inventions," Thoreau writes, "are wont to be pretty toys, which distract our attention from serious things. They are but improved means to an unimproved end, and end which it was already but too easy to arrive at; as railroads lead to Boston or New York."[67] A telegraph between Maine and Texas is useless, he writes, if "Maine and Texas . . . have nothing important to communicate."[68] Or, as you know if you've almost been hit by a texting driver, what's so all-fired important that it can't wait till you've parked? As Thoreau writes above, "If the bell rings, why should we run?"

Seeking a "realometer" can be uncomfortable, but so is every process of self-examination and growth worth the name. When it comes to technology, the have-tos of consumerism becomes downright dangerous for people and for air and groundwater, as discarded cellphones, computers, and flat-screen TVs that used to be the have-to-have thing are too often discarded to leak toxins into ground, air, and human bodies. If we really asked ourselves "Why do I 'have to' buy this? How long will I have this? And what will happen to it when I'm done?," we'd buy and discard much less than we do, and we'd be taking some steps toward our own internal "realometer" that would let us find our own bedrock of integrity and fact amid the shrieking voices of consumerist culture—heightened by smartphones, Facebook, precisely

65. Ibid., 92–93.
66. Ibid., 23.
67. Ibid., 49.
68. Ibid.

targeted advertising, and the thousand other shocks the Internet is heir to—
that we are all too apt to mistake for truth.[69]

More than a hundred years after Thoreau wrote about them, Boston
University biologist Richard Primack came with his research team to the
woods around Walden to test a brilliantly simple question: what would they
find if they compared their own notes on the first blooming/leafing/hatch-
ing dates of plants, birds, insects, and frogs in the early twenty-first century
with Thoreau's observations of these things in his famous journals? Primack's book *Walden Warming: Climate Change Comes To Thoreau's Woods*
(2014), the result of that project, gives us a new sense of what inattention
costs, and what attention might save.

Primack adapts Thoreau's "realometer" to the problem of global
warming, writing, "Despite the clear evidence that the world is already
warming due to the burning of fossil fuels and clearing of tropical forests,
most Americans still do not regard climate change as a priority. They . . .
believe that the effects of climate change will only be felt in the future and
at some faraway place and not where they live today."[70] Yet when we "[use]
Thoreau's own observations as a realometer to test for the truth of climate
change," we find some surprising facts, as this apparently distant phenomenon has some highly local instantiations.[71] *Walden Warming* teems with
case studies of plant, animal, insect, and amphibian species in the Concord,
Massachusetts area whose first and last appearances of the year, numbers,
habitats, and general health have been affected by a warming climate. Salamanders, frogs, butterflies, lady's-slipper orchids, and hummingbirds are
among the many species studied, and the conclusions are similar across
the board: the species that do survive are blooming or arriving earlier
(more than three weeks in some cases) than in Thoreau's time, and are being affected by the changes global warming and other human activity is
wreaking. These changes include earlier ice-melt on Walden Pond, rising
pond temperatures, fewer vernal pools (or temporary rainwater ponds) for
amphibians in a drought or too much water in a flood, meadows cut or
planted with trees or covered with buildings, pesticides, or lawn chemicals
that harm beneficial wild plants and insects, and many more. "[A] quarter
of the species Thoreau saw are botanical phantoms, plants that have van-
ished from the landscape," Primack writes.

> And since rare, native species are most likely to go extinct,
> and a lot of the smaller populations we recorded were both

---

69. See Shakespeare, *Hamlet* (III:i), 951.

70. Primack, *Walden Warming*, 25.

71. Ibid.

rare *and* native, we could speculate that within a few decades, if nothing is done to prevent it, those species we saw only in a few populations—a third of Thoreau's original list, remember—could also disappear. That would mean that around half of the species that Thoreau observed in Concord will no longer be present in a few decades from now; they are destined for local extinction.[72]

Temperature fluctuations also affect the complex system of cues by which birds arrive and depart during migration cycles, meaning that late arrivals may be able to find only marginal sites and may fall prey to starvation, heat, or other animals and early arrivals may freeze. Amphibians could be affected by this too, as "[t]emperatures just a bit warmer could dry up [vernal pools] in the early summer before the amphibians have completed their life cycle, causing the death of all juveniles for that year. This is particularly true for spotted salamanders, which have a long development time."[73]

What sets Primack's book apart from many other calls to action on global warming is his solution, expressed in the wonderful term "citizen science:" the marvelous simplicity of looking carefully at your local ecology, observing, and writing things down to provide a "realometer" for future studies and fuel for change. This meshes with what any good farmer or butterfly watcher already knows: you don't have to be a professional scientist, you just have to be observant, and you have to get out and look at things so you know what's normal and what's not. Primack muses on the possibility that maybe among young members of his audience is a "new Thoreau," eager to observe and act on those observations.[74] And "citizen science" can renovate perceptions at the local and national level and beyond, as environmental philosopher Philip Cafaro states: "In itself, one individual consuming less is trivial, in the context of global climate change. But that person freed from the desire for ever 'more' is now in a position to ask for a new kind of politics from his leaders and his fellow citizens: a politics of 'enough' rather than the current 'more more more.'"[75] Thoreau's realometer is chal-

72. Ibid., 39.

73. Ibid., 194. In one of the many personal anecdotes that enliven this book, Primack describes a nighttime family outing to a golf course where a parking lot and a dangerous road stood between salamanders and a vernal pool at the bottom of a hill; as the excited children "gently gather[ed] up the salamanders in cupped hands and carr[ied] them across the parking lot and access road" to get safely down to the pond for breeding, Primack notes, "This was a night to remember: a night for salamanders, and not one of the hundreds of typical nights of homework, computers, television, and reading." See ibid., 190–193.

74. Ibid., 92.

75. Ibid., 222.

lenging but inspiring, and, I argue, achievable for each of us—a practical and ethical position we arrive at within ourselves, a place we can stand to see what is and to properly assess our role in it. This is the "simplicity" that will let us examine our human systems and adjust them to meet our real human needs. Saving our world begins with paying attention to what is around us, right now, even when it brings us pain, since the presence of pain can signal—and heighten—the presence of love.

Recently I had the pleasure of Skyping with a colleague's class on environmental writing about an essay I'd published on frac-sand mining, which included a version of my "solastalgia" for my grandparents' farm as you have read it in this chapter.[76] Even on the screen, students' faces were bright and thoughtful, and their emotional investment was palpable. Their questions centered around one concern: "What can we do?" One answer we arrived at was *presence:* show up at county Board of Supervisors meetings, vote in elections, hold our politicians accountable, participate in active, peaceful demonstrations by lending your literal physical presence to your cause. Another is *witness.* Only you can tell your story of the place you love in your particular way, blending your subjective truth with the objective realities of climate change available to anyone. Stories have a power to invite us into someone else's vulnerable heart and mind and, therefore, inviting us to open our own.

In the evening just after I finished Primack's book, I hiked into the woods on a high limestone bluff above the river. His descriptive observations, and his witness to the power of seeing, had heightened my own. Molten sunset striped through the trees onto the stone as the rain melted away. A raccoon scrambled past. All around me, rich wet smells rose from the tangled banks of green stretching up the hillside above the river. A woman in an SUV went by: in the passenger seat sat a kid with head down, texting. Passing puddles in the road, I thought, *vernal pond.* Frog song came up the hill from the river and fireflies—the first of the year, I am prepared to say—blinked on, and on again, under the trees. In that moment I was fully alive in this place with the gentle presence of these other creatures—whose presence in the world I felt newly equipped to see, and to work to save.

76. Weldon, "A Miniature Handbook."

3

Tune into politics—and get involved—so you can respond to what's really being said.

ON A JULY MORNING in 2008, I climb aboard a bus headed for my first protest march.[1] We're going to Postville, Iowa, twenty-five minutes south of our town. Almost three months earlier, on May 12, federal Immigration and Customs Enforcement (ICE) agents raided Agriprocessors, a kosher meat-packing plant in Postville, and arrested 389 illegal workers, mainly Mexicans and Guatemalans. Families have been shattered, lives ruined. We on the bus—a mix of ordinary elderly and middle-aged people—don't pretend to be immigration experts. But we think this is wrong.

My fellow passengers, their hands still stained with markers and paint, are toting water bottles and backpacks and signs: *Convict the Employers. It's All About An Election. Washington, Where Is Your Heart?* In my backpack is my own sign, on a square of leftover cardboard: *Have Mercy.* It looks kind of like Sally Field's *UNION* sign in the movie "Norma Rae." My grandfather was once the company doctor at the Pepperell Mills in Opelika, Alabama, where that movie was filmed. I doubt you can be a Southerner headed off to a march anywhere—even in Iowa—and not think nervously about Norma Rae, or about the Freedom Riders and Goodman, Schwerner, and Chaney and Viola Liuzzo. People who came down to mess in somebody else's business and ended up dead.

"Makes me miss Vietnam." The sixty-something man on my right is talking to the sixty-something woman on my left. "The peace marches, I mean. Did you go?"

"No," she says, "I wasn't that political then. Did you go to the civil rights movement?"

"No," says the man, "I missed the civil rights movement, and I always regretted that."

A faraway look crosses their faces. "Such a time," says the woman. "Soldiers shooting those college students. Where was that, Ohio State?" She looks at the man. He shrugs.

1. See Preston, "Iowa Rally Protests."

"Kent State," I say.

"Oh, right," says the woman. "That was in Ohio. I had that right, at least."

"I don't know what's happened to all that idealism," says the man. "Look at the total lack of opposition, in this generation, to the Iraq War. I mean, this apathetic generation!" He pulls out this morning's *New York Times* story on Postville—"After Iowa Raid, Immigrants Fuel Labor Inquiries"—and reads. The woman's eager to keep talking (a backhanded apology to thirtysomething me?) but I'm looking out the window to quell faint motion-sickness, and more-than-faint nervousness.

Nobody quite knows what to expect down in Postville. In our town, Decorah, the region's biggest ethnic party, NordicFest, has just ended. Every year at this time, Decorah's streets are lined with booths selling Norwegian food (*krumkakke, lefse, smakaker,* and *smorbrod,* translated "delicious traditional delivery systems for starch and meat"). Costumed volunteers demonstrate weaving and knife-blade forging. A Viking ship is parked in front of the Vesterheim Norwegian-American Museum, which is stocked with treasures once belonging to the Norwegian immigrants who settled this town and much of the upper Midwest: painted immigrant chests, teapots and spinning wheels, silver wedding brooches and bridal crowns. Here, immigrants are celebrated. Half an hour away, they're arrested. Here, they're white. There, they're brown.

Before the May 12, 2008 raid, I knew only one thing about Postville: it was changing. As a new Northeast Iowan, I read Stephen Bloom's book *Postville: A Clash of Cultures in Heartland America* (2000), which describes the cultural shifts and tensions that grew after Agriprocessors, the nation's largest kosher meat-processing plant, was established there by Orthodox Jews, who then hired Guatemalans and Mexicans and Eastern Europeans as well as native Iowans. In a town where the population never topped 3,000, neighbors believed that proximity would smooth rough edges, especially since Agriprocessors had swiftly become the town's major employer. So many little American towns are dying as the agricultural economies that kept them alive mutate and collapse. Nobody wants Postville to die too.

Yet in a region known for its horror of making a scene, the May 12, 2008 raid was truly a shock. 389 illegal workers were arrested and taken away, the majority of them Mexicans and Guatemalans. Those not taken fled to St. Bridget's Catholic Church, where they sheltered in the pews and shared food hustled to the sanctuary from neighbors' kitchens and tried to get word of their loved ones who had been arrested. Outside, surveillance helicopters circled. Those arrested were scattered to jails all over Iowa—held, in almost every account, without adequate access to lawyers and translators—or released, as were many of the mothers, with electronic monitoring bracelets on their ankles. Becoming the disappeared, the *desaparecidos*. Or *las personas con brazelete*, the women with bracelets. All of them transformed, in an instant, from workers to criminals.

I hear of a husband and father who has been deported to his native Guatemala. His wife now faces a choice: stay in America to pursue an education for her two daughters—native-born citizens—or follow her husband home, where, as is the case with many returning workers, they will likely be mugged and beaten. In a desperately poor country, torn by thirty years of civil war—including the machinations of the CIA and the American corporation United Fruit Company—returning Guatemalans can become the prey of those who stayed behind.[2] (They're rich Americans now, the logic goes.) Yes, they are here illegally. They are breaking the law. But they are following even stronger laws: supply and demand. Opportunity. Survival.

Imagine: a uniformed man walks into your place of work, where you're doing the job few white Americans want. Your worst fear happens: the uniformed hand of La Migra, the immigration authorities, on your shoulder. "Come with me." *Ven conmigo*. No word to your wife or mother or children or the people who line up back home for the money you send. No way to let them know that you are about to disappear.

As our little bus pulls into Postville, we spot an all-white crowd of counter-demonstrators standing on the other side of Postville's main street, in front of the Tidy Wave Laundromat, the State Farm Insurance Agency, and the Club 51 Bar ("Your Home for All Iowa Hawkeye and NFL Football Games!"). Men with American flags hoist signs reading *Stop the Illegal Invasion*. A woman painted green is dressed as the Statue of Liberty, with a sign reading *Save the American Worker*. A preteen girl in an American flag cap circles the edges of the group, mouth stretched in an anxious smile.

In the main hall of St. Bridget's Catholic Church, babies whimper, flies nibble arms and legs, and everybody sweats. I'm wedged at the back between an elderly lady and an elderly man with HOSPITALITY badges. With a practiced gesture, the lady straightens the paper cloth on the table in front of us. We might be hungry parishioners crowding toward her after the service, ravenous for Midwestern church food: Jell-O salad, sweet corn in season, *lefse* (Norwegian potato pastry), and hot dish (here, a generic name for any kind of casserole.) There are easily two hundred people in this room, maybe even three hundred, with more crowded outside, from Des Moines, Minneapolis, Chicago, Mexico, Guatemala. Brown-skinned women in red shirts, their long black hair tied back. Brown-skinned,

2. See Schlesinger, "Ghosts of Guatemala's Past."

mustached men wearing beat-up boots and Wrangler jeans with big belt buckles and crisply ironed shirts. Phalanxes of people in matching blue Jewish Council of Urban Affairs T-shirts. *If not now, when?* another T-shirt pleads. Across the room are some of my own students. Every kind of person is here: hippie kids with dreadlocks, stocky men in John Deere shirts, elderly ladies with apricot-dyed hair.

A red-shirted Hispanic woman in front of me carries a sign: *ICE: Dejen libre mi hermano . . . nuestros padres estan sufriendo queremos justicia y una respueta. Somos trabajadores. No somos criminales.* I piece it together from high school Spanish: *Free my brother. Our parents are suffering. We want justice and an answer. We are workers. Not criminals.*[3]

The elderly man next to me fingers his HOSPITALITY badge. "Is this your church?" I ask him. "Yes," he says, "where'd you come from?" "Luther College," I say, "I teach there." We fall into the affectionate Protestant/Catholic banter of the upper Midwest. "Too bad you folks aren't going to heaven with us," he jokes. "We've got a different door," I joke back. Suddenly, he straightens. "That's all right," he says. "We're all about the same thing, aren't we?" His eyes wrinkle with tears. "That's why we're here." I pat his back, suddenly unable to speak through my own tears. *Amen.*

We pray for God to give us courage, give us hope, give us love. *Danos coraje. Danos esperanza. Danos amor.* There are readings from the Old Testament in English and Spanish, and in Hebrew—a throat-catchy, thorny, hypnotic sound. *You shall not violate the rights of the stranger or the orphans . . . for remember you were once slaves in Egypt, and the Lord your God freed you from there.* Speakers mount the pulpit one by one: a rabbi from Minneapolis, a Lutheran pastor from Postville, a rabbi from Chicago, a Catholic archbishop from Dubuque. Each speaker pauses for a Spanish interpreter to repeat, into a faulty microphone, what he's just said. The pastor wipes sweat and takes a breath. "People will say, 'oh, these folks were breaking the law,'" he intones. "But I want to say, there is a law of man and there is God's law! There is a law for the immigrant, and a law for the factory owner who exploits the workers! There is God's law!"

Amen, I murmur. We bow our heads for silent prayer, as indicated in the sweat-dampened bulletins passed from hand to hand.

Filing outside, we start our march toward the Agriprocessors plant. It looks like a prison: water tower and long low buildings, all surrounded by a high chain link fence, at the very edge of town. Three figures in long black robes—remaining Orthodox managers, on what is still a working

---

3. Thanks to my colleague David Thompson, Professor of Spanish at Luther College, for checking my translation.

day—hurry inside when they see us. NOW HIRING banners flap from the fence. "Good luck," someone mutters sarcastically.

What it must be like in that plant? Gutting chickens and slinging the guts into slimy piles that slither sideways under their own weight. Pluck, cut, toss, in that dim hot dark. This morning, the *New York Times* reports the story of Elmer L., one of more than twenty underage workers. A supervisor shoved him and he cut his arm open on a knife, then was forced to return to work although the stitches had popped open and bled. An informant said "a floor supervisor had blindfolded an immigrant with duct tape" and hit him with a meat hook. A union organizer said of Agriprocessors, "They are the poster child for how a rogue company can exploit a broken immigration system."[4]

In the marching crowd—"keep to the left side of the street!" pleads a volunteer, "*la izquierda, por favor!*"—I find a friend of mine, an Episcopal priest. We hug and I reflexively apologize for light church attendance. "Church is here," she says, lifting one hand. "Church is here." Earlier this weekend, she was helping her parishioners around Cedar Rapids and Iowa City clean up damage from last month's floods. Each time I see her, she looks exhausted but resolute, as she does now. Below her close-cropped gray hair, her priest's collar nudges the flesh of her neck. *Church is here.*

In front of us, red-shirted Mexican and Guatemalan mothers hold up a long white banner with a startlingly realistic pencil drawing of a sad-eyed child and words in Spanish I can't read. Every third woman wears an electronic ankle bracelet. We meet each others' eyes and smile bashfully, as people have been doing all day across the borders of different lives. I don't trust my awkward Spanish for what I'm wondering: *Was your husband taken? What will you do now?* I settle for smiling at the children perched on their mothers' shoulders. "Cute baby," I say, and they smile back. Then we all join in another of the chants that sweeps the line every few minutes, from the back to the front: *What do we want? Justice! When do we want it? Now! Si se puede! Si se puede! No more raids! No more raids!*

People watch us from their lawns, their faces neutral, their digital cameras ready. A tiny brown-skinned boy in glasses darts toward us, then whirls back to a cluster of Hispanic men in front of a garage. A sign on the garage wall advertises *mufflers, rims, transmissions* in Spanish and English. Even for a Sunday, businesses look forlorn. After this raid, what's left?

Bye-bye, Postville. Bye-bye, little town.

I walk for a while with a colleague and another Lutheran pastor, a friendly, bearlike guy with a long gray ponytail, a feed-store cap, and a Bible

---

4. Preston, "After Iowa Raid."

camp T-shirt. Around us are white-haired ladies, teenagers, a preacher or two. Behind us is a man with a homemade posterboard sign: *Another Wisconsin Farmer for Humane Immigration Reform.* My colleague's sign says *My Ancestors Came from Another Country—Did Yours?* "I know they told us not to," he says, "but one of those guys across the street was yelling 'America for Americans,' and I asked him where his father was born. He said 'America.' I asked him where his grandfather was born, and he said 'America.' I asked him where his great-grandfather was born, and he kind of hemmed and hawed. 'Was he born in America too?' I asked. 'What tribe? Sioux? Chippewa? Winnebago?'"

A smiling teenager hands out buttons that say *Humane Immigration Reform Now!* We pin them to our sweaty shirts and settle into a purposeful trudge. The sky darkens, the air thickens. Rain would be a relief. We tug water bottles out of backpacks, towel our foreheads with shirtsleeves.

At a neighborhood playground, brown and white children bolt from the marching line toward the merry-go-round, spinning it at delirious speeds. One falls off; the others make room for her to climb back on. More brown children, hair carefully brushed back in Beaver Cleaver flattops or curly ponytails, dash among adults' legs. Many wear red T-shirts from their elementary school, which has been devastated by this raid; in an email circulated around our community the day after the raid, a schoolteacher wrote, "We have 150 students with no parents to go home to." Superimposed on black rocket ships on each shirt's back are the words *Character is Key to Success*!

The march turns the corner onto Postville's main street. When they see us, the counter-demonstrators set up a roar. On the corner, a shouting preacher stands under a sign that reads *Ask Me Why You Deserve Hell.* A woman huddles behind a sign as tall as she is: *What Would Jesus Do? Obey the Laws.*

Jesus would have been a brown man, a Middle Eastern Jew sunburned dark as these Mexicans and Guatemalans—a man enigmatic of speech and action, whose only written words were scratched in the sand with a stick and blown away seconds later, by the feet of his followers or his pursuers or simply by the wind. Jesus rebuked the Pharisees' pettifogging whenever he saw fit. "Jesus was all virtue," wrote that radical prophet William Blake, "and acted from impulse, not from rules."[5] I remember my father's rueful face as he watched a Mexican crew at work in Alabama. "I know people have to obey the laws," he said, "but the part of me that likes to think I'm a Christian

---

5. Blake, *The Marriage of Heaven and Hell,* 80.

knows you have to have some compassion on these people. They're just trying to work hard and make a better life."

"When I pray," one immigrant woman whose husband was taken told
the *New York Times,* "I know God is close to me. I know there are laws, but
God is the judge of everything."[6]

No more raids! we roar back. *No more raids!*

Then we are back at the church, about two hours after we set out. On a
flatbed trailer pulled across the street in front of St. Bridget's, under a towering cottonwood tree, the post-march speakers assemble. The consulate from
Guatemala tells us that his country takes an interest in its people here. The
shy mayor of Postville clasps both hands in front of him and tells us that he
is going to do all he can to get families back together. A little boy waves a
sign: *Freedom for Mi Papi.* Over her father's shoulder, a tiny girl watches me,
her black eyes deepening with sleep.

The wind rises, lashing the cottonwood tree back and forth. Then the
rain comes suddenly and hard, a classic Iowa summer thunderstorm. Some
people hold their signs over their heads, but most tilt our faces back to the
rain. It feels good.

On our bus ride back to Decorah, through a landscape green and
drowsy with rain, someone instigates a sing-along: *I'd sing out love between
the brothers and the sisters, aaaa-ll over this laaaaa-nd . . . ."* I lean back and
close my eyes, fighting a bewildered weariness that's out of proportion to
what I've actually, physically done.

Simone Weil, in her classic essay on *The Iliad,* says that force is im-
moral because it reduces people to things, to objects that must be moved or
smashed if they cannot be otherwise circumvented.[7] Or, in the current lexi-
con, it reduces them to units of labor. Outside the window, cornfields roll by.
There's so much labor in the world, so much work, upon which we all float,
oblivious, in our own rickety boats. Who plants the corn, seed by seed?
Who pumps the fuel into the big tractor's tank? Who refines that fuel from
the ocean deck in Texas or Louisiana or the sandy plain in Saudi Arabia or
Iraq? Who has drilled for that fuel to begin with? What has had to happen
for us to be on this road, right now? By whose work do we live? Whose faces
are they that we do not see? And whose labor builds our American reality,
from one minute to the next?

Off Highway 52 and through the tiny hamlet of Frankville and
onto Highway 9 our bus turns, heading down the long hill into our little

6. Freedman, "Immigrants Find Solace."
7. See Weil, "The Iliad."

Norwegian-American town. And all around me, my neighbors begin to sing, in sturdy Lutheran harmonies: *In our hearts and in our minds, let peace prevail.*

We ride on, borne up by the thousands of invisible hands we hope to know, and to appease. And by whom we hope to be forgiven.

If, as Hannah Arendt writes, experience is the place where encounters with other people form our own selves, and where we become responsible to the world, then what does it mean that we have so little actual experience of politics anymore?[8] That I participated in my first public political action, this Postville march, at age thirty-four? That voting numbers—especially in midterm elections—continue to decline as corporate power in the electoral process increases? That many students have told me they don't really follow current events or don't care about politics? That even peaceful protests can be suddenly disrupted by violence? That so many of us never have a conversation with someone with whom we disagree? And that the roar of partisan media on television and the Internet has become the dominant meaning of "politics" in the average American's mind, substituting for actual political involvement, reflection, and meaning and leading to "fact-based journalism" as something we need explicitly to name in order to distinguish it from shouting talking heads?

Perhaps it's connected to the rise of the "nones"—the percentage of the US population (22.8 percent) who claim no affiliation with any denominationally named religion yet show additional signs of non-commitment as well. "Nones" also "'don't vote, don't marry, and don't have kids' at the same rate as other Americans," says Mike Hout, New York University sociologist and codirector of the General Social Survey. "They are allergic to large, organized institutions—mass media, religions, big corporations, and political parties." And demographically, the younger you are, the more likely you are to be a "none:" 36 percent of younger millennials (born 1990–1996) claim no religious affiliation, up from 34 percent of older millennials (born 1981–1989) and 23 percent of Generation X (my own generation, born 1960–1980). Perhaps this is one way to account for the creeping bewilderment and disorientation we might feel as we watch political debates, for instance: even as candidates double down on the "God Bless America" rhetoric and the accompanying demonization of their opponents, we might feel as if they're shouting into a void, playing to their base but leaving the

---

8. See Arendt, *The Human Condition.*

increasingly fragmented and doubtful majority of society—what used to be called our common life—unaddressed.[9]

We know that, as Marshall McLuhan articulated, the medium in which a message is conveyed shapes that message, and our media are reshaping not just "messages" but our whole experience of the world. The Internet is more than a mode of communication, it's a mode of thought and experience that recasts our own views of reality: "When the Net absorbs a medium, that medium is re-created in the Net's image," Nicholas Carr writes. "As people's minds become attuned to the crazy quilt of Internet media, traditional media have to adapt to the audience's new expectations. Television programs add text crawls and pop-up ads, and magazines and newspapers shorten their articles, introduce capsule summaries, and crowd their pages with easy-to-browse info-snippets."[10] We seek new shocks and pleasures to un-habitualize us through the very medium that habitually dulls us in the first place, and it becomes harder and harder to see—really see and experience—that which is not the familiarly electronic and entertaining. This has real and chilling implications for politics, and for our ability to spot and correct political problems by looking at its first sign of something gone wrong: bad language and the stories it's trying to make us believe. In the gap between an intended message and the actual language used to convey it, some dehumanizing impulses can flourish, and real understanding can suffer.

To start looking at the effects of the Internet on political language and thought, we need to look at how the Internet's initial promise has ironically been turned inside out: in practice, despite its potential for connecting us with new information and experiences, it often narrows our social and artistic worlds, making them smaller and more richly, individualistically furnished, rather than more expansive. As Nathan Heller writes, the "default mode" of our ostensibly innovative technology "is not sameness but withdrawn, hypersaturated subjectivity:"

> To be freed from the stranglehold of Big Media is, instead, to be deluged with a range of online commentary on matters big and small, a thousand click-bait headlines, a million points of irrelevant data presented in a hundred winsome graphic forms.
> It all works fine until you want to talk about the news with somebody you've never met.[11]

Therefore, technology can insulate us in private worlds of private tastes, with escalating costs to our sense of shared public values and

9. Data in this paragraph comes from Grossman, "Christians Lose Ground."

10. Carr, "Is Google Making Us Stupid?"

11. Heller, "California Screaming," 50.

language and a decreasing sense that other people and their ideas, values, and needs are as real as our own. Technology can even help us distort reality to fit our own perceptions, as seen in the flood of changes politicians' supporters make to Wikipedia entries about them.[12] We can begin to experience the sinister effect of habitualization—moral desensitization: the helpless shrug that becomes the indifferent shrug at suffering Syrians or factory-farmed pigs trampled underfoot by their own crowded barnmates, or the cliché that allows us to write off whole suffering groups ("well, those people don't know any better") or glee at the cartoonish carnage of video games and action movies—which strikes the survivors of *actual* carnage and conflict as appallingly, tragically naïve.[13] All this has real costs to community and democracy.

If a version of reality gets accepted and reproduced unthinkingly in language that becomes more or less disconnected from its original meaning, it also becomes cliché—by which I mean not just worn-out phrases but the way those phrases become intellectual shortcuts and social codes, ways to gesture lazily in the direction of assumed-to-be commonly understood ideas without actually articulating them. Yet that lazy gesture easily blossoms into a lie. Cliché is a problem not only in creative writing classrooms but in our political and social relationships, because it's a sign of one of our oldest human tendencies: we love to pay lip service to an idea or toss out a careless phrase without looking too closely at our real meaning and what the consequences of those words really are in the world. Remember Hannah Arendt's word for this—being "thoughtless." We say things we don't really mean—or the meaning of which we don't fully know—to make ourselves look smarter,

12. For example, in 2011 onetime vice presidential candidate Sarah Palin's supporters made changes to the Wikipedia entry for Paul Revere's midnight ride, trying to make it match her "confused and garbled account" of it; "what was most revealing about this episode," writes environmental philosopher Dale Jamieson, "is that it was widely regarded as an amusing, poorly executed political ploy, rather than as an attack on the very idea of truth or an expression of a complete misunderstanding of the concept." See Jamieson, *Reason in a Dark Time*, 88.

13. See Pacifique Irankunda's personal essay, "Playing at Violence." Irankunda, a survivor of Burundi's bloody civil war, is bewildered and troubled by a dormmate's taste for violent video games when he arrives at a prestigious American boarding school. "He and my other dorm mates who liked playing violent video games weren't gangsters at all," he writes. "They were just young, inexperienced, innocent. It took me some time to realize that the shooting wasn't real to them. They were just playing. For them the games were 'mindless,' as one friend told me. . . . I felt relieved, but I was also puzzled by what seemed to me like an odd sort of entertainment. How could violence so easily be turned into a game? How could companies invent such games in the first place? And how could parents buy them for their children? I lived through thirteen years of civil war. I know that violence can become almost a culture in itself, and that it twists not all but many of the people who are trapped in it."

to manipulate the opinions of others, to sound (and feel) more important or socially acceptable, or just to fill space. Yet there's a direct relationship between language and the moral self that's speaking it: clarity and honesty of language and of thought help to create and reinforce one another. When we think more carefully about what we say and how we can accurately describe what we're doing, and when we try harder to make our real intentions clear to ourselves and others, we say, and do, better things. Blurriness, unnecessary vocabulary overload, jargon, euphemism, cliché, or outright lies show that you don't quite understand what you're saying, you don't want other people to understand it, or both. ("You can explain anything to the people," wrote Frantz Fanon in *The Wretched of the Earth*, "provided you really want them to understand.")[14] Therefore, as I teach students, to revise your writing you need to start by revising your thinking, asking yourself *what am I really trying to say? What don't I understand yet?* And so to understand political actions and assumptions, we can start by looking at political language, because examples of its use of cliché can help us all be more ethical and honest.

For example, consider how in the late summer of 2012, politicians kept saying "rape" without seeming to understand what rape actually is, divorcing it from reality in a way that's the sure sign of a potential cliché. On August 19, 2012, Missouri Senate Republican nominee Todd Akin said in an interview, "First of all, from what I understand from doctors [pregnancy from rape] is really rare. If it's a legitimate rape, the female body has ways to try to shut that whole thing down." And he elaborated. "Let's assume that maybe that didn't work, or something," he said. "I think there should be some punishment, but the punishment ought to be on the rapist and not attacking the child."[15] A week later, Pennsylvania Republican Senate candidate Tom Smith, according to the *Huffington Post*, "stirred up further controversy by comparing a pregnancy caused by rape to 'having a baby out of wedlock,'" remarking, "Put yourself in a father's position. Yes, it is similar."[16] This furor churned up Internet memory of an earlier "Double Ultrasound Bill," sponsored by Idaho Republican state senator Chuck Winder in March of 2012, which would require a woman seeking an abortion, no matter what the circumstance, to undergo two ultrasounds, the first at a pro-life "crisis pregnancy counseling center." At the time, reports the *Huffington Post*, Winder also mentioned rape: "Rape and incest was used as a reason to oppose this. I would hope that when a woman goes in to a physician with a rape issue, that physician will indeed ask her about perhaps, her marriage, was this pregnancy caused

14. Fanon, *The Wretched of the Earth*, 131.
15. Eligon and Schwirz, "Senate Candidate Provokes Ire."
16. Bassett, "Tom Smith."

by normal relations in a marriage or was it truly caused by a rape. I assume that's part of the counseling that goes on."[17]

Many people across the political spectrum listened to such remarks with stunned disbelief: *they do know what rape is, right? A violent, painful criminal act more women (and more men) have suffered than anyone really knows? Why do they keep saying this?* And yet such talk continued. In June 2013, as Texas House Republicans voted "to approve a sweeping abortion measure that, if passed, would shutter thirty-seven of the state's forty-two abortion clinics," State Representative Jodie Laubenberg, a woman, opined that an exception for cases of rape or incest was unnecessary because "in the emergency room they have what's called rape kits where a woman can get cleaned out."[18] Rape kits, of course, are the sets of swabs and vials used to collect DNA evidence after physical assault, not the sort of after-rape anti-pregnancy insurance "cleaning out" seems to imply. As all this went on, the word "rape" started to enter the realm of cliché—a bit of language unhooked from lived experience, tacked into other political-talk contexts, and repeated thoughtlessly for reasons the speakers never made quite clear.

Like coded racial rhetoric, this language seemed to function as a "dog whistle" to communicate with supporters on frequencies only they think they hear.[19] (As Orwell wrote: "Words of this kind are often used in a consciously dishonest way. That is, the person who uses them has his own private definition, but allows his hearer to think he means something quite different."[20]) I can only guess that what was being "dog-whistled" about here was abortion, yet invoking "rape" to do that brought a strange mix of error and insensitivity to the debate that alienated even many voters (especially women) who consider themselves opposed to abortion. And that insensitivity, many pundits agree, was one of the factors that cost Republicans the 2012 Presidential election. As Karen Hughes, former counselor to Republican President George W. Bush, wrote at the online site Politico the day after Democratic President Barack Obama's re-election, "[T]he Republican Party has to set a tone that is more respectful, positive and inclusive . . . . And if another Republican man says anything about rape other than it is a horrific, violent crime, I want to personally cut out his tongue. The college-age daughters of many of my friends voted for Obama

17. Bassett, "Chuck Winder."
18. McDonough, "Texas Abortion Bill Sponsor."
19. See López, *Dog Whistle Politics.*
20. Orwell, "Politics and the English Language," 959.

because they were completely turned off by Neanderthal comments like the suggestion of 'legitimate rape.'"[21]

Art Ludwig, a California ecologist and graywater-systems designer, has written that "true progress actually solves problems. Most of what is commonly called 'progress' is actually the relocation of problems out of sight in space and time."[22] All this rape talk (from morally insensitive to factually wrong) kicked the can down the road in exactly this way, giving the illusion of forward political motion as these politicians—and the media—kept relocating more widespread and systemic troubles out of sight by feeding the public diversionary language. Such language functions as George Orwell and Hannah Arendt both say bad political language does—it stirs up emotion to hide, in Orwell's words, "the gap between . . . real and declared aims."[23] And it blurs our understanding of what the reality of the situation actually is. It serves politicians' careers and their popularity with their constituent political base. But, because it does not clarify our vision of human complexity, helping us see the actual causes and effects of a problem, it does not serve the truth. Given television's relentless appetite for pithy, content-free sound bites, not to mention the way words can be unhooked from context and recirculated in inflammatory and erroneous ways (or 140 characters) all around the world, it's harder but more necessary than ever to remember that when you see bad language—clichés, half-truths, blurry phrasing, coded political keywords, outright lies—you're really seeing bad thinking, the results of which may affect you more than you know.

To understand how this might be true, let's look at some moral, historical, and philosophical ideas about how humans try to use language to trick others and ourselves. The great yoga teacher B. K. S. Iyengar (1918–2014) identified choosing "dexterity instead of honesty" as a human tendency we must always work against.[24] Basically, this could refer to the million small ways we grease the wheels of our daily lives with cleverness, rather than real attention, in order to get what we want. We toy with words, manipulate people, and rig up temporary solutions rather than really addressing the problem, doing the emotional equivalent of duct-taping that leaky faucet or ignoring the check-engine light rather than getting under the hood. We seize prefabricated units of language, ideas, mannerisms, or even experiences to make ourselves feel as if we are thinking when we really aren't, or to reflect to ourselves a self-image in which we want to believe. I'm remind-

21. See Hughes, "Communication Lessons from Election."
22. Ludwig, "Principles of Ecological Design."
23. Orwell, "Politics and the English Language," 964.
24. See Iyengar, "Foreword," xii.

ed of how the writer John Berger, in *Ways of Seeing*, describes the stagy, "vacuous" quality of some sixteenth-to-eighteenth–century oil paintings, especially those depicting historical or mythological subjects, houses, or other material goods. Berger argues that these pictures "did not need to stimulate the imagination" since "[t]heir purpose was not to transport their spectator-owners into new experience, but to embellish such experience as they already possessed . . . . The idealized appearances [the spectator-owner] found in the painting were an aid, a support, to his own view of himself." Therefore, "[s]ometimes the whole mythological scene functions like a garment held out for the spectator-owner to put his arms into and wear."[25] In other words, the art functioned as cliché because it helped its owner create and sustain a lofty self-image he could "put his arms into and wear" to feel good about himself, regardless of whether that "garment" fit who he actually was.

Similarly, Arendt argued in many ways that we use language to serve our own needs, including using language to manipulate and morally numb others' understanding of reality and our own. For Arendt, cliché is both a symptom and a cause of moral blindness. Her famous phrase "the banality of evil" from *Eichmann in Jerusalem* means that under the right conditions, any one of us could accommodate ourselves to living amid great moral wrong while comforting ourselves that we're still "good people." Cliché—language that deadens thought—helps us do it; we can be moved away from moral responsibility by our readiness to slip the familiar phrase, the socially acceptable norm, over our shoulders like John Berger's "garment" and inhabit it regardless of what the voice of conscience within has to say. Significantly, the word *cliché* comes from the same place as *stereotype*: the printing shop, where blocks of type containing often-used phrases were kept together, ready for use, to avoid the hassle of assembling the same common phrases over and over again. Thus a cliché is literally a ready-made unit of words that substitutes for real thought. As we saw in Chapter 1, cliché and the brain's auto-completing habits are (to use another cliché) a match made in heaven. Dropping a familiar phrase ("it is what it is" or the tech-beloved "disrupt") into the slot where an idea should be gives us a break from the work of thinking, and, in George Orwell's words, "gives an appearance of solidity to pure wind."[26]

As we saw in Chapter 1, Orwell always believed that language and the self could create or degrade one another; his famous essay "Politics and the English Language" (1945) argues that this reciprocal relationship is as true

25. Berger, *Ways of Seeing,* 100–102.

26. Orwell, "Politics and the English Language," 967.

for nations as it is for individuals. "[The English language] becomes ugly and inaccurate because our thoughts are foolish," he writes, "but the slovenliness of our language makes it easier to have foolish thoughts."[27] However, "if one gets rid of these habits one can think more clearly, and to think more clearly is a necessary first step towards political regeneration."[28] Yet powerful forces of misinformation block our path: since war, colonialism, and other so-called necessities can only be defended "by arguments which are too brutal for most people to face, and which do not square with the professed aims of political parties," public political speech "has to consist largely of euphemism, question-begging, and sheer cloudy vagueness."[29] Therefore, cliché lets a politician talk himself and his listeners away from the truth. Anticipating his chilling image of the babbling blank-eyed man in the Ministry of Truth cafeteria in *Nineteen Eighty-Four* (published four years later), Orwell writes:

> When one watches some tired hack on the platform mechanically repeating the familiar phrases—*bestial atrocities, iron heel, blood-stained tyranny, free peoples of the world, stand shoulder to shoulder*—one often has a curious feeling that one is not watching a live human being but some kind of dummy: a feeling which suddenly becomes stronger at moments when the light catches the speaker's spectacles and turns them into blank discs which seem to have no eyes behind them. And this is not altogether fanciful. A speaker who uses that kind of phraseology has gone some distance toward turning himself into a machine. The appropriate noises are coming out of his larynx, but his brain is not involved as it would be if he were choosing his words for himself . . . . And this reduced state of consciousness, if not indispensable, is at any rate favorable to political conformity.[30]

Therefore, to keep from becoming a parrot of some exploitative force beyond ourselves, we have to tune up our own speech at the level of our own thought, making the effort to call to mind the real thing, or the real person, we are describing and choose our language accordingly. "What is above all needed," Orwell writes, "is to let the meaning choose the word, and not the other way about."[31] If you "think of a concrete object," he continues, you can "choose—not simply *accept*—the phrases that will best cover the meaning, and then switch round and decide what impression [your] words

27. Ibid., 954.
28. Ibid., 955.
29. Ibid., 963.
30. Ibid., 962–963.
31. Ibid., 965.

are likely to make on another person."[32] In my creative writing classes, I call this mental process *enfleshing an image*, and it can be surprisingly hard. Following ready-made words toward a blurry, predigested mental picture or searching for a familiar phrase to slip into like John Berger's "garment" is much easier than starting with your own mental picture first and fitting words to it. Yet making yourself responsible to your real intended meaning, and to how your listener might receive it, means making yourself responsible to people and things beyond yourself, which means, in Hannah Arendt's words, giving them "a claim on your thinking attention."[33] It means letting those "others" be real in your mind, letting them pressure you invisibly to revise your own thought and speech to be more accurate and fair—not to write them off (literally) with habitual phrases that are careless or, in political terms, actively hurtful. This is the moral heart of writing, and it is the heart of every writing class I teach: by observing in life and imagining clearly what (or who) they are describing in language, then working to be as precise as they can with their words, writers stand up for the dignity and worth of their subjects, especially since their words bring those subjects alive for readers across distances of space and time they might not initially see. Writers bear witness. It's a big responsibility, but using our language wisely may make us wise, too.

Written documents from the Nazi regime testify to how reality-softening speech, mental habits, and actions can reinforce one another and bleed into official policy based on blindness to others' humanity. Three years before "Politics and the English Language," a memo headed "*Geheime Reichssache* [Secret Reich Business], Berlin, June 5, 1942," recommended "[c]hanges for special vehicles now in service at Kulmhof (Chelmo) and for those now being built." "Since December 1941," it begins, "ninety-seven thousand have been processed by the three vehicles in service, with no major incidents. In light of observations made so far, however, the following technical changes are needed."[34] The "vehicles in service" are too big for their intended cargo, especially since the cargo space must also be filled with carbon monoxide. What *is* that cargo? Ninety-seven thousand of *what*? The writer doesn't say. Proceeding in a tone of deadpan officialese (and, significantly, passive voice, the verb tense that removes human responsibility from the picture), the memo notes that since "loading to full capacity would affect the vehicle's stability," the load space "must absolutely be reduced by a yard,

32. Ibid., 966.

33. Arendt, "Thinking and Moral Considerations," 160.

34. Katz, "The Ethic of Expediency," 255–256. Thanks to my colleague Mike Garcia, Assistant Professor of English at Luther, for introducing me to this document.

instead of trying to solve the problem, as hitherto, by reducing the number of pieces loaded." What are these "pieces?" The memo still doesn't say. Not until we reach the end of the (long) first paragraph do we start to guess at the answer: "the merchandise aboard," the memo reads, "displays during the operation a natural tendency to rush to the rear doors, and is mainly found lying there at the end of the operation." The second paragraph, here quoted in full, confirms the reader's suspicions: the "cargo" is human beings.

> The lighting must be better protected than now. The lamps must be enclosed in a steel grid to prevent their being damaged. Lights could be eliminated, since they apparently are never used. However, it has been observed that when the doors are shut, the load always presses hard against them as soon as darkness sets in. This is because the load naturally rushes toward the light when darkness sets in, which makes closing the doors difficult. Also, because of the alarming nature of darkness, screaming always occurs when the doors are closed. It would therefore be useful to light the lamp before and during the first moments of the operation.[35]

Here, syntactical and moral evasion enable one another: referring to human beings crammed into gassing trucks as "cargo" and "merchandise" and deploying the passive voice ("screaming always occurs") helps this functionary, who signs his memo only "Just," do his job by ignoring its real nature.[36] Scholar Steven B. Katz names this memo as an example of an ethical problem in rhetoric, and in life: "Here," he writes, "expediency and the resulting *ethos* of objectivity, logic, and narrow focus that characterize most technical writing are taken to extremes and applied to the mass destruction of human beings. Here, expediency is an ethical end as well."[37] And, as seen in Chapter 1, when expediency—like "efficiency"—becomes an "ethical end," to be achieved by engineering solutions to problems, no matter the human cost, language suffers along with human beings themselves.

35. Ibid., 255–256.

36. These euphemisms are also examples of what the Nazis called "language rules," code words designed to conceal the reality of their actions and their results from the outside world and, perhaps, from themselves. "[E]xcept in the reports from the *Einsatzgruppen*," Hannah Arendt writes in *Eichmann in Jerusalem*, 85, "it is rare to find documents in which such bald words as 'extermination,' 'liquidation,' or 'killing' occur . . . . For whatever other reasons the language rules may have been devised, they proved of enormous help in the maintenance of order and sanity in the various widely diversified services whose cooperation was essential in this matter. Moreover, the very term 'language rule' [*Sprachregelung*] was itself a code name; it meant what in ordinary language would be called a lie."

37. Ibid., 257.

Hannah Arendt's influential analysis of cliché in *Eichmann in Jerusalem* helps us join Orwell's idea of the "mental picture" with the role of language in Nazi bureaucracy. Behind a wall of bulletproof glass in a Jerusalem courtroom, Eichmann answered many questions with long, pointless answers or with clichés.[38] How could you *truly* not have realized, prosecutors asked him, that all those orders you were signing and those train schedules you were confirming were leading systematically to the deaths of millions of human beings? "Well," Eichmann replied, with a folksy German proverb, "nothing's as hot when you eat it as when it's being cooked."[39] Colleagues familiar with Germany have told me that this can mean "things look more extreme in the planning process than they turn out to be in reality." In using this cliché, Eichmann was trying to evade the fact that his plans had real victims, even though, as historian Deborah Lipstadt writes in *The Eichmann Trial* (2011), he knew very well and actively intended that that would be the case.

In *Eichmann in Jerusalem*, Arendt famously identifies what, for her, is the real cause of Eichmann's dexterity with a cliché: "Whether writing his memoirs in Argentina or in Jerusalem, whether speaking to the police examiner or to the court, what he said was always the same, expressed in the same words," she writes.

> The longer one listened to him, the more obvious it became that his inability to speak was closely connected with an inability to *think*, namely, to think from the standpoint of somebody else. No communication was possible with him, not because he lied, but because he was surrounded by the most reliable of all safeguards against the words and the presence of others, and hence against reality as such.[40]

For Arendt, Eichmann's use of cliché exemplified how a morally distorted society gradually leads individuals to distort their own morality in order to fit in and function within it. To help assure them they're doing the "right thing," that society may then give those people a stock of ready-made clichés to smooth over any of their lingering doubts. And any society is subject to this process. "Eichmann and his cohorts did not randomly go from being ordinary men to being murders," Deborah Lipstadt writes. "They traversed a path paved by centuries of pervasive anti-Semitism. They 'knew' this road, and, given the society in which they lived, it seemed true and

---

38. See Lipstadt, *The Eichmann Trial*, 115–117.

39. Arendt, *Eichmann in Jerusalem*, 39.

40. Ibid., 49.

natural."[41] Therefore, Arendt implies, when you see a person spouting cliché, you see a person who's bought into a morally deadening system and is using language to anesthetize any last vestiges of inner objection to that system until they disappear for good. (As Orwell writes, this person has "turn[ed] himself into a "machine.") Crucially, the longer you use such clichés to help integrate yourself with a warped social reality, the more numb you become to their real meaning, and to the connection between language and reality in general. In what we've seen is a very important word for Arendt, you become "thoughtless," unable to register reality beyond your bubble of self-reinforcing linguistic and social delusion. "[A] more specific, and also more decisive, flaw in Eichmann's character," Arendt writes, "was his almost total inability to ever look at anything from the other fellow's point of view."[42]

Yet in Arendt's analysis, Eichmann remained unaware that he was in any way morally lacking or inconsistent, since he continued to "consol[e] himself with clichés:" morality was, to him, "questions of changing moods, and as long as he was capable of finding, either in his memory or on the spur of the moment, an elating stock phrase to go with them, he was quite content, without ever becoming aware of anything like 'inconsistencies.'"[43] Even when forced to read from the transcript of his own memoir of the Third Reich, dictated to a fellow Nazi, Eichmann reached for the same comfortable cliché of self-image as John Berger's "garment:" "[When] I received orders to proceed," he read, "against the guest of the host people, I thought this over, and when I recognized the necessity to do so, I carried out these [orders] with the degree of fanaticism one expected of oneself as a National Socialist of long standing."[44] Lifted on the emotional wave of an uplifting but meaningless cliché, which gave him all the pleasure but none of the work of actual thought, Eichmann could remain insulated from what Arendt, in her essay "Thinking and Moral Considerations" (1971), would later call "the claim on our thinking attention" made by other beings' right to exist:

> Clichés, stock phrases, adherence to conventional, standardized codes of expression and conduct have the socially recognized function of protecting us from reality, that is, against the claim on our thinking attention which all events and facts arouse by virtue of their existence. If we were responsive to this claim all

41. Lipstadt, *The Eichmann Trial*, 183.
42. Arendt, *Eichmann*, 47–48.
43. Ibid., 55.
44. Lipstadt, *The Eichmann Trial*, 137.

the time, we would soon be exhausted; the difference in Eich-mann was only that he clearly knew of no such claim at all.[45]

Although compassion fatigue is a real danger of ever-present empathy, a lack of awareness, an inability to "think from the standpoint of somebody else," is worse. "A life without thinking," Arendt wrote later, "is quite possible; it then fails to develop its own essence—it is not merely meaningless; it is not fully alive. Unthinking men are like sleepwalkers."[46] (She deliberately echoes Socrates's famous statement that "the unexamined life is not worth living," for the same reasons.) Therefore, if we aren't giving reality beyond ourselves a full "claim on our thinking attention," we don't just make bad art or cliché about it—we kill it because we don't really *see* it, and (in ironic circularity) the deadening language we keep using about it helps us keep on destroying it, with less and less attention. (Remember, even Tolstoy had to keep himself awake to remember whether he'd dusted that divan.) Cliché is a symptom of inattention that can deepen to exploitation, consciously or not, in any one of us. Therefore, we always need to be aware, in our individual lives and in our political systems, of how linguistic and moral thoughtlessness damage our capacity for judgment, justice, and care.

For both Arendt and Orwell, clear language enabled and signified the moral clarity needed to recognize and to act with and for other people. "The great enemy of clear language is insincerity," Orwell wrote in "Politics and the English Language." "When there is a gap between one's real and one's declared aims, one turns as it were instinctively to long words and exhausted idioms, like a cuttlefish spurting out ink."[47] To those who would defend politicians as "misspeaking" or having been made a falsely "political" issue, Orwell would likely snort in disbelief. "In our age there is no such thing as 'keeping out of politics,'" he declared. "All issues are political issues, and politics itself is a mass of lies, evasions, folly, hatred, and schizophrenia. When the general atmosphere is bad, language must suffer."[48] And when language suffers, people can too. Words can hurt, in more ways than we think, by encouraging and enabling human thoughtlessness.

Of course, Democrats aren't immune to cliché that springs from failure to imagine—or to communicate—reality. (No politician is, because no *human* is.) On June 25, 2013, President Barack Obama unveiled a new plan to help America address the results of climate change. Even admitting that climate change is real represents an historical improvement for the White

45. Arendt, "Thinking and Moral Considerations," 160.
46. Arendt, *Life of the Mind: Thinking*, 191.
47. Orwell, "Politics and the English Language," 964.
48. Ibid.

House. But Obama made no definitive statements against the Keystone XL pipeline, which would cross the Ogallala Aquifer and other environmentally sensitive areas to transmit fossil fuels and signal, in the words of climate scientist James Hansen, "game over for the climate" because of the massive amounts of tar sands it would open to burning.[49] Additionally, although he said "energy independence" and "natural gas" many times—touting natural gas as a means of "domestic energy independence" in our post–September 11 context—he never said "fracking," or even "hydraulic fracturing," the recognizable and controversial method by which "natural gas" is produced. This went beyond euphemism toward a lie of omission. Decoupling "natural gas" from "fracking" decouples an apparently clean solution from the messy and distressing costs of its production. As many articles, studies, and documentaries have shown, fracking—which blows apart underground shale formations with a high-pressure injection of water, sand, and toxic chemicals to release natural gas upward through a pipe—brings sickness to animals, humans, and land wherever it goes. It pollutes water and air. It destroys property values and homes. It has been linked to earthquakes. Its intended consequences are highly global, but its actual consequences, particularly the negative ones, couldn't be more local. More and more of us in "rural America" (another political cliché) have learned firsthand what fracking means and connected it with real costs in the real world, even if our elected officials haven't.

Fracking remained a fearsome but abstract issue for me until I learned, in October of 2012, that a frac-sand mining company was sniffing around my corner of northeast Iowa.[50] Frac-sand, the fine-grained, pure-silica sand used in fracking, occurs in natural abundance under the green hills and high river bluffs of northeast Iowa, western Wisconsin, and southeastern Minnesota (aka "the Driftless region"[51]), and the fracking boom elsewhere

49. The veil of "economic good sense" and "toughness" in which President Obama often veiled his environmental statements—in an attempt to appease the obstructionists in business and government around him—depressingly reminded me of the typical middle manager Matthew Crawford describes, a "corporate dramatist" who must "produce the stage props of a profit-maximizing" for her superiors in order to "get the official cover she needs to do the right thing by her workers" (see *Shop Class as Soulcraft*, 141).

50. See Weldon, "A Miniature Handbook."

51. This area is called "the Driftless region" because during the last great ice age, the glacier that moved roughly north to south and scraped away soil in its path swerved and missed this area, leaving intact our bluffs—and the silica sand underneath them, which is very geologically old. That's why we are "driftless"—we didn't experience the same glacial drift—and that's why so much of the land to the west of us is flat, because it was ironed out by that glacier.

in the country represents an economic opportunity for some (few) investors to come here and mine it. The fracking industry seeks the sand for use as a proppant: when mixed with water and chemicals (which are usually proprietary and highly toxic) and blasted into shale below ground, the sand rolls into cracks in the rock and holds them open to allow natural gas to flow up and out. Frac-sand mining is a different process from the gravel and agricultural sand mines we've always had here, and its results are much more dire and enduring. Typically for mining and extractive industries, it does not bring more than a handful of unsustainable jobs to an area. But it does bring blowing silica dust, which is much finer and therefore more dangerous for humans and animals to breathe than ordinary dust; water tables depleted and polluted from washing the sand (which takes a million gallons of water a day); carcinogenic chemicals (acrylamides) left in (sometimes leaky) surface pools of used sand-washing water; destroyed roads and bridges; the constant noise and danger of big truck traffic on small rural roads; vanishing property values; and the helplessness that homeowners feel as they watch the land around them literally disappear. Having attended many community groups, Boards of Supervisors and Planning and Zoning Commission meetings, and other events connected with this issue, I can testify that this issue knows no political boundaries. People who would otherwise place themselves all over our political spectrum came together in opposition to this industry, because in so many ways frac-sand mining is bad for us and for the place in which we live. If a mining company can get a landowner to sell or lease them the rights, they can come in and scoop a giant hole in the ground right next to your farm.[52] Then you can watch your property values, your clean air and water (for yourself and your animals), your personal enjoyment of your property in beauty and quiet, and your safety on your public roads (torn up by multiple semi-truck loads of frac-sand trucks) disappear. And under current regulatory frameworks, all of this is legal.

In August 2013, to help ourselves understand what we were fighting, Winneshiek and Allamakee County Protectors (our anti–frac-sand–mining community groups) organized a bus trip through Chippewa and Trempealeau Counties in Wisconsin to see these mines in operation. Our guide was a cattle farmer whose land now borders a frac-sand mine. The sights were staggering: railroad cars lined up; sand spilled on tracks; washing and loading facilities; conveyor belts and piles; and trucks zooming past on narrow country roads every two or three minutes. Piles of the washed frac-sand itself, with an eerie, pearly gleam. And giant mines like tan scars ripped

---

52. See local activist Robert Nehman's documentary "Frac Sand Land.: The Incredible Story of the Vanishing Hills" (KnoMor Productions, 2012), which features interviews with the farmers under threat.

out of hillsides, destroying the lovely green hills for good. Above heaps of sand waiting to be trucked away floated a sign with a discreet corporate logo: EOG, or Enron Oil and Gas—yes, the same Enron that, back in 2001, bankrupted all of its employees except its CEOs.[53] Western Wisconsin was being hauled away, little by little.

The sight of what I don't want our land to become made me see again that the work against fracking and frac-sand mining, like our overall work to survive as a species in our post-peak oil, global warming era, is a struggle between two opposing voices that shape our behavior, that we see externalized in society at large, and that we carry within ourselves every day. One voice says, "I know I'm not the only creature on earth, and others will come after me, so I need to live with humility and decency." The second just snarls, "I want *mine*, right now." What's *mine*? Convenience, safety, pleasure, sweet salty somethings to rip out of a bag and scarf down before flinging the bag out your car window and speeding away—and money. Freud's model of the human mind would say the first voice is the superego, and the second is the id, which growls and shouts from down in the basement, deaf to everything except itself. In between, of course, is the ego, where we all live, struggling to reconcile our obligations and ethics and our greed. Because we're human beings, we can and must make choices not to let that id—whether at the personal or the corporate, profit-seeking level—run us, like a border collie runs sheep. We're humans. We can make choices. We have to look at the corporate and social landscape around us and see how our choices are enabled or constrained by the structures in place, with or without our consent.

Commercial cliché helps feed our desires for "convenience," and by betraying our rural places and the people who live there, it reveals just how deeply "rural America" is itself becoming an exploitable cliché, tagged by Democrats and Republicans with every new Iowa caucus cycle. Corporate ag giant Monsanto, for instance, rolled out a series of pious billboards and blog entries about "being thankful for America's farmers."[54] Yet, like frac-sand mining, Monsanto—which has sued farmers for copyright infringement when they found its genetically modified seed accidentally growing on their land—has also acted as yet another of the extractive, exploitative industries preying on rural America.[55] I'm a woman with a garden. I grew up on a cattle farm in Alabama. I live in an Iowa town of 8,000 people. I love land that's under threat. I believe human beings are here on earth

53. Now known as "EOG Resources."

54. http://monsantoblog.com/2010/11/22/being-thankful-for-americas-farmers/

55. See Harris, "Monsanto Sued Small Farmers."

to do justice and love mercy, not to stack cash. Those facts of my identity are the aquifer through which everything I learn from news and reading and everyday life and travel all over the world filters down and settles into meaning in my mind and heart. So when I look at every corporate wealth-extraction method deployed in rural America—drilling and fracking in the Marcellus Shale and on public lands, mountaintop-removal mining in West Virginia, the mining of silica sand for use in fracking, and so many more—I see a recapitulation of every shameful thing done in the name of wealth and power to the bodies of the poor and powerless, from the deep past to the present, all over the world. Split open. Forced apart. Ripped and discarded. Stuffed with engineered product. Poisoned. Lied to. Exploited for the benefit of other people far away. These things are done to the poor from Bangladesh to Bolivia to the tiny farming towns in your state and mine, and these things are done to their land. Like the rest of us, those in eerily named "sacrifice zones" are experiencing in their individual bodies the same things done to the body of their land, our land, our Earth.[56] For example, food deserts and big-box stores combine in the weird paradox of malnutrition, obesity, and diabetes in poor rural communities (often all present in the same person), where getting food often means getting in the car to drive to the Walmart in the next town over, because your local grocery store isn't there anymore. Here in Iowa, I see many farms with fencerow-to-fencerow corn but no vegetable garden or chicken coop or orchard. I once heard that before World War II Iowa produced half—*half*—of all the food produced in America, because each farmstead used to have its own means of food production for itself as well as for the market. Not anymore.[57]

Yet rural people are still so often matter-of-fact and stoic about the way things are. They keep on with multiple jobs (including the off-farm job to support the farm, turning on their tractor headlights to work at night), and counter posts at the convenience store and beauty parlors in their garages. They look for jobs after the mill or the lumber company or the manufacturing plant has shut its doors and moved overseas for greater profit (or replaced them with robots, as we saw in Chapter 1). Their kids move to the city and don't come back. Methamphetamine, that dismal rural scourge, corrodes lives.[58] But people still keep on, in tidy houses in tiny towns like the

56. See Chris Hedges and Joe Sacco, *Days of Destruction, Days of Revolt*.

57. See Dan Barber's *The Third Plate: Field Notes on the Future of Food* for a promising new model of "eating the farm" and of raising on individual farms the range of foods needed for a meal—including chickens, grains, dairy, and vegetables.

58. See Nick Reding, *Methland: The Death and Life of An American Small Town*, which describes Oelwein, Iowa, a small town about 45 minutes south of Decorah. Fayette County district attorney Nathan Lein, profiled in Reding's book, is a Luther College

ones we rolled through in rural Wisconsin, decorated with wind-spinners and flower baskets and Green Bay Packers flags. They are the people Monsanto and frac-sand–mining company CEOs claim to see but never do. And many of the rest of us ostensibly salt-of-the-earth–respecting Americans don't see them, either. When I looked at those trainloads of frac-sand ready for shipment to Pennsylvania or Ohio or North Dakota, I thought about the mythical giant Atlas, holding up the earth on his shoulders. Those grains of sand—the literal substance of rural America—get blasted into cracks to hold them open while the stuff that actually makes money flows up, out, and away. The sand will stay down there, in the dark, holding open the rock. Atlas does not complain. This is the way things are.

But there's another fact: our land is our home. In his 1871 poem "Homesick in Heaven," Oliver Wendell Holmes wrote, "where we love is home, / Home that our feet may leave but not our hearts."[59] You see the difference between the way we feel about our homes and the way the industry feels about them when you look at the language of mining and fracking as compared to the physical realities of land and people who live on it. The layers of trees, soil, grass, and other types of sand scraped away to get at silica are called, in the mining industry, the *overburden*. The condition in which you may own your land but not own the mineral rights beneath it (which is legal and quite common) is called *split estate*. When you see such Alice-in-Wonderland, matter-of-fact distortions of reality surface in words (Trees and soil are nothing more than a "burden?" The layer of your land on which you live and in which you grow your food is less important than what's underneath, and can be *separated* from that?) you can be sure there is something dirty at work—a "split" of body from spirit and brain, money from value, you from yourself and the deepest, truest things you know. In Christian theology, sin arises from such a fundamental separation, and no matter what your tradition, such alienation is a sign of ill health, physically and morally; remember Hannah Arendt's idea that conscience involves being able to live in the same interior "house" with yourself as a whole person of integrity. But for some people, this split is very profitable. And in order to keep those profits flowing—and their consciences clear—businesspeople and the politicians they have bought keep the bright, cheerful, ostensibly neutral language of concealment and exploitation flowing too. This is why writing teachers say "avoid cliché:" it short-circuits the hard work of rendering what you see into language that does justice to the realities of the thing seen and to the complex, socially located self that's seeing it.

---

graduate.

59. Holmes, "Homesick in Heaven," 147.

Yet we can resist cliché, especially the media disseminated and distorted kind, by getting involved in politics ourselves, so we can build a body of personal experience to counter it. Even in the face of Supreme Court decisions enshrining corporate donors as "people" who will always outearn and outspend me, I do believe this action has power. Even attending a city council or Board of Supervisors or school board meeting, or door-knocking for a candidate, or talking to friends about a local issue, can break the spell of distance that so often hovers around politics in our minds—the notion that politics has nothing to do with and cannot be affected by us. As Eduardo Nesi describes the power of standing up at a political demonstration, "what counts is one's body: its extension to become a thought, its ambition to stand in for even those who aren't or couldn't be there."[60] But in order to get out there, we've got to take a look at what might be inside ourselves that holds us back.

In the fall of 2011, I attended the first meeting of our little town's branch of the then-national Occupy Wall Street movement, featuring a spectrum of voters from red to blue. (Yes, there were Occupiers on the right, here and elsewhere; out-of-control corporations in politics, financial systems, and our lives were our common concern.) We gathered on the courthouse steps, scattered with golden maple leaves that crunched underfoot, with signs reading *Power to the Peaceful*; *In God We Trusted, In Wall Street We Busted*; *Reinstate Glass-Steagall*; *I Don't Want To Buy the Kochs A World*; and *We Are The Ones We Are Waiting For*. Despite its inevitable imperfections, the Occupy movement was really about looking closely, discerning the real motivations bubbling underneath the surface of our economy, and putting ourselves and our human choices back in the equation—and, crucially, about examining our own complicity. When I walked down the street, carrying my homemade signs—one said "CORPORATIONS ≠ PEOPLE," one said "CHERISH THE LOCAL *(vote with your dollars, support sustainable economies)*," I noticed that something about that felt really weird. Yet what *is* it that makes walking with a sign feel "radical?" And what does that say about our political future together?

That semester, I was teaching Charlotte Bronte's classic novel *Jane Eyre* (1847) to first-year students amid a spate of anti-Occupy Wall Street sentiment flying around the Internet. Juxtapose the two and you could see an odd, revealing faith that separate spheres, public and private, were still the right thing to maintain, especially since they protect some people's power and money just fine. If Wall Street's working in your favor, it suits you to scoff at Occupiers as naïve, "unwashed," or "refugees from a Phish

---

60. Nesi, *Story of My People*, 148.

concert," implying something distasteful about them which led them to take to the streets at all. If you have money, you can buy your own lobbyist, your own politician, your own revisions to the language in the clean air or anti-fracking or banking regulation bill. You can circumvent the legislative systems ordinary people access only through the ballot box and the letter to an elected official. You don't have to put your own body under the windows of Wall Street skyscrapers or the White House or the Capitol Building or the Pentagon to claim, with your physical presence, the attention of those inside, because you're already inside that building too. You've bought your place at the table. You've moved from door to door in your own private car, wrapped in a thick green blanket of money.

The Victorians considered the private sphere society's moral center. Significantly, it was also the place where traditional—particularly male—power was most philosophically unchallenged, even though as a domestic world it was also associated with proper femininity. Home was the place the businessman came to rest his world-weary feet and defer to his wife about (to him, relatively unimportant) things to satisfy her that she needn't ask to be recognized in other places and other ways; she had "power" in her home, and that was supposed to be enough for her, even though she couldn't be legally recognized as a person in the public world. We still live with this idea and many others of what historian Daniel Smail calls "'ghost theories,' old ideas that continue to structure our thinking without our being fully aware of their controlling presence."[61] We still rely a little too much on a notion of "home" as totally separate from the rest of the world. If you can buy your own private bubbles, you may have trouble seeing yourself as part of a public, or responsible to a common good. Yet, as the great social activist and Nobel laureate Jane Addams wrote, "the good we secure for ourselves is precarious and uncertain, is floating in mid-air, until it is secured for all of us and incorporated into our common life."[62] And our Constitution does give us the right to get out there and ask, peacefully, for our common good: think of suffragettes campaigning for the right to vote, Martin Luther King, Jr.'s March on Washington, Black Lives Matter, anti-Keystone XL and anti-Dakota Access Pipeline work. Further, political philosopher Matthew Crawford reminds us that a person who clings blindly to a concept of himself as closed away, separated in his own life from the concerns of a larger world and not responsible to that world, is literally an idiot, as "[t]he Greek *idios* means 'private,' and an *idiotes* means a private person" who "lacks the

---

61. Smail, *On Deep History*, 3.
62. Addams, "The Subjective Necessity."

attentive openness that seeks things out in the shared world . . . . At bottom, the idiot is a solipsist."[63]

Therefore, we citizens have to refuse the notion that stepping into the public sphere with peaceful political intent is somehow inappropriate, because it's not. It's our constitutional right, and our moral one. Retreating to our private worlds, trusting that "they" will "take care of it," means giving up control over who will step into the silent gap between government and us. Lobbyists and corporations with the money to bypass the legislative channels you and I use—especially in the wake of the Supreme Court's decisions in Citizens United vs. Federal Election Commission (2010) and McCutcheon vs. Federal Election Commission (2014), which removed campaign contribution limits for corporations and enshrined their legal "personhood" for that purpose—can't be trusted to have our best interests at heart. Despite the new phenomenon of "B Corps," which are "for-profit companies that pledge to achieve social goals as well as business ones" (such as Patagonia, Seventh Generation, and Etsy), it is not the nature of corporations to be moral; it is the nature of corporations to make money.[64] I can understand that fact, although I'm wary of it. But I can't accept a wildly uneven governmental playing field that lets the corporation's "rights" overrun my health, my consumer choices, and my clean air and water, because I am a real person, and a corporation is not. This is the old legal principle *quod omnes tangit, ab omnibus decidetur*, or "that which touches all requires everyone's agreement."[65]

I've been heartened to see multigenerational crowds at all the public political events I've described here and more, with many college and high school students present and taking the microphone to speak. Yet young people may face a special set of problems in engaging with public issues: although they're fluent in online communication and can be readily involved in "clicktivism" for that reason, they can falter when asked to be bodily present in public because of a fear of the public sphere many have learned from their parents. Sociologist danah boyd usefully points out that for many teenagers, intense involvement with friends in online worlds substitutes for real-world interaction because teenagers receive messages (from parents, police, teachers, and other authorities) that the public space is not safe for them, or that their presence makes a space unsafe for others. "Many American teens have limited geographic freedom, less free time, and more rules," boyd writes. "[T]he success of social media must be understood partly in

---

63. Crawford, *Shop Class as Soulcraft*, 98.

64. See Surowiecki, "Companies with Benefits," 23.

65. Scarry, *Thinking in an Emergency*, 7.

relation to this shrinking social landscape. Facebook, Twitter, and MySpace are not only new public spaces; they are in many cases the only 'public' spaces in which teens can easily congregate with large groups of their peers. More significantly, teens can gather in them while still physically stuck at home."[66] Meshing with another parenting fear/social phenomenon—named the "overprotected kid" by one writer[67]—the exclusion of children and teenagers from public spaces drives them into online worlds where the dangers of predation may be even greater than in real life. And despite their fluency with their devices, many teenagers—including some of my college students—aren't very informed about privacy settings, search terms, and the reality that their profile photos on Facebook can be viewed by more than just their "friends:" "as sociologist Eszter Hargittai has quipped, many teens are more likely to be digital naives than digital natives."[68] This means, I think, that young people need not overprotectiveness but careful, sensible leadership and role modeling from adults—including appropriate exposure to public events and the public sphere. And therefore we adults will have to get better at making public spheres of discourse and interaction more safe and constructive for everyone.

Quaker activist, teacher, and writer Parker Palmer describes democracy as one of five "cultural creations" that help humans transcend the fight-or-flight responses that cause us to approach others with defensiveness or fear. Therefore, it helps us grow toward a quintessential adult ability: being in the presence of uncertainty without seeking an immediate or superficial solution. In *Healing the Heart of Democracy: The Courage to Create A Politics Worthy of the Human Spirit* (2011), he writes, "Like language, the arts, religion, and education, democracy does not propose to bring life's tensions to an end. Instead, it offers us a process for using them creatively, providing political structures that promise to turn the energy of tension toward constructive ends. Because it holds out that promise, life in a democracy can trigger a 'tend and befriend' response that some biologists believe to be as deep-seated within us as the fight or flight instinct."[69] Yet as he notes, "industrialization and the centralization of power that would come with it" are greater threats to the "associational vigor" of democratic communities than we might realize. He quotes Alexis de Tocqueville's famous *Democracy in America* (1835–1840) as being prescient about such dangers:

66. boyd, *It's Complicated,* 21. The lack of capitalization in the author's name is her personal preference.

67. Rosin, "The Overprotected Kid."

68. boyd, *It's Complicated,* 22.

69. Palmer, *Healing the Heart of Democracy,* 85–86.

> It is easy to foresee the time [Tocqueville writes] when men will be less and less able to produce, by themselves, the commonest necessities of life. The task of the social power will therefore increase endlessly, and its very efforts will make that task bigger every day. The more it takes the place of associations, the more individuals will lose the idea of associating and will need its assistance. These causes and effects engender each other without end.[70]

Indeed, Palmer writes, "The privatization of life that has come with our growing dependence on centralized power, economic as well as political, makes it all the more urgent that we do what we can to develop democratic habits of the heart in every setting available to us"—or, in other words, that we don't let our community-building skills atrophy as we polarize centers of authority in our lives between either the private home or Washington, DC.[71] "Habits of the heart," here, refers to the inward attitudes and orientations that make civil conduct in our daily "associations" possible—and that, as I noted, may be damaged by the literal habits of our lifestyles and media consumption, which can exacerbate existing prejudices and fears.

My (guarded) optimism about our power to come together in public politically at the local level may seem to be counteracted by the data, and by the way each election seems to carve (and reveal) deeper, angrier rifts in our republic. Environmental philosopher Dale Jamieson, describing what he calls "the deep cynicism that characterizes public life in contemporary America," writes that "we are no longer surprised to the depths to which others will sink."[72] Yet perhaps language can help to heal us. Let's start with the word *liberal*—which faculty and marketing teams at liberal arts colleges like mine routinely have to defend and define. Like *conservative*, *liberal* describes a set of intellectual virtues worth embodying. Throughout the nineteenth century (and before), *liberal* indicated a certain curious openness to the world, along with a sense of generous trust toward others and a willingness to give them the benefit of the doubt. (By contrast, *mean* originally meant *stingy, grasping, and fearful*, particularly with money, in a way that still shapes the word's modern connotations of spitefulness and cruelty.) "One of the earliest uses of the word 'liberal,'" writes Matthew Crawford, "was to draw a distinction between the 'liberal arts' and the 'servile arts.' The former were those pursuits befitting a free man."[73]

70. Ibid., 86.

71. Ibid., 87.

72. Jamieson, *Reason in a Dark Time*, 88.

73. Crawford, *Shop Class as Soulcraft*, 109.

In American history, *freedom*, of course, has meant not only an ideal of independence and self-direction but the legal status that empowers one to regard oneself, and be regarded, as an independent person. When Frederick Douglass (c. 1818–1895), the great abolitionist, author, and former slave, met his former master, Thomas Auld, Auld was near death, yet Douglass could use the word *liberal* to describe the qualities of masculine fairness he both extended to and expected from Auld. As Nick Bromell writes in his essay "The Liberal Imagination of Frederick Douglass," *liberal-minded* means for both Douglass and Auld a sensitivity to personal context and a shared past: "in all of [these scenes of reconciliation]," Bromell writes, "the former slave and his former masters relinquish their resentments, recognize each other's vulnerabilities, and behave with empathetic compassion," meeting on a common ground as mature adults.[74] This is not to say the pain of slavery, its brutality, or its multilayered abuses—which any reader of Douglass's autobiography knows—should be quickly or easily forgiven: "'I am no minister of malice,' [Douglass] told an audience in 1871, 'but . . . may my tongue cleave to the roof of my mouth if I forget the difference between the parties to that . . . bloody conflict. . . . I may say if this war is to be forgotten, I ask in the name of all things sacred what shall men remember?'"[75] Yet in behaving with "liberal-mindedness" and accepting this same attitude from his former master, Douglass not only expands that term to include black men as well as the white "gentlemen" with whom it was usually associated, but he "dramatize[s] the qualities of mind and feeling that would make possible a genuinely ethical reconciliation on a national scale."[76] Therefore, *liberal* can be reclaimed not just as an epithet but as a marker for a system of values everyone in a democracy can uphold. As the critic Lionel Trilling writes in his landmark critical work *The Liberal Imagination* (1950), "The word liberal is a word primarily of political import, but its political meaning defines itself by the quality of life it envisages, by the sentiments it desires to affirm," as in the standard political term *liberal democracy*.[77] Similarly, the word *conservative* can benefit from similar scrutiny: at its best, it means exercising a prudence, caution, and humility that comes from a knowledge of human limitation, especially valuable in judging the actions of the present through the lens of history. At its best, conservativism—like liberalism—insists what human beings always need to remember: that the single self and its needs, in the present moment, are not all there is or will be, or that the world is not a story about you.

74. Bromell, "The Liberal Imagination of Frederick Douglass," 39.
75. Ibid., 41.
76. Ibid., 42.
77. Trilling, *The Liberal Imagination*, xvii.

Ultimately, I think, serious but fundamentally civil discourse and higher intellectual standards for our consumption of information can help us rediscover these common and necessary values. Environmentalist Terry Tempest Williams writes, "We are aching to come together, and I think it has little to do with liberal or conservative discourse. I think it has to do with increasing disconnection with what is real and soul-serving."[78] Let's keep an eye on that important word—*soul*—and remember what our job is here on Earth: seeing each other as full and dignified human beings. Nineteenth-century political philosopher John Stuart Mill described a symbiotic relationship between ourselves and our political opponents, saying "that the prayer of every true partisan of liberalism should be, 'Lord, enlighten thou our enemies . . . ; sharpen their wits, give acuteness to their perceptions and consecutiveness and clearness to their reasoning powers. We are in danger from their folly, not from their wisdom: their weakness is what fills us with apprehension, not their strength.'"[79] I like the suggestion here that we have more to fear from each other's bad ideas than the good ones, and that our good ideas may be a common meeting ground upon which we can build. I'm not saying this will take all passion, conviction, or anger out of politics, or that this means we should simply set aside our convictions and emotions, which can alert us to something truly wrong with the situation in front of us and the need to act on it. There's too much at stake for "making nice" to be sufficient; as Hannah Arendt wrote in *Eichmann in Jerusalem*, "politics is not like the nursery; in politics obedience and support are the same."[80] But we'll never change anything if we can't quit biting the hook of political cliché and asking ourselves where that emotion is really coming from—defensible moral principle or some less defensible form of habit, spitefulness, or hate.[81]

Consider author Eboo Patel's model of religious pluralism, described in his book *Acts of Faith* (2007)—taking another's faith seriously does *not* mean "being converted" but talking with other believers to find connective ground on the questions common to *all* faiths. What does your tradition say about what it means to be human, and how we should live in relationship to other humans and to the non-human world? Every tradition has some version of "the golden rule," or *do unto others as you would have them do unto you*—how is yours expressed? What does your tradition consider "progressive" or "fundamentalist?" What are some issues connected to translation

78. Gay, "The Rumpus Interview with Terry Tempest Williams."

79. Trilling, *The Liberal Imagination*, xvi.

80. Arendt, *Eichmann*, 279.

81. "Don't bite the hook" is an admonition (from Pema Chodron's work) not to grasp at habitual reactions and thought processes.

of your sacred text, and what does it actually say? How do you pray? What is your tradition's relationship to social justice? To women's rights? To homosexuality? To "strangers?" To silence? Students who have participated in interfaith discussion groups like this report that "understanding another's faith deepened my experience of my own," helping them to see past cliches toward fellow humans, all walking a path in the presence of mystery.

My own experience gives me hope that when we get together around common causes and values at the local level, we can agree—and "we" can surprise ourselves by who "we" turn out to be. Our Occupy group soon morphed into a Local Economy Working Group that explored alternatives to economic systems like those we'd just seen crashing Wall Street. One of the members of the group was a cattle farmer and chairman of the local Tea Party; I've been friends with him and his wife since I've lived here. The political and economic discontents Occupy had raised—especially the influence of corporate power and money in government—continued to percolate among all of us, and when the threat of frac-sand mining, which I've already mentioned, came along, we discovered common ground. Property rights and property values are two of those points. So are clean air and water, and our responsibility not to ruin these things for our descendants. Opposition to frac-sand mining blossomed in a series of meetings, letter-writing campaigns, discussions, working groups (Winneshiek County Protectors and Allamakee County Protectors), and other forms that included my Tea Party friend and many others who might not call themselves *liberal* but saw no reason why the interests of businesses should be allowed to overrun the constitutional rights and ecological contexts of citizens, and why money from corporate donors in politics should shut the ordinary citizen out of the process. (That's in interesting contrast to what's becoming the default political practice of *both* parties in our society, which can make questioning the will of any corporation that wants something from us seem more "un-American" than questioning the government itself.) Paul Hawken in *Blessed Unrest* (2007) describes the rise of countless small groups like ours working on local issues all over the world—united loosely by concerns for social justice, ecological health, and resistance to corporate globalization—as the largest social movement in history. "If there is a pervasive criticism of global capitalism that is shared by all actors in the movement," Hawken writes, "it is this observation: goods seem to have become more important, and are treated better, than people. What would a world look like if that emphasis were reversed?"[82] Asserting the value of *the commons*—entities like air and water, which nobody can own but every-

82. Hawken, *Blessed Unrest*, 14.

body needs—can assert a set of powerful, if endangered, shared values over and against those of corporations and special interests. Common good. Common interests. And—heartbreakingly urgent in our era of hate crimes and Twitter trollery—common decency.

All this is to say that if you get out into your town and work on a public issue, you may discover that the great and looming divisions you had imagined between you and your "opponents" can shrink, or even vanish, in practice. Sure, there will be disagreements. But there will also be conversations, and old labels will be revealed as the cliches they really are. I think the climate of partisan media, stoked by talking heads and their talking points and the tremendous advertising dollars to be gained from fear and anger, contribute to fears of having nothing to say to *them*. Shut away in your own house, with your own television and your own computer, it's easy for your anxieties to swell into anger (much easier to deal with than fear or loneliness.)[83] As our community groups worked on issues (particularly our opposition to frac-sand mining), we discovered that our values lined up in unexpected ways. When you cut through the (tremendously profitable) fear and distortion and identify what's *really* at stake—which for us was the right of property owners and residents to control the safety, beauty, and value of our own land—you discover that the actual issue is not reducible to sound bites. This is yet another reason not to surrender the public political sphere to professional politicians and the corporations who buy them: they represent reality to us, through the media and through a ginned-up fear of our "opponents," in a way that is simply not true. As Arendt wrote, "the common world . . . remains 'inhuman' in a very literal sense unless it is constantly talked about by human beings."[84] Her analogy of public life is a homely one: "To live together in the world," she writes, "means essentially that a world of things is between those who have it in common, as a table is located between those who sit around it; the world, like every in-between, relates

---

83. As the Pew study "Political Polarization in the American Public," available at http://www.people-press.org/2014/06/12/political-polarization-in-the-american-public/ indicates, conservatives are more likely than liberals (by 75 percent) to prefer a "community where the houses are larger and farther apart, but schools, stores, and restaurants are several miles away." Liberals are 77 percent more likely to prefer a "community where the houses are smaller and closer to each other, but schools, stores, and restaurants are within walking distance." Architecture and space shape psychology and culture very powerfully; I don't think it's an accident that political conservativism of an isolationist stripe, or preference for a relatively isolated home space (where you travel in your private car "into town" to where you need to go, then come back, without perhaps engaging any neighbors in spaces other than commercial ones) can reinforce one another and, in practice, often do.

84. Young-Bruehl, *Why Arendt Matters*, 33.

and separates men at the same time."[85] Public life depends on conversation within the polis, continually reinvoking community, democracy, and decency in order to keep them alive.

Winneshiek County Protectors and Allamakee County Protectors soon came to share some membership and goals with another group that grew out of anti–frac-sand–mining efforts: the Community Rights Alliance. The concept of community rights has great potential for achieving our biggest legal need: enshrining the rights of citizens, towns, and the "commons"—air, land, and water—to stand up against the "personhood" and rights of corporations. To make the case very simply, under current law, if a corporation wants to bring fracking, frac-sand mining, toxic waste disposal sites, or other things that suit their needs (but not yours) into your town, you have no legal power to stop them unless you can point out some error in their permit applications. According to the major community rights organization, the Community Environmental Legal Defense Fund (CELDF), community activists have therefore focused on finding errors in those applications. This defeats our own purposes, though, since the corporations then correct those problems and resubmit the applications, which then cannot legally be denied. A community rights approach, by contrast, seeks to change the underlying legal ecology by helping communities to write and pass ordinances that enshrine their own "personhood" to preemptively protect our rights over and against the rights of corporations. In 2013, tiny Mora County, New Mexico (population 4,481) became the first county in the United States to ban fracking through community rights–based legal strategies like these.[86] As of June 2014, according to CELDF, more than 150 communities across the country have established community rights–based ordinances to limit or prohibit "a range of harmful practices, from shale gas drilling and fracking to the land application of sewage sludge." As community rights activist and teacher Paul Cienfuegos says in his workshops—several of which he's held in our town, to enthusiastic crowds—"We the people are more powerful than we dare to believe."

One of the great promises of community rights is the way it builds sustainable local economies through the practices of good business: you

---

85. Arendt, *The Human Condition*, 52.

86. See the 2012 documentary "Rooted Lands (Tierras Arraigadas)," by Nancy Dickenson and Renae Roberts, and the 2010 documentary "Split Estate" by Debra Anderson. In the West, "split estate" laws often apply (you own the above-ground portion of your property, but not the mining rights to what's underneath, so a gas company can legally drill under your property regardless of effects on your water table, for instance.) This is one of the many ways a company's actions can affect the property values and rights of the landowners around it.

must make a plan, exercise due diligence, and follow it, accounting for your own costs and by-products rather than externalizing them onto the government, your neighbors, or the environment. (Walmart, whose "associates" frequently have to apply for federal food stamp benefits, fails at this, as many of the small businesses it replaces do not.) Your growth is controlled by the checks and balances of the human and environmental ecosystems in which you are embedded—thus you avoid what Wendell Berry calls the great ecological sin of pride, the belief that limitless growth and wealth will always be possible, with no limits ("growth for the sake of growth," ecologist Edward Abbey observed, "is the ideology of the cancer cell.")[87] Cradle-to-grave manufacturing techniques, which require you to account for every stage in the life cycle of your product so you don't get to simply "throw away" your waste at someone else's expense, are gaining greater presence and attention domestically and overseas.[88] Increasingly, businesses that externalize their operating costs or waste in the form of pollution (including noise pollution), expecting their neighbors (human and nonhuman) to cope, will find the philosophical, economic, and social burden too great to continue, and their opposition will not come only from usual-suspect "liberal" activists but from entire communities. This is the promise of community rights: the power of people to organize themselves and pressure corporate entities to remember they are embedded in and responsible to communities.

Claiming your power as an individual begins, fundamentally, with getting past your fear of being "irrelevant" or "improper" or "ignorant," going to meetings, asking questions, and educating yourself. Your presence alone at a meeting can be a powerful vote. Yes, online activism is powerful, but ultimately (especially at the local level) it does not have the impact of bodily presence in a public space, face-to-face with our elected leaders. As the old activist saying goes, "we are the ones we have been waiting for"—no one is going to give us what we need if we don't stand up and ask for it.

During my Winneshiek County Protectors work, I attended multiple Planning and Zoning Commission meetings in our county and in the county next to ours on issues related to frac-sand mining and rock/sand quarry expansion and permits. Personal appearances matter: you are in the room with county officials, where they have to look at and listen to the people they serve. Physical presence has a weight and dignity of its own, a gravitational force, especially when you have overflow crowds and head counts of 200-plus in courthouse rooms where planning and zoning commissioners

87. Abbey, *The Journey Home*, 183.

88. http://www.compositesmanufacturingblog.com/2013/01/whats-your-cradle
-to-grave-story/

sit around a table, in rooms with humming overhead lights and open windows, where citizens speak to the people they have elected to represent them. Commissioners look into their constituents' faces, listening to one voice after another. Neighbors stand together and hear each other's stories. Discussion is serious, passionate, civil; sometimes there's even affectionate laughter. And at the end of the evening, we can see the tangible results of our public presence in—or use that same presence to register opposition to—the commissioners' votes, which don't always go the way the public comments would wish but sometimes—perhaps surprisingly often—do.

One moment from one of those meetings stays with me. A white-haired, respected community leader asked the crowd in that courtroom, "Please stand if you are in favor of a moratorium on frac-sand mining." Except for mining company representatives and a few ladies with bad knees, everyone in the room—retirees, businesspeople, teachers, teenagers, farmers—rose to their feet. It was a rustling like wind in a stand of trees, or water down a streambed—the active presence of human beings in the place they love, dignified, determined, and irreplaceable, in a way that even the best-designed online petition will never be.

4

Practice an art, and let it change the way you see.

> The little that I have learned about the world, and, more important, that I have learned about myself, has been absurdly expensive, but I have always thought it more than worth the price. There is no other way. The miracle of the world, the miracle of a rebirth of the senses, the miracle of an accepting heart can only be paid for with blood and bone. No other currency has ever been acceptable.
>
> —HARRY CREWS[1]

IN OUR ALABAMA CHILDHOOD, my sister and I loved to make pottery. Hunkered next to a little creek that filled up only when it rained, we'd pry slick, jagged chunks of clay out of the side of the bank and work them into pots: pat them round and deepen the centers with our thumbs, or roll long coils and wind them up. Sometimes we pressed pebbles into them, jeweling them like goblets for queens; sometimes the drying clay gripped the jewel and sometimes it loosened to drop the stone like a tooth. As with our drawings, and as with the wild pokeberries we crushed and painted on our fingernails, we could never be sure what our materials would do.

Thirty years later I took a real pottery class for the first time. The studio in Luther's Center for the Arts was a big, bright, concrete-floored space with lots of shelves and rows of tough old Brent wheels with yellow plastic rims and accelerator pedals attached to the engines with thick cords. Lugging my new box of clay to my wheel and selecting a plastic wheel cover from the stack, I sat down on my stool, clad in rolled-up jeans and Chaco sandals, just like the students. I'm on sabbatical, I told them, and I'm here to learn, just like you.

---

1. Crews, "Introduction," 15.

Being a student promised to be refreshing. As a writer and writing teacher, I thought I'd learned the truths of doing and making: don't expect perfection; let the material take shape in front of you, then go back to bend or trim it; take another run at it. Change takes place over time, sometimes a lot of time. Any amount of forward motion, in the place where you are now, counts as progress, and that's okay. All these things are true of art making as I know it. I've been living them out for years. But it's hard to remember them when you're learning something new.

At first, shucking off my professor identity felt easy, but then bad student habits filled in that place. I congratulated myself on accepting the fingermarks along the bottom of my hand-built bowl and smoothed the breast of my little bird figure, hoping for our teacher to pause at my work-space and praise me. I stayed late on the first day to throw what turned out to be a chunky little vessel somewhere between a pitcher and a bowl, with a plump bottom and poked-out lip. Next stop—I congratulated myself—would be mastery!

Yet by the end of the second day I was stuck, and getting really mad. Over and over I centered the clay on the wheel and pressed my thumbs down and watched dumbly as the clay wobbled and the sides unfurled. I cursed. I tried again. But the more I thought about how to drop the notch of my thumb and finger along the rim, how to pull up the spinning clay, or how to fetch more water on my fingers without tugging the nascent shape out of line, the less I could do anything. I clenched my foot to the pedal. "Maybe ease up on the gas a little," my teacher offered. But by then the pot was too far gone, slung out of balance by my over-anxious speed. The frustration lingered for the rest of the day. *I have a $%^*g PhD and I can't do this?*

And then, on the morning of my thirty-eighth birthday, at the beginning of my sabbatical, a package dropped onto my porch: my novel manuscript had been returned, with the kindest and most encouraging letter any writer could hope for from the editor I'd been working with over two incarnations of that draft. But still—she said no. Four years of work had come to what felt in that moment like nothing.

That afternoon, trying to put the novel out of my mind, I drove to a nineteenth-century Lutheran church at the edge of a cornfield to read Shakespeare's Sonnet 116 in the wedding of two of my former students. Wind tossed the wildflowers in the ditches. Their friends played guitar and handed out programs. Standing at the altar I looked down into the eyes of the bride and groom, trying hard not to cry. *Let me not to the marriage of true minds admit impediments . . . .* All the loud hurt in my blood receded, and something about the world on that bright early fall Saturday became very clear. I thought about love and loss of family and others, the way the world twisted and turned around me as I moved through my twenties and into my thirties, the way my plans have and have not worked out, the fact that I would not go backwards by even five minutes, the way my writing has broken my heart and brought me back to it over and over, the gratefulness I feel for every single year. Grateful? I am. As bewildering as it can be. As hard as the surfaces of disappointment can feel when you are pressed against them, with what feels like nothing else to touch. As keenly as emotion bites into you, wry and sweet and deep and wrenching. I am grateful.

The next day, I biked to school and centered and threw my first success-ful bowls: thick-walled, crude-bottomed, wobbly, but recognizable. When I set them in the window to dry, I noticed they were accidentally right—three sizes all in a line, all slanting up and to the right. Ascending bowls. Hollow vessels, equally exposed, inside and out. But always leaning up.

I kept working and got better. The vessel walls got thinner, the shapes more centered and even. But increasingly, there was no more self-congrat-ulation, only equanimity: only the desire for hands in clay, a need to let it absorb from my skin what it wanted and throw back its stored light, because clay *is* stored light—energy held deep in the particulate scales that are bro-ken and released into new shapes by your own working hands. I just wanted to sit at that wheel and let my hands see if they could feel a shape before my mind knew what it was. And again and again, they did. The less I plotted and diagrammed in advance, the better the finished piece would usually be. And the better my failures were, too. Lifting one of the drying bowls to paint it with red oxide powder, I snapped a chunk out of the rim. But it was all right. I dropped the bowl in the scrap-clay bin, to be recycled at the end of the semester. There will always be more to come along behind the broken, the rejected, the disappointing ones. There will always be more. And every-thing in your life changes when you recognize this fact.

I wrote in an online essay about all of this.[2] Then, in a four-page handwritten letter, another former student told me how much my words had meant to her. My ideas about emotion and humility and whatever the next thing is were helping her as she waited out post-graduation blues, working a hometown job, trying to keep on writing in the mornings and the afternoons. This student wrote two different novel drafts under my supervi-sion and completely restructured each one. She's persistent. She took from me advice that—I know, because I got it too—is hard to hear: *it isn't working, break it down and build it up again, from the beginning.* She will be a writer. She wants it that much.

2. See Weldon, "The Spinning Self," which grew out of my earlier blog entry at *The Cheapskate Intellectual.*

Telling this story reminds me how small our efforts to control any stories can be, because their formation—like the formation of our selves and lives—depends on the accidental, serendipitous, awkward, stressful, or graceful interventions of other people, more than we admit. My dear students think I am stronger and wiser than I know I am. It's too easy to get caught up in the notion that perfection is possible, and desirable, and to get caught up in the illusions of one's own power and competence. That's why I have to show them, and myself, my failures, hesitancies, and vulnerabilities, lest we all believe that story. I'm no writer and no writing teacher if not immersed in craft, trying and failing and moving forward any amount. I'm no teacher if I am not being humbled, reminded that I'm really just another writer on the path, with these people alongside me. The practice of hands in material rewires the body, and the body and the brain learn to listen to reality. It will or will not crack, gel, bend, or break. It is or isn't there. You can't always make it what you wish it was.

As with "attention," though, the flip side of deep engagement with a craft is self-confrontation and pain. I put this on the table explicitly in my Advanced Creative Writing class: writing will challenge you in deeper ways than struggling for the right word. Being a writer, as novelist Sonya Chung says, means accepting a tolerance of difficulty and uncertainty as the basic fact of life and craft.[3] Routinely now I begin my creative writing classes with this fact: you will confront, here, your own limitations and insecurities and arrogances in ways you never expected to, and you will be changed, because when you write, that's just what happens. You'll get little to no external reward—even I write and get rejected and keep going. But you'll have to decide, for yourself, whether and how to keep doing it because it's worth it. Every semester more students come to understand that you can find out what you really think by writing. In Biblical terms, you can be transformed by the renewing of your mind. You can bring clarity and dignity to your relationships with yourself and others. And you can help yourself grow up.

One student in the very first creative writing class I ever taught—a bright, kind business major who confessed she had never thought of herself as a writer before—told me at the end of the semester that she now thought creative writing should be required for every student, no matter what their major was, because it teaches students to see themselves, and other people. I tend to agree with her. Struggling with the materials of art, particularly difficulty and imperfection, helps us in our struggles to accept ourselves, and the world. It helps us to keep asking for something more than the cliches that make so much money for so many people. Using good words involves

3. Chung, "What We Teach When We Teach Writers."

beholding—fully imagining, inside yourself—the reality of bodies, selves, and lives, and struggling to help your language reflect those things. As Orwell says in "Politics and the English Language," before you can write it, you have to find a way to see it and feel it inside yourself: a way to make it real to you, so you can make it real to others too.

Because language is rooted so strongly in the body and the physical world, new bodily experiences can enrich our art and our language. I learned this again a few years ago during a student-run tour of my college's human anatomy lab. Students set a divided heart into my hands. And then they handed me a brain. I cupped one hemisphere in each palm, then opened them book-wise to study the cross-sectioned cerebellum, the separate lobe down low at the base of the brain. A pattern branched through the tissue there, like a fern fossilized in the limestone cliffs that circle this town. "Look!" I exclaimed. "It looks like a fern, a tree—"

"*Arbor vitae,*" one student explained to me, "the tree of life."

I stared at the hidden tree until my tears blurred my sight, overwhelming me with wonder. A cadaver's ears, the lab professor had told me, should be covered when showing new students the lab; ears, faces, and hands are hardest for first-time visitors to see. "Unless they're pianists," she added, "and they really want to see the hands." I learned later that these students' hands did other work in this laboratory: the student who had showed me the "tree of life" was also a potter, and he had made the urns into which the students placed the cremated remains of their cadavers—a man and a woman—at the end of the semester. In a little ceremony, they cradled those urns in their hands, saying *thank you* and *goodbye.*

On the stretchers, the cadavers were long shredded shapes in beige and brown, flesh and bone laid open where blue-gowned students bent over them in white light. *Carcass* was a word that seemed, guiltily, right— *plucked, skinned, flayed.* These bodies were utterly material, inescapably tissue and bone that would rot if it weren't bathed in chemicals. Yet traces of human life remained; the acts and processes of living, doing, and making had reshaped that matter and made it, in motion, something human, in a way that lingered even in this lab. Those bodies were marked by childbirth, osteoporosis, and smoking: I could touch the visibly thickened intercostal muscles that had labored to push each breath away and bring the next one in.

Art is woven through with this struggle to engage with the real and let it reshape us and our bodies, the medium through which we encounter the world in the only life on earth we'll ever have. Consider the humblest forms of art we practice: daily types of making, and of craft. Plants come up in a garden and you can see how the seeds fell, where the hand was more open in sowing them. My clay bowls show thin places where my fingers pressed too hard, fingerprint smudges on wet sides, graceful accidental shapes no machine could replicate. Handwriting on a page pins our thoughts from multiple dimensions into two, keeping us from being forgotten as long as that page survives. Consider how it is to live in a world of things made and marked by bodies in space and time, how at home in it our own body can feel. And consider the world of the machined and mass produced, where artifice (in Jay Griffiths' term) rules, where consumerism levitates us subtly up from the realm of the actual and toward the realm of the desired, the always-a-little-more, the never-quite-enough—replicating the way cars speed us over the landscape and foster our fatal illusions of invulnerability, shaping around themselves the towns in which we live and the places where we can walk, or not. ("Hurrah!" remarked the Italian futurist Filippo Marinetti in 1909, celebrating the racing car. "No more contact with the vile earth!")[4] But as we've been exploring, the earth is our home, in multiple senses of the word—the grounding-place of our language, our bodies, our emotions, our hearts.

To start thinking about these ideas, let's consider this: great art is made and apprehended with the body and the senses, which means that it is a very inviting meeting place for minds and selves across apparently unbridgeable gaps of time, culture, and space. Hannah Arendt calls the public daily life, the space people are shaped by our encounters with others on the street or in school or work, the *polis*.[5] For all of us—citizens, theologians, artists—the world of the senses is our *polis*, creating and feeding the ongoing inner conversations that shape our selves. We learn by experiencing delight, discomfort, challenge, or success, through our senses, our bodies, and our encounters with people and things that aren't ourselves, every day, in ways large and small. The body is the home in which we live: a compass and guide, the place to which we can return to listen for signals of whether our actions are good or bad. (We don't call them *gut reactions* for nothing.) They signal what's out of place or out of balance in our environments and our psyches. And our modern world, which urges us constantly to exchange the sensual for the artificial and technological, endangers these self-creating inner conversations every day. Yet art—which we can engage as practitioners and spectators—renovates our attention through the body and the senses because it relies on them, intrinsically. "[I]t is only in the world of objects," T. S. Eliot writes, "where we have time and space and

4. Griffiths, "Artifice vs. Pastoral," 25.
5. Arendt, *The Human Condition*.

selves."[6] As I tell my writing students, "the senses are the common language we share with our readers, across all of place and time. So speak to us in our common language."

Language takes its savor, its texture, and its impact from its connection to our bodies and our senses, which is why struggling to keep our language rooted in a sensory world means keeping ourselves fundamentally responsible to and aware of that world. This starts at the level of the qualities of language: one of the first things we discuss in my creative writing classes is the difference between sensory and specific language—which summons up sense memories in the reader's mind and often has tasty sensory qualities of its own (*snap, crackle, pop* are good verbs for specific motions but also sound like what they mean, a quality called *onomatopoeia*)—and editorial language, which tells us how to feel about something (*beautiful, scary*) rather than giving us the sensory information we need to make that decision on our own. Editorial language holds the reader at a distance from the world you're trying to summon in her mind, shortchanging her independence within and experience of that world by insisting that she see it through the judgment you've already passed. It turns you, the writer, into a bossy doorman at a dance club, handing each entrant a pair of earphones to muffle the same music they came to hear. Yet choosing specific rather than editorial language can seem counterintuitive for beginning writers, who often think of vague adjectives like "beautiful" as giving the reader the freedom she needs to imagine a person or thing for herself (or making the work "relatable."[7]) However, specific detail opens up your mental imaginings by giving you a place to stand, based on the broad sense memories and processes of perception you and that writer share as humans; this is why I refer to "our common language" in conversations with my students. As Jay Griffiths indicates, "The human spirit needs language, shimmering and liquid . . . [and] [l]anguage needs the natural world, each word has real 'roots.'"[8] For instance, the name for a metrical unit of poetry, the dactyl—one long syllable followed by two short ones—takes its name from the Greek word for *finger,* which has one long bone and two shorter ones.[9] If I ask you to picture a character's "hardworking" hands, you may wander all over a map of possible "hand" images

6. Kaag, "Books' Fragile Bodies."

7. One of my least favorite words ever, for reasons well-described by Rebecca Mead in "The Scourge of Relatability": "But to reject any work because we feel that it does not reflect us in a shape that we can easily recognize—because it does not exempt us from the active exercise of imagination or the effortful summoning of empathy—is our own failure. It's a failure that has been dispiritingly sanctioned by the rise of 'relatable.'"

8. Griffiths, "Artifice vs. Pastoral," 26.

9. Freeman, *Searching for Sappho,* 13.

in your mind: dirty, callused, male or female, old or young, in action or still, playing an instrument or saddling a horse—it's hard to know quite where to go. By contrast, if I show you the character's hands in action, "red and rough from the cold, tugging on a rope," your mental picture gets much more focused and immediate; you are invited into and included in my imaginative world in a way more general adjectives don't help you achieve. "Words are effective," writes graphic designer Peter Mendelsund,

> not because of what they carry in them, but for their latent potential to unlock the accumulated experience of the reader. Words 'contain' meanings, but, more important, words potentiate meaning . . . . *River*, the word, contains within it all rivers, which flow like tributaries into it. And this word contains not only all rivers, but more important all *my* rivers: every accessible experience of every river I've seen, swum in, fished, heard, heard *about*, felt directly, or been affected by . . . . This is a word's dormant power, brimming with pertinence. So little is needed from the author, when you think of it. (We are already flooded by river water, and only need the author to tap this reservoir.)[10]

As aesthetic philosopher Elaine Scarry explores in *Dreaming by the Book* (1999), authors can create the effect of an imagined scene, even a moving one, in a reader's mind by triggering certain sensory modes that are easier for us to imagine and combine than others are. Therefore they "duplicate the phenomenology of perception," or the way we actually form and envision images in our minds, "by taking what the imagination is best at (dry, thin two-dimensionality) and enlisting it into the operation."[11] For instance, Scarry writes, "the glide of the transparent over the surface of something underneath"—an effect used by Marcel Proust as he describes the reflections of "the ever-changing view of the sea" on a wall of glass-fronted bookcases—can become a "way of achieving solidity."[12] It's easier for us to imagine a wallpapered wall in an upstairs bedroom, for instance, when we're also asked to imagine the shadow of a windblown curtain floating *over* that wallpaper. We draw on static images as well as motion to picture an image and bringing it to life. Thus language rooted in the body's experience of the sensual world also calls upon the body as partner in its process of making meaning.

Engaging your readers' senses more richly in your writing means tuning in to the senses yourself, re-grounding yourself in the textures of the world in

10. Mendelsund, *What We See When We Read*, 302–303.

11. Scarry, *Dreaming by the Book*, 23.

12. Ibid., 15, 22.

order to be able to evoke them in words. In the first week of our creative writing class, students and I list ten specific things—no matter how small—we've seen, heard, tasted, touched, or smelled that week. Our responses can be a revealing place to start: one adult student stared at the page in dismay. "I can't remember *anything*," she said. "Have I *really* been such a sleepwalker?" This is the first step, I think, in becoming a writer or other type of artist—noticing what's around you, and noticing what keeps you from noticing. Sometimes we take walks around campus together, peering into the interiors of the spruce trees around the library to see if we can find any nests. Later, everyone writes a description of something they know how to do with their hands, then selects another student's activity to research as needed and write into a scene in a way that gives shape to a story (she is cutting back raspberry canes in her garden as she's thinking about her mother, and how do the verbs and sensory details in the present deepen the emotional subtext? He is carving a wooden spoon with a knife; how does the tension in his hands enrich the emotional tension in the scene?) Even in non–creative-writing classes, we try to connect body and word: when first-year students and I read Zora Neale Hurston's description of Janie Crawford's reverie under the blossoming pear tree in *Their Eyes Were Watching God* (1937) or Charles Darwin's description of the "Tree of Life" (as quoted in Chapter 2), we go outside to lie in the grass under the big cottonwood tree outside Main Building and read the words aloud. Sensory observation builds a sensory imagination, a mental bank of images and impressions you can draw on as a writer to enflesh the world on your page or your canvas. It expands the space inside yourself that seeks the sensual world, and seeks responsibility to it. You continue to wrestle with your medium—language, paint, your own body and voice—to seek your own vivid, direct angle of vision, voice, and vernacular. By contrast, how strangely infantilized you become when perfectly entertained, technologically cosseted from even your senses' simplest reports. And how deeply at a loss for words you are, because words, and the world they render unto your body, have been lost to you.

Like I said in Chapter 2, sensory delight can still carry pain on its shadow side, and practicing art brings us up against uncertainty and difficulty as well as joy. Yet the story of John Keats (1795–1821), one of the greatest poets ever to write in English, shows us how, yet sensory, specific language can bear all these emotions and more. Keats was a young English hostler's son and medical student, who left medical school because he wanted to write poetry but also (some biographers think) because he identified too intensely with his patients' pain. And early nineteenth-century medicine was, literally, a world of pain. Anesthesia was still uncommon, so barbers—the earliest practicing surgeons—gave their patients sticks wrapped in white bandages to grip. (White bandages, red blood: that's where we get the familiar barber's pole.) One of Keats's jobs as a "dresser" was to empty and refill the boxes of sawdust kept under operating tables to soak up the blood. Yet as scholar Alan Richardson has wonderfully traced in *British Romanticism and the Science of the Mind* (2005), Keats's poetry never stopped drawing on what he'd learned about the living, responsive body. The poet Dean Young has imagined Keats as a medical student, staring down with "sad, electric eyes" at a patient undergoing an amputation on the table, and filmmaker Jane Campion, in *Bright Star* (2009), depicts him as borne up, ecstatic, in a blossoming tree.[13]

In fact, even among the charismatic Romantics—my own favorites— Keats is one of the easiest poets to imagine as a living man, because he compressed such sensory life into his five-foot–tall frame. He walked all over England and Scotland with his friends. He liked dirty jokes but could also be carried away by beauty. (My favorite sketch of him, by his friend and roommate Charles Brown, shows him raptly self-forgetful, listening to music, chin on hand.) In an era when daily life by its very nature offered little or no insulation from physical reality—cold, death, sun, shit, heat, rot—Keats not only accepted but sought sensory immersion in the present moment, even imagining himself into the lives of other creatures. "I scarcely remember counting upon any Happiness," he wrote his friend Benjamin Bailey in November 1817, "I look not for it if it be not in the present hour—nothing startles me beyond the Moment. The setting sun will always set me to rights—or if a Sparrow come before my Window I take part in its existence and pick about the Gravel."[14] Encounters with other creatures expand his own consciousness. "I go among the Feilds," he wrote to his brother and sister-in-law in the spring of 1819,

> and catch a glimpse of a stoat or a field mouse peering out of the withered grass—the creature hath a purpose and its eyes are bright with it—I go amongst the buildings of a city and I see a Man hurrying along—to what? The Creature has a purpose and his eyes are bright with it. But then as Wordsworth says, "we have all one human heart"—there is an electric fire in human nature tending to purify—so that among these human creature[s] there is continually some birth of new heroism— The pity is that we must wonder at it: as we should at finding a pearl in rubbish—[15]

13. Young, "I See A Lily On Thy Brow," 111.

14. Keats, *Letters*, 38.

15. Ibid., 229.

Many of Keats's letters are like this: an ongoing rush of observed detail lifts and carries him to a literary or aesthetic observation that seems deceptively simple until you really look at it and notice how generous it truly is. Indeed, generosity opened by curiosity is a quintessentially Keatsian imaginative state: in this letter, he hurtles like a comet through and across the spaces between himself and what is not himself, carried on by his own forward-leaning curiosity and burning a bright track of connection through and across all these disparate modes. The act of perceiving and rendering into language and communicating to others what he sees so that it can change them as it changes him are all one thing for Keats. And all of it is embodied in the act of writing, which fuels the next thought in the process of channeling the first one from the eyes to the brain and down to the scribbling hand. For Keats, like Lord Byron in the unfinished epic poem *Don Juan* and like William Blake a generation earlier, "Energy is Eternal Delight"[16]—the act of making art carries the artist forward in a state of flow that accelerates to rapture. Even on paper, he's intensely alive: his letters and poems bristle and breathe with dashes, sinuous enjambments, idiosyncratic spellings, swift and fluid handwriting. Like his forbear Wordsworth, he abandons himself to the intense humming "life of things" and because of that self-abandonment—a fundamentally generous and open state, a precondition to ethical engagement with the world—he carries his readers there too.

It's a hard choice, but perhaps my favorite Keats poem is "To Autumn," composed in September 1819:[17]

1.

SEASON of mists and mellow fruitfulness,
   Close bosom-friend of the maturing sun;
Conspiring with him how to load and bless
   With fruit the vines that round the thatch-eves run;
To bend with apples the moss'd cottage-trees,
   And fill all fruit with ripeness to the core;
     To swell the gourd, and plump the hazel shells
With a sweet kernel; to set budding more,
   And still more, later flowers for the bees,
   Until they think warm days will never cease,
     For Summer has o'er-brimm'd their clammy cells.

16. See Blake, *The Marriage*, 70.
17. Keats, "To Autumn," 360–361; text also widely available online.

2.

Who hath not seen thee oft amid thy store?
  Sometimes whoever seeks abroad may find
Thee sitting careless on a granary floor,
  Thy hair soft-lifted by the winnowing wind;
Or on a half-reap'd furrow sound asleep,
  Drows'd with the fume of poppies, while thy hook
    Spares the next swath and all its twined flowers:
And sometimes like a gleaner thou dost keep
  Steady thy laden head across a brook;
  Or by a cyder-press, with patient look,
    Thou watchest the last oozings hours by hours.

3.

Where are the songs of Spring? Ay, where are they?
  Think not of them, thou hast thy music too,—
While barred clouds bloom the soft-dying day,
  And touch the stubble plains with rosy hue;
Then in a wailful choir the small gnats mourn
  Among the river sallows, borne aloft
    Or sinking as the light wind lives or dies;
And full-grown lambs loud bleat from hilly bourn;
  Hedge-crickets sing; and now with treble soft
  The red-breast whistles from a garden-croft;
    And gathering swallows twitter in the skies.

This marvelous ode illustrates how poetry achieves a double, triple, even quadruple life in the senses and the body: it's meant to be both spoken and heard, savored as words in the mouth and images in the mind that recall sense memories. Repeated patterns of rhythm and sound twine through the poem like the late-blooming flowers on a vine, or the other types of fruit-bearing "vine" (grapes? Hops?) that twist around a cottage roof, holding the poem together and propelling it forward while never lapsing into a simplistic jingle of rhyme. "To Autumn" balances its own integrity of craft and structure with freedom for readers to enjoy their own pleasure in imagining and speaking these images. (Read it aloud yourself and you'll see what I mean.) Sensorily, the sound and feel of the words as we say them reward us and catch us off guard and reward us again with satisfying textures of speech and sound. And they mean sensually satisfying things, stirring up images of food, wine, lounging in the sun: *Ripe. Swell. Plump. Sweet. More. More. More.* Saying them, we hum, we bleat, we drone, we dream, we doze off into a "drowse" of poppy- (or wine-)infused sleep (a recurring image for Keats), and we are thoroughly drawn into the spell of this autumn world—the same rueful golden warmth of the dying year that Southern writer Elizabeth Spencer, more than a hundred years later, would name as "the dusty stir of autumn in the twilight," with the indescribable "quality beneath the eagerness and color that tried to speak and could not."[18] And we seem to taste the late-bearing fruits of an underrated season: the nuts, the grapes, the apples, and the cider that are matured with time. We luxuriate in a sensual world, the sensuality of which is heightened by its closeness to winter, to death and decline. We love this time of year although—or maybe because—we know it's a sign the year is drawing to a close, about to die. (As Grace Paley beautifully wrote in her poem "September," "Then the flowers became very wild / because it was early September / and they had nothing to lose.")[19] We settle into and linger in a difficult but necessary space, where adults must learn to live—paradox, where more than one thing can be true at once.

Keats described the genesis of "To Autumn" in a letter of September 21, 1819 to his friend John Hamilton Reynolds: "How beautiful the season is now—How fine the air. A temperate sharpness about it . . . I never lik'd stubble fields so much as now . . . . Somehow a stubble plain looks warm—in the same way that some pictures look warm—this struck me so much in my sunday's walk that I composed upon it."[20] What the letter doesn't say—because his friends didn't need to be told—is that the beauty of autumnal richness and decline may have struck Keats so deeply because he was dying too. Early in 1820, only a few months after composing "To Autumn" and his other major odes, Keats coughed blood onto his bed pillow—undeniable evidence, especially to a former medical student, that he was suffering from tuberculosis, the same disease through which he'd nursed his mother and his younger brother Tom before their deaths. He was in love with Fanny Brawne, the girl next door, who lived with her mother and siblings on the other side of the duplex he shared with them and his roommate Charles Brown. He knew, as he wrote, that he "would be among the English Poets after my death."[21] He was going to die; tuberculosis, then called consumption, could not be cured. And he was twenty-four years old.

Yet in "To Autumn" as in his other great odes, Keats plunges himself, through poetry, into the reality that the human body—our mortal, suffering, sensual home—is still our instrument to enjoy, understand, and even transcend the physical world. The body is nothing to scorn, or escape, or

18. Spencer, *The Voice at the Back Door*, 185.
19. Paley, "September," 70.
20. Keats, *Letters*, 291–292.
21. Keats, *Letters*, 161.

condemn, or shun. It is a means of knowledge and delight that will somehow linger even after we die, in the art we make from the impressions it has made upon our senses, our nerves, in all the channels of our blood and bone. Look at how the poem itself asks you to linger on the wrenching beauty of that slow fade, as night comes on and the light falls: "gathering swallows twitter in the skies." Nothing is "darkening"—creatures of a different stage of day are "gathering." The year is dying; so are the plants, the swallows and even the bees, dazed by their overload of honey. So are we. Yet the world lives on, in radiant, irreducible delight.

Art is what takes us directly into the heart of that paradox and pain— our limitation, our short sweet time on lovely, troubled Earth—to guide us in the direction of the wisdom waiting on the other side. When we enter into the world of a work of art, and let it live in and speak back out through us— when we let our own perceptions become the carriers for what someone else saw in this moment—that moment as rendered in art literally comes alive in us, right here, in our own brains and hearts and mouths. Art needs our human bodies, to be made and to come to life. When bees tickle and swarm on my sedum and salvia and phlox in the fall, I always hear Keats's words: *. . . to set budding more, / and still more, later flowers for the bees / Until they think warm days will never cease / For summer has oe'r brimm'd their clammy cells.* And down into the hive, across the border of species skin and space, I travel. Something new is then being seen, or born, under the eye of the mind slipped loose from conscious, controlling agendas and intentions. Imagination is both active—it can "[p]aw up against the light, and do strange deeds/ Upon the clouds"—and quiet, waiting for what Keats also called "the repetition of its own silent Working coming continually on the spirit with a fine suddenness."[22] And this can happen anywhere, if we're paying attention. My father once said his favorite place for prayer—the sort of prayer that is nearly wordless, *coming continually* on the listener for God—was out on his tractor, bush-hogging pastures. Small creatures leap and scuttle away; rusty-crowned white egrets stalk lizards; the ground drinks rain; the grass comes back short, and green, and soft. The farmer comes to the field and goes away and comes again. *The creature has a purpose and his eyes are bright with it.* What he hears, when he listens, is his God, is his spirit, is the fine suddenness of all that lies breathing just beyond the surface of what we can touch and see. And what the attentive artist hears is the breath of other artists and their works, long dead, coming to life again in her.

22. "Paw against the light:" from Keats, "Sleep and Poetry," 37. "Repetition of its own . . . " from letter to Benjamin Bailey, 22 Nov. 1817, in Keats, *Letters,* 37.

Keats developed his famous idea of negative capability, I think, out of just this sort of crossing-over between the self and the world, being in two places and two states at once without seeking to clarify it—being on a border, being in that place of what Maurice Merleau-Ponty called *chiasm*, of presence and responsibility to the other thing (which can also be the place of eros; how unresponsive is desire to any conscious goal!) and waiting to see what's there.

> ... several things dovetailed in my mind, & at once it struck me, what quality went to form a Man of Achievement especially in Literature and which Shakespeare possessed so enormously—I mean Negative Capability, that is when man is capable of being in uncertainties, Mysteries, doubts, without any irritable reaching after fact & reason—(to George and Thomas Keats, December 1817)[23]

A child seeks the simple resolution, the absolute rule, the black or white. An adult knows it's more complicated. Twentieth-century anthropologist Gregory Bateson, who was steeped in the Romantic poets, might have been thinking of negative capability when he said, "An animal should be thought of as a tangle of ideas that have to live together in him, more or less."[24] We are always caught in a "tangle of ideas" and pressures in multiple directions, what we want and know we should do, what we act on knowing we shouldn't. Yet even when that tangle seems insoluble, that's not the end: "on the other side," Bateson says, "through that double, twisted, what we called a double bind some years ago, there is another stage of wisdom."[25] It is a type of wisdom attained by patience and presence, and, as Harry Crews said, known in and paid for with blood and bone.

Throughout his poems and letters, Keats plunges into this intense absorption in the senses, even as he's dying. His friends took up a collection to send him someplace warm to die—all you could really do for a consumptive in 1821—and his friend Joseph Severn made the long, agonizing trip with him away from England, both knowing Keats would never come back. In a boarding house at the foot of the Spanish Steps in Rome, he lay in a narrow bed, staring at a pattern of carved and painted roses on the ceiling, heaving his chest up and down under the airless weight that sat on it like a nightmare beast, thinking about the ridicule of his poetry, all the years he would not get to live, the gaping emotional gash where Fanny Brawne, the girl he loved, had been torn away and left back in England, the love that would hurt

---

23. Keats, *Letters*, 43.

24. See the documentary film "An Ecology of Mind," dir. Nora Bateson, 2010.

25. Ibid.

and yearn without ever being able to take rest in its object. He was sick, he was poor. They couldn't get married. And he'd never really leave that room again. He lay there and stared at that ceiling and took this knowledge, in and out, with every breath. All of it.

In that same boarding house at the foot of the Spanish Steps, on a January day almost two hundred years later, students and I came to visit for the first time. We studied artifacts: the bust of Shelley, a scrap of Byron's bed-curtain, a lock of Keats' light-auburn hair. One by one we slipped, alone, into the narrow room where John Keats died. Outside, a sudden rain beat the steps even as the morning sun continued to shine, peach and gold.[26]

And when we looked up at the ceiling, we saw the same painted daisies at which Keats had stared. *Tell me, Severn*, he asked, about the Protestant cemetery at the edge of town, where he knew he'd be buried. *What's it like out there?*

There are daisies growing there in the grass, Severn reported back, *even in the winter*.

Keats lifted his eyes to the ceiling and smiled. *I think*, he said, *I can feel them growing over me even now*.

That afternoon, we filed into the Protestant Cemetery and gathered around the pair of stones—Keats's and Severn's, which still stand together. Sunlight filtered through the tall pines; the sky was an intense Botticelli blue. I read "Ode on a Grecian Urn" aloud and then joined a silence the students kept. We balanced notebooks on wrists or knees, scribbling. Someone sniffled. All our eyes were filled with tears.

If I could have trusted my voice, I would have read this poem instead:

> When I have fears that I may cease to be
> Before my pen has glean'd my teeming brain,
> Before high piled books in charactry
> Hold like rich garners the full-ripen'd grain;
> When I behold upon the night's starr'd face,
> Huge cloudy symbols of a high romance,
> And think that I may never live to trace
> Their shadows with the magic hand of chance;
> And when I feel, fair creature of an hour,
> That I shall never look upon thee more,
> Never have relish in the fairy power
> Of unreflecting love;—then on the shore
> Of the wide world I stand alone and think,
> Till love and fame to nothingness do sink.[27]

26. See Weldon, "Keats-Shelley House," which draws on this visit too.
27. Keats, "When I have fears," 166.

Keats wrote this in January 1818, when he was twenty-two years old, with three years and one month left to live.

Around his grave, little white daisies sparkled in the grass. A student fell into step with me as we slowly moved away. "The daisies *are* blooming," she whispered. "Severn was right. He would have come out here in January to report back to Keats. And it's January now."

In that moment, that student crossed. She was seeing what Severn saw and what Keats knew he would be bodily present with if not able to see—what he imagined from staring at those same painted ceiling flowers on which our eyes had rested, too. The truth of his experience, as he felt and knew it, came alive again in her, colored with her own perceptions and memories and processed in her own particular self. "Axioms in philosophy are not axioms until they are proved upon our pulses," Keats wrote in a letter to Reynolds in May 1818. "We have read fine things but never feel them to the full until we have gone the same steps as the Author."[28]

Even professional "artists" like me, a college creative writing and literature teacher, need to try new forms of art to keep ourselves fresh, and to experience both success and failure from new angles. We've all got to use our senses' unique powers to cut through the noise of our daily social landscape—especially the noise of technology and media, especially because the moneyed interests that govern both of these would blind us to the real results of our actions so that we stay calm and keep shopping. Practicing an art renovates the sources of an interior self that can help us make and remake our world in just that image, by increasing our capacities for not only wonder but also difficulty, perseverance, sensuality, and mystery. "I'm not an artist," you may be thinking. "I don't have any talent." But I'm here to say—as I do to all my students—that it's less about "talent" than about practice, play, and giving yourself a chance to discover something new, which anyone can do, no matter what background or age.

Over what's now almost a decade of practicing it, I've found that Iyengar yoga reaches deeply into the net of self, emotion, and body the way art does—in its own way, it, too, is a craft. The point is to position your body properly in a pose and stay there, adjusting by knowledge and by feel, to develop a discipline of aligning your bones and your muscles and your thoughts. It's not about weight loss, "toning," or even "religion"—it's about a very, very old practice of using your body to tune into what's really happening inside your mind. Our classes attract men and women, from sixty-something financial advisors to football players to students I recognize from my creative writing classes, because yoga makes a real difference in your

28. Keats, *Letters*, 93.

range of physical and mental motion and strength. My teacher says that it can ameliorate the supposedly inevitable ailments of aging—ground-down hip sockets, a flat-footed osteoporotic shuffle—by helping you straighten your limbs and retain space and mobility in your joints. Despite my typing-focused writing and teaching life, yoga keeps my arms and shoulders from contracting into a permanent hunch. More than that, it helps me chill out and open some room in my head.

One day in class, we moved through a series of standing poses involving not only strong work with the legs but a strong emphasis on keeping our shoulders back and twisting our bodies to open and raise our chests. In *uttita parsvakanasana* in particular—body in a deep lunge, one leg extended and one leg bent, one arm stretched down and one up and overhead—I was twisting my torso and ribs upward to look at the ceiling and extending both legs out and down and into the floor, more deeply and correctly than I ever remember doing before. My whole body was active, and I wasn't really thinking about anything. Near the end of class, we did some deep, seated forward bends, and when I straightened up, an unnameable wave of sadness flattened me. For the last few minutes of class I could only lie still, hoping the other students didn't see the tears leaking down my face. Was it Man X who didn't call? Was it Recent Emotional Disappointment Y? Was it a voice from some chamber of pain or guilt or doubt or loneliness I don't even know how to touch directly? I don't know. When we talked about it later, my teacher wasn't surprised, with all the chest- and heart-opening poses we'd been doing. "People think the heart is where we hold love," she said, "but it's actually where we hold pain, and sadness." Twisting, bending, and staying there, then moving to take a different position and go at it again, will wring dark little pools of anger or grief up out of your body as thoroughly as two hands on a rag, twisting one direction and then another, leaving the whole cloth evenly damp. It'll make you clear of emotion without being clean of it, aware of what has been, or maybe still is, living in you, even if you can't give it a name. And that's a good thing.

It may be best to talk about the big emotion yoga always works on in me—fear—by talking about one of the poses I struggle with the most: head balance, or *salamba sirsasana*. The first time I tried it, in my fifth year of practice, it seemed not only impossible but terrifying. To go into head balance, you kneel on the floor and make a triangle with your forearms and interlinked hands on the floor, resting your knuckles against the wall. You nestle your head into your hands so that the back of your skull fits against your fingers and the crown of your head is in full contact with the floor, pointing straight down. Then you rise on your toes, straighten your legs, and walk your feet slowly toward your now-upside-down face.

(The closer your knees get to your nose, the better—it helps your head get in the right position.) Your hips rise into the air and more and more weight comes onto your head and your shoulders, which you should keep lifting up to counterbalance the pressure. You walk your feet forward a little more. And then—I still can't say exactly how this happens—you kick your legs upward, one leg slightly in front of the other, and bring them to rest against the wall. Now you're upside down, your body's whole weight supported by the triangle of your shoulders and arms. The work is to keep straightening and lifting your spine and your shoulders—asking them to reach up rather than sink down to bear the weight, so that you don't collapse onto your neck and your head—and straighten the rest of your body without clenching it. And then, you stay there. My teacher urges us to aim for ten minutes. "You come to crave it," she says, "the way it settles and rebalances you." Even in my own struggles with it (a minute and a half is a really long time!) I can tell she's right.

Nevertheless, the pose is not without risk. You shouldn't try any of these steps without proper training and preparation, because you could *really* hurt yourself. Of course, you could also hurt yourself or your teacher or fellow students when you first try head balance—swinging your legs up only to have them fall back down, kicking backwards like a panicked mule, afraid you'll topple over on your neighbor. This was me, cursing under my breath. Suddenly I was caught in my old childhood humiliation at being the one kid who never could figure out how to kick up high enough to do a cartwheel. I seldom forgot that I was a "fat kid"—tall, earthbound, and alienated from the body at which I usually felt only fury and shame. I could, when I was fifteen or sixteen working our haying crew in the summer, snatch a square bale by the strings, heave it almost completely over my head, and pitch it up into the loft to be caught and stacked by the boys. I look at pictures of myself now and think, *You weren't fat.* But when you can't fit into the cute miniskirts all the popular girls are wearing, and your feet are really big, what consolation is your reliable body's humble, quiet strength?

Eventually my teacher took pity on me and helped lift my legs into position; then I was doing head balance at last. Except I wasn't. Head canted back at the wrong angle, neck stressed, I felt flooded with a sense of total panic. I was upside down, all my blood rushing to my head, my face breaking out in cold sweat. I dropped down and huddled with my forehead to the floor, breathing hard, unable to move for fear. I couldn't imagine ever doing that again. Some voice all through me shrieked *you're going to DIE!*

Of course, that's exactly why you do head balance. When you do it right, it teaches your body and your mind that fear may come but it's a temporary thing, and that even under stress you can still learn to pay attention to what's *actually* happening. Head balance rubs this knowledge into deep, deep levels of your nervous system and your self-awareness, and it's not until you find yourself able to stay calm and not freak out somewhere else that you realize how deeply it's soaked in, like some kind of really good hand cream. You get nervous or angry or start to lose your temper and something inside you sets a calming hand on your arm: *Calm down. You're not going to die. The danger isn't real.*

This is a skill for life, and it's a skill and practice of the spirit: don't be hounded by your emotions, obedient to and driven by them and whatever imaginary stories they lead you to tell. We live in a world of fears that will invade us inside and out if we listen. Be able to stop and look at them—like little Danny Torrance in Stephen King's *The Shining*, shouting at the Overlook Hotel's ghosts "False face! Not real!"[29] Yoga and writing have been essential parts of the ongoing process of growth and thought and prayer and reaching for the invisible realities I know to be true. And I have learned it not just in my mind but in my body, which is always there to remind the mind, gently, *remember, you are not in here to face the world alone. I'm here too. And I know more than you sometimes want to think.*

---

29. King, *The Shining*, 475. I'd love to teach this novel someday alongside William Faulkner's *Absalom, Absalom!* (1936) and Alfred Hitchcock's *Psycho* (1960).

5

Ask for more from your education by asking more from yourself—before and after graduation.

> "Specific knowledge is not education . . . . Education is learn-
> ing how to live and on what level. And you must learn that
> or everything else is useless."
>
> —JAMES SALTER (1925–2015), *LIGHT YEARS*

LIKE MANY SCHOOLS, THE University of North Carolina at Chapel Hill, where I taught for eight years as a graduate student in English, has a summer reading program for first-year students. In 2003, when I was a twenty-nine-year-old PhD candidate, the book chosen for the then-relatively new program was Barbara Ehrenreich's *Nickel and Dimed: On (Not) Getting By In America* (2001.) Ehrenreich, an investigative journalist, goes undercover in a series of minimum-wage jobs, including Walmart stock clerk, hotel maid, Merry Maid, nursing home cafeteria worker, and waitress, in three different cities (Key West, Florida, Portland, Maine, and Minneapolis/St. Paul, Minnesota) to test the theory that those being removed from welfare rolls—especially women—could support themselves with plentiful minimum-wage jobs. "The idea," she writes, "was to spend a month in each setting and see whether I could find a job and earn, in that time, the money to pay a second month's rent."[1] She sets herself some ground rules: she will not "fall back on any skills derived from my education or usual work," she will "take the highest-paying job that was offered me and do my best to hold it," and she will "take the cheapest accommodations I could find."[2] Musing on the project, she wonders if she "would discover some hidden economies in the world of the low-wage worker . . . . Maybe I would even be able to detect in myself the bracing psychological effects of getting out of the house, as promised by

1. Ehrenreich, *Nickel and Dimed,* 6.
2. Ibid., 4.

the wonks who brought us welfare reform."[3] Yet what she found was that even with two jobs, an emergency startup fund, no children, good health, and a car—advantages most of her co-workers lacked—she couldn't make a living. In fact, she could barely make enough to eat on every month, and not enough to pay the deposit on and rent an apartment. "Something is wrong, very wrong," she writes, "when a single person in good health, a person who in addition possesses a working car, can barely support herself by the sweat of her brow. You don't need a degree in economics to see that wages are too low and rents too high."[4] Many students and faculty, including me, found this book riveting and sobering. Ehrenreich's accounts of co-workers sleeping in their cars and fainting from hunger during Merry Maids shifts reminded us how lucky we really are to have been able to leave jobs like this behind in high school or college, or to never have had to work them at all. "I never knew Walmart thinks twenty hours a week is 'full-time,'" one student said to me. "And I will never under-tip a waitress again." Another student said, simply, "Good God." A student group used *Nickel and Dimed* as support for their campaign to raise wages for UNC housekeepers.

But other students objected to *Nickel and Dimed* on the grounds that it was yet another example of what they called the university's historically liberal bias. A campus group called the Committee for a Better Carolina took out two full-page advertisements against *Nickel and Dimed,* one in the student newspaper, *The Daily Tar Heel,* and one in the *Raleigh News and Observer.* The ads invited "all North Carolina residents" to contact then-UNC Chancellor James Moeser and "demand academic fairness and intellectual honesty at UNC-CH," and the group attracted support from a number of Republicans in the North Carolina General Assembly. In a soon-to-be-familiar confusion of genres, a Republican senator called *Nickel and Dimed* "intellectual pornography with no redeeming qualities" and expressed disappointment that "my alma mater can't find a book that's no more academically and intellectually challenging than that two-bit novella."[5]

In the summer and fall of 2003, we graduate students referred to the *Nickel and Dimed* "controversy," in quotation marks, because the furor around the book had such an unreal, ginned-up feel. Arguments against the book were dizzyingly weird, often because their starting facts were incomplete or wrong or they relied on a premise the arguer was determined to cling to, no matter what. Claim 1: *Nickel and Dimed* shouldn't have been required because it is "not scientifically factual" and "just one

3. Ibid., 3–4.
4. Ibid., 199.
5. Kluttz, "Reading Debate," 1.

person's opinion." Where, then, does that leave—just for starters—literature, religion, philosophy, and investigative journalism, the genre *Nickel
and Dimed* proclaims its allegiance to from the beginning? If we're to read
nothing that's not "scientifically factual," then farewell to Jane Austen, Zora
Neale Hurston, Dietrich Bonhoeffer, Socrates, Plato, Shakespeare, Milton,
and even, some might argue, the Bible itself. College exposes you to a range
of academic disciplines, including but not limited to the "scientifically factual," to show you the ways in which people have reached for knowledge
and understanding over time in a variety of intellectual languages. *Nickel
and Dimed* doesn't claim to be anything more than what it is: one journalist's account of her experiences in trying to tell a story about the invisible
lives of the poor, just as nineteenth-century journalist Nellie Bly exposed
the shocking state of mental institutions by getting herself admitted as a
patient. Claim 2: Ehrenreich "didn't do her research." What about the foot-
notes, the citations, and the rich detail of Ehrenreich's own experiences?
What deeper "research" can there be for a project like this than testing the
truth about welfare reform and minimum-wage labor for herself? Other
objections depended upon careless or willful misreadings of the book and
the use of dog-whistle terms like "biased," as if there *were* another point
of view to the fact that surviving on minimum wage in the early twenty-
first century is difficult. Generating a convincing-sounding objection to the
book meant kicking up a cloud of tautologies, undefined terms, contradictions, and assumptions based on a political point of view connected to a
personal one. And as a teacher, I needed to engage with both.

In my literature and creative writing classes, one of the first questions
my students and I ask of a story or poem is "What is this really about?" It's not
a bad tactic with politics as well. The fevered yet forced quality of the *Nickel
and Dimed* opposition made me suspect that this was about something more
than met the eye. Most obviously, it was the latest eruption of long-standing
tensions between the university and the rest of North Carolina. But *Nickel
and Dimed* had come into a freshly charged atmosphere. In the wake of
September 11, 2001, the previous summer's reading selection, *Approaching
the Qur'an* by Michael Sells, had touched off a firestorm of national media
attention, including pieces on "Good Morning America," CNN, Fox News,
the *New York Times*, and even a satirical segment from Comedy Central's
"The Daily Show." Although many students seemed glad of the chance for
more insight into the terrifying September 11 attacks, the *Qur'an* controversy had primed legislators to scrutinize the red-headed liberal stepchild in
their midst, the First State University and the first in political conflict, once
again. And the *Nickel and Dimed* "controversy" obliged them.

But the objections weren't only about unthinking arrogance, and this fact showed me something more complex about my students and about teaching. Let me tell you a story about one of the best students I ever had at UNC, a friendly, smart girl I'll call "Jane," from Charlotte, North Carolina. Jane is one of those people who makes you smile, who draws others to her and motivates everyone around her to do better and feel better. I first met her when she enrolled in my composition class during the fall of 2003, during the *Nickel and Dimed* furor. Within a week, her in-class work group was working more consistently and happily than any other. Jane dropped by my office to talk about her papers or just to visit, as I invite students to do, and she liked to talk about current events. "Yeah, I vote Republican, although I don't agree with everything they say," she said. "My parents always have, though, and the majority of my beliefs do fall there. But I like to talk to anyone. I'm not one of these people who yell." Although her group included students to both the left and the right of Jane—including a conservative male student and a liberal, openly gay male student—Jane became friends with all of them, and particularly with the gay student. She was and is an intelligent seeker, a real thinker and a respecter of individual human lives.

So I was pleased when Jane enrolled in my discussion section for a large lecture course called Film Criticism the following semester. For the documentary unit, the professor in charge of the course chose Michael Moore's *Bowling for Columbine* (2002). During discussion, students were passionately but respectfully engaged, exchanging ideas without much prompting from me. There were Republicans, there were Democrats, there were people who rejected both labels, all talking meaningfully to each other. It was great. But Jane wasn't talking. Her expression said she was working something through on her own. When class ended and all the other students had left, Jane stayed rooted in her chair. And then she burst into tears. "I didn't kill those people!" she blurted, referring to Moore's painful montage of soldiers and civilians dying in Vietnam and elsewhere. "I love America but I didn't want those people to die! I resent this man telling me I am a bad person because I love America!"

Aside from the pain of a student I respected, this was about much more than the film. In Jane's sobs was not only the desolate shock of moral confrontation but also an emotional shock that hits like lightning at moments like this: *if everything I thought I understood is not true, I am not safe. Have I been lied to? What can I believe? What if all of it is wrong?* In her outburst was belief unshaken, and belief shaken, all at once, and there was the rupture and the weaving of political and moral identity. For young students in particular, a challenge (actual or perceived) to political identity *is* a rupture, the impact of which we can't underestimate. The social and political identities with which our students enter our classrooms are not always just what we might label "provincialism" or "unwillingness to learn." Particularly for first-year students, political identity is tied to the places and people they fear, deep down, they are betraying when they go to college, and behind that lies any child's oldest fear: my parents will stop loving me if I act up, if I disagree. Even what we would consider reasonable debate or criticism can look to these students like a blow to this essential part of themselves, especially if they don't come from homes where disagreement was modeled well.

This doesn't mean professors can't and shouldn't nudge students further along the path of critical thinking (of which more later) and intellectual growth. But we should do so mindfully. Illogical and inaccurate statements can and should be challenged on those grounds, but we should also look at what's underneath them. The desperation in the construction of arguments, the insistence on terms even when their use is unclear, can be a sign that underneath the rhetoric is a student trying to shield himself against the frightening existential face of change. And, as the poet Rainer Maria Rilke said of angels, change is terrifying.[6] "Look through the sign to the thing signified," Robert Browning wrote.[7] Particularly at what our students signify to us.

I saw all this later. In the empty classroom, with the late-afternoon light striping the floor and footsteps echoing away down the hall, I just saw a student in pain. I sat down next to Jane and patted her on the shoulder. (I should have chucked protocol and given her a hug.) She sniffled and her sobs gradually wound down. We sat together in the classroom for a while. "You are anything but a bad person," I said. "You see something that bothers you, and you take it seriously, because it *is* important. You let yourself feel it and think seriously about it. And that is the right thing to do." From our talk, I saw she was considering not so much politics as she was morality. That's still her concern, even today, as a bright and successful woman who still keeps in touch with me and of whom I am very, very proud.

Every single note in this story—global geopolitical reality, curricular tug-of-war, legislators tossing red meat anti-intellectualism to their constituents (especially to generate rationales for cutting university budgets), and teachers and students trying to make sense of it all and learn something anyway—has only intensified in the years since then. I've been a real professor for eleven years now, and therefore I feel constantly called on to discuss and defend the embattled institution I love: *college*. It's still a place where transformation

---

6. Rilke, "The First Elegy" (*Duino Elegies*), 151.
7. "With Bernard de Mandeville" (1887), part VII, line 192; pg. 163.

happens between students and professors in a physical space, together. But the questions are inescapable, particularly from people outside that space. Why does college cost so much? Isn't it *really* just about indoctrinating the innocent young into our sinister political cabal? Why are there more administrators and adjuncts and fewer tenured and tenure-track professors these days? Can't those professors who *are* left just deliver their "content" online? What are students really supposed to *get* out of college? Given the changes in our economy and employment prospects—accelerated by the forces I discussed in Chapter 1—will a college education help students get jobs? And the biggest question of all: what is college really *for*?

Higher education is a large industry, if not always a profitable one (particularly for teachers). According to data from the Associated Colleges of the Midwest (ACM) Institute on College Futures in the summer of 2014, there are currently 4,314 higher-education institutions in America, with 3.4 million employees and 21 million students enrolled. Forty percent of these institutions are public and educate 76 percent of undergraduates, while 38 percent (like Luther, my college) are nonprofit private institutions, educating only 15 percent of all undergraduates. Both public and private are watching for-profit private institutions take some of our "market share," to coin a phrase—for-profit institutions currently educate 10 percent of students, a number that seems to be growing. However, the experience of students and faculty in actual classrooms at actual colleges—particularly at small liberal arts colleges like mine—demonstrate over and over that economic "value," like other terms from the business world, is inadequate as a single measure by which to approach an individual college education or higher-education reform in general and plays right into something we've already seen to be fatal to thinking—cliché.

No doubt about it: college is financially expensive, and that creates real issues for students. For 2014–15, tuition, room, and board at Luther College, where I teach, is $45,260; at St. Olaf; $51,200; at Carleton, $60,102; at Macalester, $57,691 (just to compare us with other small private liberal arts colleges in our region).[8] However, once scholarships and financial aid are factored in, many students at many small colleges end up paying half (or less) of the "sticker price," even before student loans are added; the "dis-

8. For the 2014–15 academic year, or closest available figures on their websites, the University of Minnesota charges $12,060/year for tuition alone (excluding room and board); the University of Iowa estimates $17,693/year for tuition, room, and board for an on-campus, in-state student; the University of Wisconsin-Madison charges $17,693 for the same. At Harvard, the tuition, room, and board cost for an on-campus undergraduate is $58,607. To compare Luther with other nationally known small liberal arts colleges, Williams College (MA) charges $61,070 for its comprehensive fee; Middlebury (VT), $58,753; Davidson (NC), $58,146.

count rate" for college tuition, scholarships, and other sources of funding can mean that, like airplane passengers, one student is effectively paying a different tuition rate than the student sitting next to her in class. Yet I know and see the financial pressure students experience. At our school, it's more rare to see a student *without* a job (on or off campus) than one with. I see the same pairs of jeans worn again and again, the pinch as the money goes through the financial services office before registration, the rueful looks in students' eyes as they survey the nonrequired books they can't afford to buy. And we're not alone; some campuses now run food pantries—for their students.[9] Among ourselves, colleagues and I discuss the reality that first-generation college students form a larger percentage of the Luther population than many of our peer institutions, who can therefore rely on parental pockets a little deeper than we can. International students from the United World College and similar schools make their way here as well, to bring a joyous variety and texture to our small Northeast Iowa world, yet they also are not immune from money worries. I know some students whose parents are custodians and other students who are the children of single parents working very, very hard to keep them at school. I knew a student whose home in India had a dirt floor and another whose family fled the genocide in Sudan. I knew a student who augmented his wrestling scholarship with road-crew work back home in the Iowa summers. They are all here. They all want an education. And—even though money and time are tight for everyone, and getting tighter (including for faculty)—we are privileged to help them achieve that.

Luther College is a small private liberal arts college affiliated with the Evangelical Lutheran Church of America (ELCA), a moderate-to-progressive Christian Protestant denomination. We were founded in Decorah, Iowa in 1861, on the eve of the Civil War, to train English- (rather than only Norwegian-) speaking Lutheran pastors to serve the growing Norwegian-American community around Decorah, which is still the proud home of the Vesterheim Norwegian-American Heritage Museum. Luther seldom has more than 2,500 students on campus at any one time; the average size of our first-year class is around 600 students. I was proud to see that in his book *Where You Go Is Not Who You'll Be: An Antidote to the College Admissions Mania* (2015), *New York Times* columnist Frank Bruni singled us out for praise. Describing otherwise normal kids maddened by Ivy League fever, Bruni argues that we need to look beyond the Big-Name Schools to consider what education is really for. "Now more than ever," he writes, "college needs to be an expansive adventure, propelling students toward unplumbed

9. See Kolowich, "How Many College Students Are Going Hungry?"

territory and untested identities rather than indulging and flattering who they already are. And students, along with those of us who purport to have meaningful insights for them, need to insist on that." On page 127 of Bruni's book, there we are:

> [S. Georgia Nugent, former president of Kenyon College] has come around to the firm conviction that for undergraduates, [small and midsize independent liberal arts colleges are] ideal environments: especially approachable, uniquely nurturing. She said that each has a much greater bounty of programs than its size might lead an outsider to expect. And she noted that the colleges as a group present an extraordinary spectrum of options, with distinctive colors for individuals who take the time to notice.
>
> For instance, Luther College, a school in Decorah, Iowa, that's affiliated with the Evangelical Lutheran Church of America, has proven to be a surprisingly sturdy cradle for winners of some of the most prestigious academic prizes. Although it has an endowment of only $116 million [*actually, more*] and just 2,500 students at a time, it has produced eight Rhodes scholars and, since 2009, sixteen Fulbright scholars.

Those are good numbers for those scholarships, which are gold standards of academic achievement anywhere. And of course, they aren't just numbers. One Fulbright recipient worked with a colleague of mine who is one of the top Reformation historians in America (his wife, also a colleague, is another.) A recent Rhodes scholar (a chemistry major) took the same pottery class I'd taken in Luther's Center for the Arts. Faculty here (in a twelve-to-one student ratio, 93 percent of whom hold terminal degrees in our fields and 84 percent of whom are tenured or tenure-track) live the reality that "it takes a village to raise a child." Even if we don't know students from our classes, we know them by sight and by reputation, from casual conversations after lectures or in the caf. We send them to each other's offices and write recommendations and smile when we pass on the sidewalk. Luther's small enough for all of us to know each other as people, not numbers, even when the numbers are pretty good. This helps us make college an "expansive adventure" for every student who accepts the challenge.

Yet like any small college, we are more expensive—not just expansive—than big state schools, primarily because that high tenure-track faculty number means higher costs in salaries and benefits, which represent most of the budget at small schools like ours.[10] When a professor gets tenure, she has job

---

10. I want to point out here that Luther staff members at all levels also take justifiable

security, which is conferred after a rigorous, multistage vetting process and is meant to protect intellectual freedom against vindictive administrators or the cultural storms that regularly sweep our society (remember the "Red Scare" of the 1950s?) Tenure is good for students because it means the institution has invested in a professor who's therefore able to repay that investment with an institutional knowledge that deepens over time, governance power over and commitment to the value of the school's curriculum (and thence to the value of the student's degree), and, most importantly, rich knowledge of students themselves. (When first-year students come looking for me two years later to write them recommendation letters for medical school, I'll still be around, and I'll know them well enough to either write for them or counsel them on how to make themselves better candidates.) By contrast, the sticker price at big state schools is lower not only because they're subsidized by taxpayers in a way we aren't, but because they externalize more of their labor costs onto adjunct faculty and graduate students, whose positions are usually temporary, poorly paid, and benefitless. "Well," said one prospective student's father when I explained this to him, "I guess college is like anything else—you get what you pay for." At small colleges like mine, what you are paying for is our people and our investment in our students—including that father's son, whom I've seen happily engaged in classes and conversations around campus as a student here ever since.

In spite of cost, our students (and their families) make an effort to be here because they believe in a type of value that dollars alone don't account for, a value that is deeply intertwined with the value of the faculty and the mentoring and experiences we provide. When I ask students why they chose Luther, they often say the same thing first: they prize their relationships with professors, who get to know them very well, who advise them closely, and who are professionally rewarded primarily for our work with them. Teaching is at the center of our work here, as at most small liberal arts colleges: a full-time load for a Luther faculty member is six courses per year, while four courses (or fewer) per year are typical for Research I faculty. Although scholarship and artistic activity and service connected to our faculty's governance of the college and curriculum are still important

---

pride in the way they contribute to students' growth. I've never forgotten a bit of advice I received from a senior colleague in my early years at Luther, when I was learning the ropes of academic advising, which is done here by faculty starting in a student's first year. "If you see a student struggling, and you know they have a work-study job in the cafeteria," she said, "talk to the 'caf ladies.' They get to know the students really well, and students will tell them things they won't necessarily tell professors." I've taken that colleague's advice on several occasions, and it's reinforced to me the value of a college culture based on people who've been supported and maintained in their positions over the years.

and factored into promotion decisions here, our professional lives are centered on students—in teaching (including class preparation and grading) and advising (formal and informal, including academic and personal work with students and their organizations.) We see our research and creative work as energizing our teaching and developing the professional connections that can benefit our students too. Even administrative work ultimately circles back to the question of "how does this serve students, and our mission?" As a denominationally affiliated college, we place values, ethics, and living a good life—without church-college narrowness but with consideration of what *good* really means—explicitly on the table here. Our mission statement links us to our namesake, Martin Luther, whose statue stands at the edge of campus:

> In the reforming spirit of Martin Luther, Luther College affirms the liberating power of faith and learning. As people of all backgrounds, we embrace diversity and challenge one another to learn in community, to discern our callings, and to serve with distinction for the common good.
>
> As a college of the church, Luther is rooted in an understanding of grace and freedom that emboldens us in worship, study, and service to seek truth, examine our faith, and care for all God's people.
>
> As a liberal arts college, Luther is committed to a way of learning that moves us beyond immediate interests and present knowledge into a larger world—an education that disciplines minds and develops whole persons equipped to understand and confront a changing society.
>
> As a residential college, Luther is a place of intersection. Founded where river, woodland, and prairie meet, we practice joyful stewardship of the resources that surround us, and we strive to be a community where students, faculty, and staff are enlivened and transformed by encounters with one another, by the exchange of ideas, and by the life of faith and learning.[11]

Yes, it's earnest and maybe a little corny. But it's sincere, and to paraphrase Martin Luther himself, I stand willingly here next to it. I believe in the liberal arts college ideal and the possibilities it represents for students and for our world, and I believe in the work we do here. Defending the value of the liberal arts is a hard sell in an era when *liberal* has been twisted into an epithet. But I believe in it, for the reasons I discussed when I unpacked the term in Chapter 3. An expanded human capacity—a bigger and more

11. http://www.luther.edu/about/mission/.

generous self, which leads you to a bigger and more generous life—is at the heart of Luther's mission, as stated and as lived by faculty and administration. Perhaps it's this notion of mission I should point to—and put alongside *liberal*—in helping to explain why I'm so insistent that college is not, and shouldn't, and can't be, all about the money, and in helping, therefore, to shatter some of the cliches that keep students and the rest of us from seeing what college is really about.

Maybe the best display of college cliché is the John Landis film *Animal House* (1978), still beloved by generations of students (and me), for the way it both celebrates and undercuts those cliches. Starring John Belushi as "Bluto," a seventh-year senior with Bacchanalian appetites and a 0.0 GPA, the film affectionately spoofs hippie English professors, uptight deans, and a range of Greek-system social types at the fictional Faber College (motto: "Knowledge is Good.") Filmed at the University of Oregon at Eugene, the movie hits the visual notes associated with college too: imposing brick buildings, wood-paneled libraries, ivy-covered walls.[12] It neither quite praises nor quite condemns the epic partying of Bluto's fraternity, the underdog Deltas, but it does show the ways in which college is just like the "real world:" full of crooks, prissy hypocrites, truants and troublemakers, and a few decent people. Yet at the end of the film (written by the graduates of some "prestigious" colleges, including Dartmouth) we're left wondering: what has all this really been for? What will a college degree mean? Especially since Bluto, riding victoriously into the sunset with his 0.0 GPA and a kidnapped sorority girl, becomes a United States senator? At a time when college is seen as more necessary for more people than ever, *Animal House* still makes us ask: what is being a college student really about?

John Belushi's famous sweatshirt reading simply COLLEGE—reproduced on a million dorm-room posters—is a brilliant deadpan picture of our reality: in twenty-first–century America, college is a brand, not just in terms of individual schools (which have their own brands to manage and market) but as an amorphous, and often amorphously understood, mental image that has become an equally amorphous commodity. It's a next-level maturation experience, lasting somewhere from three and a half to five years, involving classes, teachers, a somehow-improved shot at a somewhat-higher socioeconomic status, and that longed-for thing, a social life. It's a chute into something like adulthood waiting on the other side. It's

12. My Luther English Department colleague Martin Klammer, who was then an undergraduate at Oregon, appears as an extra in the film.

the experience gestured at in the shirt's block letters, deliberately generic and excited—not college but "college," in which one four-year-ivy-walled-classroom-'n'-parties experience is much the same as any other. College is an experience to purchase, a phase of life with its own archetypical images, and therefore a commodified and often poorly understood experience, even as it remains what is perhaps the only social maturation ritual our culture now offers, a socioeconomic necessity in many cultures and work climates, and the last systematic educational experience many people will ever have. Therefore, college is at risk of becoming a cliché.

Parental expectations and fears—and even good intentions—can shape the unknowability of college: as anthropologist Margaret Mead noted, American society's relative lack of folkways and traditions leads to both freedom and anxiety for parents, who know they need to prepare their children to "leave [them]" and move into the future but can't know what the future will look like. "In a very short while," Mead writes, "[children] will be operating gadgets which [a parent] does not understand and cockily talking a language to which [s/he] has no clue." (As current as this sounds, it was written in 1942!)[13] As parents experience the financial realities of the recession, their anxiety shifts to a key even sharper than students', for good reason: *will this degree help my child get a job?* Thus money is added to the muddle of images clustered around college: it is about (intangible) self-development but also about (tangible) material reward; it is both as a preparation for "the rest of your life" and a removal from your life: you go away for a semi-monastic "retreat" for study and contemplation, far from the distractions of the world (which literally is the reason why so many colleges are located at some remove from cities or large towns) yet are regularly warned that the "real world" waits at the bottom of that idyllic, contemplative hill.[14] Yet you also know college has huge power to shape your personal and professional identities and, even more, the ideas with which you'll navigate your future, good and bad. And you aren't wrong.

13. Senior, *All Joy and No Fun,* 136.

14. You can see a similar marketing based on a philosophical ideal (even cliché) of college, meshing uneasily with consumerist preferences for college as entertainment, at High Point University (NC). As Jeffrey Selingo writes in *College (Un)bound* (2013), "when you start the [campus] tour [by golf cart], faint sounds of classical music are piped in from hidden outdoor speakers as you pass life-size statues of Galileo, Jefferson, and Aristotle" (32). Yet this veneer of "college"-cliché intellectualism is belied by the numerous consumer amenities—"a first-run movie theater, a steakhouse, outdoor hot tubs, and free food all over campus, including a roaming ice cream truck (part of the $39,800 list price)"—and the school's financial status: "Moody's Investors Service has downgraded the university's debt rating to junk status and calls it one of the most highly leveraged universities in the country" (33).

In his 2009 book *Shop Class as Soulcraft: An Inquiry into the Value of Work*, political philosopher and motorcycle mechanic Matthew Crawford critiques the American educational system as producing a vague type of "knowledge worker" who fits right into a corporate environment that divorces processes from products and people from real, satisfying work in a physical world about which—the real danger is—they'll eventually stop caring. The corporate world requires higher and higher degrees of credentialing, yet "[w]hen the point of education becomes the production of credentials rather than the cultivation of knowledge," Crawford writes, "it forfeits the motive recognized by Aristotle: 'All human beings by nature desire to know.' Students become intellectually disengaged."[15] And no wonder, when the end result of college credentialing is far too often white-collar work that's morally and practically meaningless, as Crawford describes it, there is no daily demand upon one's intellect, upon one's critical abilities or best self. Crawford, who left a white-collar job at a think tank to develop a much more satisfying career as a motorcycle mechanic, writes that "knowledge" and "education" need to be rooted in the world of material objects, actions, and consequences—which, as we've seen, can root a person in the world of meaningful and necessary encounters with that which is not herself. Elsewhere he quotes Marge Piercy's poem "To Be of Use" to evoke this deep human need: "The pitcher longs for water to carry / and a person for work that is real."[16]

Yale professor William Deresiewicz discovered a similar need in himself and in his students, yet, he argues, their Ivy League educations are distancing them from the non-Ivy world and from their own deepest desires, goals, and capabilities. In his essay "The Disadvantages of an Elite Education" (2008), which became his book *Excellent Sheep: The Miseducation of the American Elite and the Way to a Meaningful Life* (2014), he describes being "struck dumb by my own dumbness" when trying to talk to the plumber working on his house.[17] "Elite institutions are supposed to provide a humanistic education," he writes, "but the first principle of humanism is Terence's: 'nothing human is alien to me.' The first disadvantage of an elite education is how very much of the human it alienates you from."[18] Elite students get alienated, Deresiewicz argues, not only from the non-Ivy-League world but from themselves, which defeats the entire purpose of education. "[T]heir sense of self has been built around their ability to succeed," he

---

15. Crawford, *Shop Class as Soulcraft*, 147.
16. Crawford, "The Case for Working With Your Hands."
17. Deresiewicz, "The Disadvantages."
18. Ibid.

writes. "The idea of not being successful terrifies them, disorients them . . . . But if you're afraid to fail, you're afraid to take risks, which begins to explain the final and most damning disadvantage of an elite education: that it is profoundly anti-intellectual."[19]

Although Deresiewicz doesn't say it, I do: the Ivy League and the magical rocket pack of privileges it straps onto any student who wins the admissions battle is becoming a cliché nested within the larger cliché of "college," the hazy visuals and expectations for which it has helped to shape. (Our images of "college" look like the Ivies, which in turn look like Oxford.) But if you buy Deresiewicz's analysis, you'll also buy something he and I agree on: the best and most genuinely transformative education, with the barnacles of cliché scraped off, is happening at small liberal arts colleges. This is one of several truths bubbling into sight in the higher education landscape now. Another is Crawford's idea that contemporary American higher-ed credentialing will lose its value if sought uncritically by college students and corporations as a badge of professional readiness rather than of intellectual growth. Still another is his contention (subtly echoed by Deresiewicz) that if we decouple white-collar "college-degree" work from blue-collar "physical work," and say white-collar work is the only kind worth seeking, we'll shortchange the vocations and abilities of many intelligent, able people who might not want to go to a four-year college and who would otherwise be served by the shop classes and community industrial colleges being cut all over the country. Split head from heart from hands and all three suffer.

Put all these ideas together and you get a grim view of how college may be propping up the increasingly unsustainable reality of American capitalism: a few super-rich "elites" and millions of "knowledge workers" somewhere in the middle, managing the transfer of the actual making of things to physical workers somewhere in the Third World and leaving more and more people optionless and angry at the bottom. (Especially, as we saw in Chapter 1, if their jobs have been replaced by robots.) Meanwhile everyone's increasingly unable to see and protest the way this order of things is making the world of things blurry, opaque, and distant. We can't fix our own cars, cook our own food, make our own clothes, or enter into what Crawford calls the "kind of spiritedness that is called forth when we take things in hand for ourselves, whether to fix them or to make them."[20] In Marxist terms, we're alienated from our own things, from the material conditions of our own lives, and therefore at some level from ourselves: "what ordinary people once made, they buy; and what they once fixed for themselves, they replace entirely or

19. Ibid.
20. Ibid., 2.

hire an expert to repair, whose expert fix often involves replacing an entire system because some minute component has failed."[21]

As a college professor, I'd also like to see college become more of an arena for hands-on, experiential work and learning, real encounters with real ideas and things, producing people who can challenge the blue-collar/white-collar distinction in our economy and in their own lives, able both to understand Plato and to make their own dinners and fix their own bikes. I believe in college as a place of opportunity not just to improve your own life but to improve the systems around it by analyzing them and seeing what's wrong. I'd like to see less of a bifurcation between types of schools and more of a healthy, full-spectrum notion of what learning is. Perhaps this looks like two-year Deep Springs College in California's remote high desert, where about twenty-six students at a time (currently all men) run their own herds of cattle, shoe their own horses, and immerse themselves in Hegel and Cormac McCarthy, or like Berea College in Kentucky, where tuition is free and students work on the college's farm. Perhaps it looks like Reed College in Portland, Oregon, where as part of its serious intellectual emphasis, students receive detailed feedback on their work and "although grades are recorded for all classes, they are not routinely reported to students."[22] Perhaps this looks like Luther College's own internship, study-abroad, and social-justice involvement opportunities (where social work students visit prisons and education students teach in schools before graduating), or like the college gardens students manage every summer. But most likely it looks like what any college can offer, or any college student can find—personal transformation that creates a thoughtful, self- and socially critical person who has something constructive to say and is willing to take equally constructive action to make herself heard.

Unfortunately, finding this sort of transformation may mean swimming against the tide of the college admissions process itself, particularly the habits of self-creating busyness it fosters, which persist well into many students' college careers and are maintained by campuses themselves. Starting (dismally) early, college dangles before ambitious teenagers' eyes as the next step on the ladder of personhood, the motivating engine of continued work, the dream of membership in the community of the like-minded beyond what so many experience as the jocks-'n'-princesses small-mindedness of high school. But to get into college, you have to be not only academically successful but also "well-rounded"—or rather well-armored, with a high

21. Ibid.
22. http://www.reed.edu/about_reed/history.html.

GPA and participations in sports, music, clubs, community service activities, or all of these and more.

What this means in theory is that colleges will be admitting delightful
young people who have already begun to develop gifts in a number of fields
and are looking to us to help them develop even more. What it means in
practice (amazingly often) is that we're admitting delightful but frazzled
and fearful young people who, often without realizing it, have substituted
"involvement" for intellectual interests, because the former is much easier
to measure (especially in a test- and numbers-driven educational system)
than the latter. Many have also (again, without realizing it) learned to play
a teacher- and parent-pleasing game called "school" which checks boxes
while leaving heart and mind untouched. In her engaging book *I Love
Learning, I Hate School: An Anthropology of College* (2016), Notre Dame
professor Susan Blum writes, "The *game of school* involves mastering the
rules and behaving in ways that maximize one's advantage, like collecting properties in Monopoly," yet "[l]earning to act simply in response to
another's goals, while presenting them *as if* they were one's own, teaches
that action is hollow. There is no solid core of motivation. It is all designed
as a performance that will yield rewards."[23] And, as Blum writes, this "in-
authenticity," which "comes from being for others," has costs students will
recognize if given the chance.[24] Often, in my conversations with first-year
students, their real feelings tumble out: "I came to college to discover my
real passion, because even though I'm 'successful in school,' I have no idea
what I really care about. I do so many things I don't know what's really
important to me anymore. I can't remember the last time I read a book that
wasn't assigned for class. I'm in college—now what?"

Students choose a variety of responses to these questions of meaning. Some keep up their overinvolved high-school habits, clinging to clubs
and activities rather than coursework as attachment points to campus life.
Some fall into social life, and stay there. The lucky ones (guided by the
faculty advisors they have a much better chance of connecting with at small
colleges) discover an intellectual passion that fuels curiosity for further
learning in school and in life. They learn to choose activities that will feed
their souls and give them energy for their ongoing pursuit of an education,
not become substitutes for the coursework they're here to complete. They
learn to ask, early and often, "Why am I here?" In the process, they learn
what education really means.

23. Blum, *I Love Learning,* 36, italics original.
24. Ibid.

So if you're a college student, you'll need to think your way through these mixed messages toward the truth. If you come in with a vague enthusiasm for "college" and expect to gulp down everything you need for a degree without letting it touch the rest of your brain, you're in for some unpleasant surprises. (And, needless to say, only in *Animal House* world—or Skull and Bones, sons-of-presidents world—does Delta-style partying carry no consequences.) As our current dean of student life says, students can't just expect to "get on the people mover" and be conveyed through all four years, then spit out into a job at the end—they have to take active roles in their own educations.[25] To come here, you don't have to know what your major will be or what you're going to do after college. One feeling is enough—"I want more, I think there must be something more out there for me"—but you've also got to accept that looking for more is going to challenge and change you in some pretty deep ways. If you do this thing called *college* right, you will be different at the end than you were at the beginning. Therefore, everything I say in this chapter will be centered on one plea to students: take responsibility on yourself for going to college, not "college," by taking the time to discover what it really means for you, and why you are really here. Faculty and administrators share this responsibility with you, and if you accept it, you will be well-placed to work alongside us during your time on campus, to hold us accountable to our own stated ideals when we fall, and to carry your education out into the world to meet its deepest needs, and your own.

So what is college really about? When I ask myself what it is that I *really* teach, in all my classes—literature, creative writing, our first-year common course, study abroad—I always come back to this: college, like education in general, is about *becoming a self with something constructive to say*. This is less about discovering a single unchanging identity (who is ever the same at forty as they are at nineteen, or *wants* to be?) or job training that will set you on a fixed career path (the average person changes careers at least three times in her life) than about building and strengthening a flexible and dignified "core" of self-understanding at the heart of your own spirit and mind. That core is fed by a wide-ranging curiosity that helps you see yourself as part of an ecological, artistic, historical, and political version of Indra's Net, never bound to the childish delusion that the world is only a story about you, and prepared intellectually and socially for a world where change is the only constant. You may get here in ways that neither you nor I expect. You might revise your ideas based on classmates' discussions or reading or your own experience. You might disagree with people you otherwise respect:

---

25. Thanks to my colleague, Dean of Student Life Corey Landstrom, for this phrase.

your friends, your parents, your professors. That's normal. What matters is that you open yourself to the process of learning, and be willing to stay there, even when it gets uncertain and painful. Perhaps *particularly* then, because if you can't deal with difficulty, complexity, and change, you won't deal that well with the rest of your life.

One of my students' favorite texts is Plato's "Allegory of the Cave" from his *Republic*, because of the way it asks us to unpack what education and enlightenment really mean. The setup is simple. Inside a cave, prisoners are chained with their faces toward a blank wall, onto which are projected the shadows of objects carried past a fire burning somewhere behind them. Now imagine that a prisoner who's spent his whole life in the cave is suddenly released from his chains, then dragged up out of the cave into the sunlight to stand there until his eyes have adjusted to what we would call the "real" world. In the voice of his old teacher Socrates, Plato posits that after the prisoner comes to see and understand the world outside of the cave, even though the process has been physically and psychologically uncomfortable, "he'd feel happy about his own altered circumstances, and sorry for [the other prisoners.]"[26] Coming to see how deeply he'd misunderstood the nature of reality while chained in the cave, the ex-prisoner, despite his uncomfortable adjustment to the outside world, "would go through anything rather than live that way" again.[27] If the prisoner returned to the cave, however, and sat in his old spot, he'd find his eyes struggling to readjust to the darkness, and the other prisoners, still enslaved to their old system of values and rewards, would mock him and "would say that he'd come back from his upward journey with his eyes ruined, and that it wasn't even worth trying to go up there."[28] Chillingly, Plato asks, "And wouldn't they—if they could—grab hold of anyone who tried to set them free and take them up there, and kill him?"[29] Glaucon, the student and straight man in this dialogue, responds (accurately, we are to understand), "They certainly would."[30]

Students take this text deeply to heart, especially in their first year of college, when every day they're adjusting to new ways of learning, thinking, and socializing, and, therefore, new ways of confronting oneself. Here, many find that suddenly, "school" is reaching into more areas of their lives and hearts than it ever has before. This challenge can lead to some personal derailments if a student is not able to dig into the challenge (with the help of

26. Plato, *Republic*, 242–246.
27. Ibid.
28. Ibid.
29. Ibid.
30. Ibid.

advisors and professors), stay with it, and continue to grow into the Platonic reality that growth causes, and requires, uncertainty. I've seen this process in action a lot. An attractive, charming athlete/class clown/class beauty discovers that the social cushion and just-enough study habits that floated him/her through high school evaporate on contact with college, dropping him/her to the ground. A straight-A student from a small rural high school finds that in the first college semester s/he's a B student, and that some next-level critical-thinking and argumentation skills (as well as a lot more study time) are necessary here. A conservative Christian student befriends an openly gay (and also Christian) student. An avid video gamer learns (the hard way) to leave his games at home over Christmas break.

Properly designed, college courses can give students the tools they need for this kind of intellectual and imaginative growth. A Luther student's career begins with a two-semester interdisciplinary introduction to college-level reading, writing, and thinking called Paideia, after the Greek word for "education," and designed to teach the intellectual habits they'll need from here on out. In the first week of Paideia, I walk my eighteen brand-new college students through a series of steps to give them a common understanding of what critical thinking means and why it matters. Step one: What's your first reaction to this (novel, current event, Facebook post, annoying text from your mom)? Step two: What are some questions you can ask in good faith to complicate that first reaction, to see around corners, to get more information? Step three: How might your response change based on answers to those questions? Step four: Putting all these things together, what's your reaction now? "Feeling these muscles moving in your brain in this order," I tell them, "is critical thinking." I'd think this was overkill if not for the testimonials students give in their final papers of the year, when I ask them to reflect on what education means to them now and how their understanding of it has changed. More and more, students tell me that in high school "getting the right answer," "regurgitating information," or "teaching to the [national or state standardized] test" was the focus of class, splitting off intellectual pleasure (such as reading) into something students pursued on their own, with "fun" being something very different from school. They find that when they get to college they are being asked to stretch in more directions, three- or even four-dimensionally, and in contrast to earlier grade focus, a B can be okay if it reflects the new orientation to thinking and work.

Most of all, critical thinking as college asks for it is often something new in students' experience of what Susan Blum calls the "game of school." A history major wrote that in her big-city public school, chopped and changed in redistricting and budget-cutting, critical thinking was almost entirely downplayed in favor of right-or-wrong answers and test scores that could raise the school's profile and divert more money in its direction. An art major wrote of feeling bored to the point of rage in high school classrooms, isolated not only from peers but from teachers by the desire for "school" to mean something more transformative than filling in blanks on test sheets. Another young woman wrote of negotiating the illusions put forth by well-meaning family members that "an education is just about getting a degree, and then a good job" and is worth pursuing mostly "because going to college is the respectable thing to do." Rather, she discovered, an education allows people to "have a voice and stand up for themselves, as well as fight for the truth and what [is] right." A student athlete described his struggles to get his work done as a member of one of our college's best-known and most demanding sports teams; he had come much closer than I'd known to dropping out in his fall semester, wondering "whether all this was worth it," but had now connected his athletic and academic experiences to understand that difficulty and struggle could pay off, and that his reserves of persistence could be called on in non-athletic areas too. Still another young man, who remarked in his first week of college that he wasn't worried about online threats to his privacy because he wasn't "doing anything wrong," had changed his mind by the end of the year: "now I see how *Nineteen Eighty-four* could be connected to me personally," he told me, "and it sends a shiver right down to my bones." Every first-year student seems to get to this realization: *this year has shown us that "college" and "education" are more than we thought—and that's as it should be.* They've discovered what psychiatrist and Holocaust survivor Victor Frankl famously wrote in *Man's Search for Meaning* (1946) that a certain amount of difficulty and tension is not only inevitable but necessary in life: "If architects want to strengthen a decrepit arch," he wrote, "they *increase* the load that is laid upon it, for thereby the parts are joined more firmly together." Therefore, those whose lives might feel purposeless "should not be afraid to create a sound amount of tension through a reorientation toward the meaning of one's life."[31] Similarly, as novelist James Blaylock writes, "[t] o learn the truth is to make things fall apart. Knowledge [is not] a cement, a wall of order against chaos; it [is] an infinitude of little cracks, running in a thousand directions, threatening to crumble into fragments our firmest convictions."[32] Studying the ideas of people who have come before us can help us feel a sense of stability, however, even amid this necessary uncertainty. As William Deresiewicz writes, "To study the past is to continually have the experience of realizing, Oh, so that's why I think that. That is what is speaking through me when I say that. The critic Northrop Frye remarked

---

31. Senior, *All Joy and No Fun*, 254.
32. Martin, *Masking Hegemony*, 32.

that a liberal arts education ought to lead to a recognition scene, as at the climax of a play. But in the study of the liberal arts, he said, the thing we come to recognize is ourselves."[33]

That's not to say that Luther students—or any students—are perfect, or that embracing difficulty is an easy sell, to them or to anyone (including ourselves.) As I've mentioned, we as humans can tend to prefer inertia, inattention, and comfort rather than the friction of challenge, and the social and technological structures in which we spend our days may reinforce that preference. Beyond a certain point, teachers can't control when, how, or if a student engages with the material: to borrow my grandfather's analogy again, we have to put the hay down where the goats can get it (making the hay as tempting and fluffy as possible), and trust the goats to make the choice to step forward and eat it. (Sorry, students—I know you are not goats, or sheep, although you *are* excellent.) Professors are about furnishing minds, and selves, with the sort of flexibility, plenitude, and perspectives—not to mention literal information—that will help a student keep herself good company throughout her life. But this is an inherently un-monetizable, hard-to-define, nuanced and delicate ideal, easily ridiculed—like many ideals—as impractical in light of the language of values swirling around us in the marketplace, drowning out the quieter voices that can be hard for nineteen-year-olds to hear. That's why we professors get so angry when we hear higher education referred to in the language of "product" and students as "consumers." We're not just making and selling some object. We hope to build not only selves with something constructive to say but selves with a complex, resilient, irreducibly human grain to them—a texture that develops over time, like the hearts of rare trees.

Of course, as transcendent and universal as we like to think this goal is, it may be inflected by historical contingencies, just like other higher education goals. Historically, though, college curricula have attempted to enshrine some version of this complex, critical selfhood even in the face of changing industrial and social realities. As former Harvard president Derek Bok describes in *Higher Education in America* (2013), "From the colonial era through the Civil War, most colleges embraced a highly prescribed course of study known as the classical curriculum," which "emphasized mental discipline attained through a rigorous study of classical subjects and texts coupled with moral discipline achieved with the aid of a strict disciplinary code, compulsory chapel, and a capstone course on practical ethics often taught to the senior class by the college president."[34] Focus on chal-

---

33. Deresiewicz, *Excellent Sheep*, 164.

34. Bok, *Higher Education in America*, 166.

lenging classical texts was thought to prepare students for other intellectual demands; as instructor William Allen wrote in 1890, "the student who has acquired the habit of never letting go a puzzling problem—say a rare Greek verb—until he has analyzed every element and understands every point in its etymology, has the habit of mind which will enable him to follow out a legal subtlety with the same accuracy."[35]

Inculcating "habit[s]" of mind and morality in hopes they would equip students for unknown future challenges is still reflected in the "three large, overlapping objectives" Bok defines as common to the last century of American undergraduate education: preparing students for careers either through specific vocational skills or broadly applicable intellectual skills; helping "students to be enlightened citizens of a self-governing democracy and active members of their own communities;" and "[helping] students live a full and satisfying life by cultivating a wide range of interests and a capacity for reflection and self-knowledge."[36] A 2011 survey of professors showed "a strong consensus among American professors on a number of specific goals that can contribute to one or more of these larger purposes," including critical thinking and evaluating information (which 99 percent rank as "essential" or "very important"), tolerance for differing views (78.9 percent) and "developing students' creative abilities" (79.4 percent).[37] As a professor myself, I'd say this breakdown of our goals reflects my own aims and experiences; a flexible, tolerant, intellectually curious mind will be able to survive, even thrive, just about anywhere. Columbia University professor Andrew Delbanco echoes this goal in his own list of "certain qualities of mind and heart requisite for reflective citizenship" that he thinks college should help students develop, including, "1. A skeptical discontent with the present, informed by a sense of the past. 2. The ability to make connections among seemingly disparate phenomena. 3. Appreciation of the natural world, enhanced by knowledge of science and the arts. 4. A willingness to imagine experience from perspectives other than one's own. 5. A sense of ethical responsibility."[38] Therefore, it seems fair to say that the goal of college is to develop students' knowledge bases and critical abilities in such a way as to develop their minds and their selves.

Yet the dangers to college as an institution and to the intangible goods it is designed to transmit and communicate are everywhere, acquiring new edges each year—especially dangers to the habits of mind we try to instill.

35. Ibid.
36. Ibid., 167.
37. Ibid.
38. Delbanco, *College*, 3.

Lutheran scholar and educator David Tiede defined some of them to me and my faculty colleagues as what he called "the Five Disruptors" of higher education today: 1) the student cost-and-debt spiral; 2) the digitization of learning; 3) the regrouping of American communities, including faith communities (a particular issue for us as a college of the ELCA, as we can't count on common understandings of "Lutheran" or even "Christian" in the way we once did); 4) the changing profile of prospective students, including changes in backgrounds, needs, and goals for college; and 5) the measurement of educational excellence by learning results, symptomatized in the testing mania that's such a regrettable feature of the K–12 public educational landscape in America today. Reflecting on these, I realized that one in particular seemed most intimately and problematically linked with the others: the digitization of learning, which ties students into a network of increasingly commercialized, complexity-flattening assumptions about what college is and should be and reinforces the worst effects of each of the other "disruptors." Faculty aren't immune to these effects, either. We too often assume that technology, as it makes its way into our classrooms, our admissions efforts, and our and our students' lives, is part of "progress" and therefore cannot (or should not) be resisted; that adapting the latest device or platform is necessarily productive in all areas of our lives and work; and that electronic media are cognitively, socially, and pedagogically neutral, always able to complement without co-opting the nature of the work we are privileged to engage in on our campuses. I believe each of these assumptions is wrong, and that playing into them means playing a corporatized game that we, our students, and higher education itself will lose.

The notion that using technology is inevitably a marker of progressive thinking and good teaching seems to me to be one of the last unchallenged assumptions in higher education. This is especially ironic—and sad—for an enterprise that depends for its life on leading all of us to see and reevaluate our paradigms and assumptions every day. Yet even as many of us shake our heads at K–12 initiatives to put an iPad in every student's hands (at the same time as arts programs and library budgets are cut), we accept far too often that digital media are inevitably necessary and helpful in our work as they are in our lives beyond the classroom—to say nothing of their "necessity" for marketing purposes. However, to accede too easily to prevailing modes of being and doing could mean acceding to what educator Lowell Monke has called "a common disregard for one of schooling's most important tasks: to compensate for, rather than intensify, society's excesses."[39] Since college is one of the last (if not the last) places where our students can be helped

39. Monke, "Is It Time To Unplug Our Schools?"

to examine cultural norms and their effect on individual minds (including the constant demand for entertainment and small bites of information that the Internet and electronic devices have helped create in them), we owe it to them to point out what else is possible for them, and what they are missing in a life conducted largely online. As I've been arguing, the Internet is far from neutral in its effect on our capacities for attention and therefore on our personal, educational, and civic lives. Our students, often without quite realizing it, are seeking other ways of seeing, thinking, and being in the world than what has become their "new normal" of techno-stimulation and subsequent jadedness. If we, their college professors—especially within the liberal arts tradition of inquiry towards richer meaning in our world—can't show them alternatives, then no one can, or will.

As I type this, I'm smiling ironically: I use online course information modules, email, and overhead projection from a computer screen in my classes almost every day, and I do accede to two realities: these techniques do enable student learning that wouldn't otherwise happen, and they enrich my own perceived market value as a teacher and a writer. Tech-based education reformers love to decry the pontificating professor who lectures from yellowing notes. But as seen in UC San Diego professor Elizabeth Losh's book *The War on Learning: Gaining Ground in the Digital University* (2014), educational technologies can take us too far in the other direction. "In an effort to get more of the two hundred plus enrolled students in my large lecture class participating in class discussion," Losh, a specialist in online rhetoric and theory, writes that in January 2011, she "chose a hashtag on Twitter, #cat125, and invited a roomful of otherwise silent and passive UC San Diego seniors in the Culture, Art, and Technology program to tweet for thirty minutes and thus add their comments to a free form evolving stream of text in the public record."[40] This in-class experiment was designed to augment Losh's lecture on disability and social media, including a presentation by a guest scholar, and to engage "otherwise silent and passive" students—one of the most crucial yet challenging things for a teacher to do in a large lecture hall. "Once the experiment started," wrote Losh's graduate student teaching assistant, Tara Zepel, "a handful of isolated tweets did address the topic of the lecture. After watching a YouTube video created by a young woman with autism, one student wrote, "#cat125 I have always kind of wondered what it might feel like to live inside an autistic mind, at least now I have seen it . . . in some form."[41] Yet the Twitter feed soon degenerated into comments on ceiling tiles, the smell of food one student had brought to the lecture hall, and a group effort to drop

40. Losh, "Who Was The Experimenter in the Twitter Experiment?"
41. Zepel, "Revisiting the Twitter Experiment (In Context.)"

pencils, then escalate disruption: "i say at 2:30 we all randomly start cough-ing . . . the proff isn't tweeting so she won't know whts going on hahaha."[42] Other students chimed in: "lezz doo itt! #cat125" and "#cat125 2min left guys! The countdownnnnnnn haha."[43] When she realized what was going on, Losh stopped the experiment, tweeting, "@_@ why is everyone coughing #cat125?"[44] The ringleader of the coughing effort later justified her actions as an effort at social self-empowerment similar to the Arab Spring, writing that it was "my way of testing the limits of this social experiment and demonstrat-ing our presence as students."[45] (Yeah, right.) Another student tweeter was disgusted by her classmates' behavior: "I remember that from eighth grade. This is why we can't have nice things!" Another was self-satirical: "I feel guilty to have made this twitter account during class . . . but I blame new media for my ADD."[46] Still others seemed lost: one "wrote this plaintive farewell: 'I didn't know what to say . . .'"[47]

In her account of the experiment, Tara Zepel notes an apparent con-tradiction: in her small-group discussion after the lecture that afternoon, students overwhelmingly "voiced that they expected some level of direc-tion, especially in a lecture setting" and "[s]ome even felt that such direct guidance was a necessary element of education," complaining that "[Losh] didn't tell us what to do."[48] Students complained, also, that "because they had to divide their attention between the Twitter screen feed on their phones or laptops and the lecture material on the projection screen, they could not effectively pay attention to either." Yet, Zepel writes, "While this perceived tension may allude to a valid criticism of new technology and suggest the need for a degree of coherence when using networked media for pedagogical purposes, it is also a bit perplexing. Without exception, in the CAT 125 lecture hall and in every other classroom I have sat in since laptops and cell phones became regular attendees of university classes, stu-dents routinely have some communication or entertainment technology running in the background."[49] So what was so different—and so overtly misbehavior-prompting—about multitasking for class purposes? Zepel

42. See Losh, *The War on Learning*, 41–42, and Losh, "Who Was The Experimenter in the Twitter Experiment?"

43. Zepel, "Revisiting the Twitter Experiment (In Context.)"

44. Zepel notes that ""@_@" is a common emoticon used to express disbelie[f], not amused, or disapproval."

45. Losh, *The War on Learning*, 43–45.

46. Losh, "Who Was The Experimenter."

47. Ibid., 42.

48. Zepel, "Revisiting the Twitter Experiment (In Context.)"

49. Ibid.

suggests that maybe "context" was the key: "It seems," she writes, "that as a group, the students chose to partially shed their identity as students in a classroom precisely because the request did not fit within their expectations of the roles and responsibilities teachers and students should have in a university context, in general, and a lecture class, in particular."[50] I think this makes sense, but it makes me wonder: why, then, do students subvert their *own* experience of the "roles and responsibilities teachers and students should have" by Facebooking, texting, or playing computer games in class when they think the teacher can't see them? Sure, part of that is plain old school rebellion, part of individual and cultural memory from the ancient Greeks to Charles Dickens and Pink Floyd. Maybe it's also what a colleague told me about something she'd recently learned: part of late-adolescent development is a desire, rooted in brain development, to turn away from parents or authority figures and turn toward peers. Yet Zepel's and Losh's accounts, which register these and other contradictions, make me think that the #cat125 Twitter experiment has revealed the same problem I've been wrestling with in this chapter—students don't always think through, or held themselves to account for, what their "college" education really involves and how their own choices may enrich or dilute its value.

The story of #cat125 exemplifies how thoughtful colleagues challenge themselves pedagogically, as all professors should. It reminds me that we can't control every aspect of students' experiences in our classrooms, and probably can't expect to. But it also warns me not to succumb to the quintessentially capitalist logic of using technology to "add value" to a college experience by adding a layer of complexity that can be meaningless and even patronizing to students, who are quick to spot that it can be just an effort to woo them with new toys and/or subvert instruction with their devices, while—every instinct tells me—still not really believing that these devices will help them learn.[51] As we've seen in Chapter 1, devices can also reveal, even exacerbate, students' naïveté; when Zepel told the students their Twitter disruption could be interpreted as disrespectful to Professor Losh and to the guest lecturer—particularly since the guest lectures and videos, exploring autism and deaf culture and language, were connected to a campus-wide Diversity Day, and several guests were in the audience—students were "horrified." Yet "the students simply did not take the disconnect with the lecture content into account. It simply didn't register."[52]

50. Ibid.

51. For the reasons discussed in Chapter 1—particularly data exposure—I'm also wary of making social media participation a condition of success in an academic course.

52. Zepel, "Revisiting the Twitter Experiment (In Context.)" Of course, it's not only students who behave badly on Twitter during lectures. See Parry, "Conference

In *The War on Learning*, Losh describes a fall 2002 mass distribution of "700 wireless-equipped HP Jornada handheld Pocket PCs"—forerunners of smartphones but less user-friendly and practical—to first-year college students at UC San Diego as an experiment that came to an ignominious end: neither instructors nor students could find workable, pedagogically effective ways to use the devices, and "many of the Jornadas were relegated to e-waste."[53] Nevertheless, device distributions continued on other campuses: Duke gave more than 1,600 students their own iPods in 2004, and Seton Hill gave all faculty and full-time students iPads in 2010. (Losh notes that this was "an important institutional marketing opportunity for the small Pennsylvania university, which is often confused with the larger Seton Hall in New Jersey;" I suspect that device distributions like this *are* often more about marketing than pedagogy.[54]) Both distribution efforts met with mixed—and, in the case of Duke, largely indifferent—results. In reading about this, I find myself thinking: So much work (and e-waste) for so little reward. So much fancy spinning up of illusion and tech-cliché enthusiasm to justify our own existence. So much replication of the errors of the K–12 "computer for every student" initiatives which are so easy to mock until we're the ones making the same mistake. And so much avoidance of our real, hard task as students and teachers: digging in to articulate and then to carry out the value of encounters among people and ideas, never allowing the mechanism of conveyance to obscure the thing conveyed or our responsibility to treat colleagues and classmates with respect. Overall, technology is still just a tool, to be deployed with exceptional care.

My own always-evolving technology-in-the-classroom approach asks students to take charge of their educational experience and quality of attention and decide what's at stake for them in doing so by engaging with the questions of value: what is their education worth, and what opportunities do they want not to miss? And how can they avoid tuning out or succumbing to old bad habits once difficulty hits? I try to head off a screen-based default mode—which is fatal to small discussion-based classes like mine—by being direct and thoughtful about technology and encouraging students to

Humiliation," and Losh, "Who Was The Experimenter" for stories of Twitter-enabled social insensitivity exhibited by professionals and academics, including back-channel rudeness and cruelty during a 2009 talk by digital media scholar and sociologist danah boyd (who's cited elsewhere in this book.) In *You Are Not A Gadget*, Jaron Lanier writes that he asked the audience for one of his talks to avoid tweeting or blogging during his speech so that "what was tweeted, blogged, or posted on a Facebook wall would then be *you*," since "[g]iving yourself the time and space to think and feel is crucial to your existence . . . you have to find a way to be yourself before you can share yourself" (ix).

53. Losh, *The War on Learning*, 170, 181.

54. Ibid., 183.

do the same. It starts with the literal classroom setup: as much as possible, I move desks into one big circle (*not* rows) so we can all see each other, distribute the desks to avoid that bunching-at-the-back-of-the-room effect ("y'all scooch forward a little!" I've been known to urge), and position the table holding my own materials so that I can escape the "teacher zone" in front of the board and walk out among the students.[55] I also believe in using the syllabus as a teaching tool. "Yes, it's long," I say, "but it tells you everything you need to know to succeed in this class"—course policies (absences, etc.), course expectations (including "be professional and responsible, respecting your classmates' views and the value of their time and helping to create a classroom environment in which everyone can work and learn"), the students' rights (including "to be treated with professionalism and confidentiality by me and by your classmates"), my philosophies on writing and grading, what plagiarism is, and some other things to bear in mind about college, including the fact that you may someday be asking professors for recommendation letters, so you should give them the impressions of you they'll need to write good ones. (First-generation students, navigating academia's unspoken codes, particularly appreciate all this.)[56] I make my expectations and reasoning as clear as I can: laptops and phones should be off, stowed, and/or not used for non-class purposes, because, especially in small classes like ours, they hinder your educational experience and the experiences of students around you.[57] I even ask students to go out in the hall if they want to use their phones *before* class: if you're in the room, please talk to other people. Here's the current version of my technology policy on my first-year Paideia syllabus:

SOME NOTES ON TECHNOLOGY

When we need to use computers as a class (such as posting drafts of paragraphs to [course webpage] forums for group critiques), you'll be able to use your laptops, and I'll let you know that in advance. However, I prefer that you *not* use laptops in class unless specifically requested or permitted. You may worry that you'll miss something if you aren't typing, but research shows students are more fully present in class activities and discussions if they're listening, speaking, and writing by hand.

55. If the classroom's not that way when we arrive, we—and I do mean *we*, because the students also take ownership of it—make it that way.

56. See Weldon, "Claiming Your Right to Say No."

57. Obviously, I can work with particular cases and medical needs, but I ask those students to speak with me and to document their need through the appropriate college support centers. My syllabus includes the information necessary to do that.

Among many other things, Paideia is about learning to see and judge the invisible filters—such as technology—that shape how you see the world. Therefore,

- Please don't use computers unless specifically requested or permitted.

- As soon as you enter the classroom, please remove headphones, silence your phone, put it away out of view, and turn your attention to your text, your notes from our previous class, the view from the window, or the people around you.

There are cognitive and pedagogical reasons for this. As you can see in the studies I've linked from our section's course page, scientific research and common sense show that laptops in class distract you and those around you more than they help. The sound of clicking keys and the ease with which any of us (including me) succumb to non–class-related distractions on screen detract from the environment we're creating in Paideia—in which we, the text, and our ideas about the text are the center of attention. Plus, since ours is a small, discussion-focused class, getting to know each other before class starts builds a community spirit that builds everyone's learning, too.

And there are larger realities at stake. We're all making some pretty big investments of time and money to be here, and we want to take advantage of the chance college gives us to learn and grow and be more than we ever hoped. Habitual laptop use can divert your participation energy to the machine you're literally placing between you and your colleagues. As for smartphones, I really can't think of a purpose for them in Paideia other than momentary fact-checking, which can be handled later (and comes up much less than you'd think.) Stash 'em and tune in to the other people sharing this unique moment with you. It's one small piece of your "one wild and precious life" (poet Mary Oliver's words) as it passes by.

Sometimes I also do some simple calculations. If Luther's comprehensive fee is $45,260/year, that's $22,630/semester. If the semester includes (on average) 13 weeks of class, then that's a cost of roughly $1740/week. At three class meetings a week (for Paideia), that's roughly $580.26 per class—a lot of money to be paying for a half-attentive, surreptitiously-keyed-in-to-a-private-screen hour of opportunity you will never get back. Fundamentally, I try to help students see what unprofessional or inattentive behavior costs, then leave the decision about their own behavior up to them, letting them experience consequences as they happen and actively "policing" only when behavior threatens other students' concentration. Students aren't stupid. As Elizabeth Losh's Twitter experiment shows, even alongside a class-disruption stunt or plain old tech-enabled inattention lurks the knowledge that they *are* wasting money, time, and opportunity this way—yet the consequences of that waste may not seem fully present to late-adolescent brains unless professors explicitly foreground them.

The value a student is missing by Facebooking during class isn't only financial, and isn't only in the short term. My syllabi also include a statement (at the request of senior students, who have found this helpful) that beginning with your first semester, you're building relationships with professors that might someday lead to graduate school recommendations or professional connections, and most professors (including me) won't write letters unless we can write positive and specific ones.[58] We discuss some big truths of college: a) if you don't take charge and help yourself, no one else will, b) technology isn't neutral in its effect on your education, your anxiety levels, and your social life, c) breaking habits of "checking" the screen now is one of the ways you can build your attention and your relationships with professors and colleagues, and d) your big project as a person is becoming a self with something to say, and professors are here to help you.

How do students respond to all of this? Very well. There's some initial bewilderment ("What do you mean, technology's doing things to my brain?") followed by dawning realization ("It's true—it *does* feel different in my head when I take a walk with no headphones!) and increasingly far-reaching and thoughtful personal transformation ("Clicking away to Facebook while I'm writing has gotten to be a bad habit—now I don't open that window at all" or "I've never kept a notebook and pen in my pocket to write things down before—now I notice more *and* do a lot more writing because of that.") Interestingly, no one has ever objected to any of the policies in my statement above, and the social norm in my classrooms, which, luckily, are small enough to make this possible, has shifted to mean that the students, chatting happily before class, give a texter the side-eye until he puts away his phone. (Shy students also seem more likely now to join into that chat rather than hiding behind a screen.) We take walks outside in the middle of class sometimes, and break into small groups for instant workshops and discussions, always trying to vary and engage pedagogical methods but also to keep the fresh surface of student awareness pressed against the textures of the living world, human and nonhuman. These students have come a long way toward the independence of thought and capacity for self-analysis that will make them flexible, curious people for

58. See Weldon, "Claiming Your Right to Say No."

the rest of their lives, able to navigate changing worlds based on internal rather than merely external compasses.

Yet for corporations—which are alarmingly influential in higher education, as in government—passivity, credulity, and adherence to the needs of the moment are profitable and desirable, and independent thinkers are not. Almost the first thing one reads in Jeffrey Selingo's *College (Un)bound: The Future of Higher Education and What It Means for Students* (2013), is a quote from Jennifer Fremont-Smith, described as "the cofounder of Smarterer, a Boston-based start-up that offers technology for validating technical skills on everything from social media to Microsoft Office programs." "In other industries, 'those who don't innovate go out of business,'" Fremont-Smith says. "Higher ed shouldn't be different."[59] This quote is surrounded by descriptions of anxious universities partnering with industry to tailor curricula to that industry's needs, producing workers for that industry: in 2011 Stanford professor and tech entrepreneur Sebastian Thrun (CEO of for-profit MOOC company Udacity) "and Google's "director of research, Peter Norvig, offered their graduate-level artificial intelligence course online for free" and drew 160,000 students—the top thousand of whom were invited to send the professor their resumes so he could relay them to Silicon Valley tech companies.[60] The University of North Texas "called in the management consulting firm Bain & Company, famous for helping corporate America restructure its operations, to assist the university in designing the college of the future for its branch campus in Dallas. The model shaped by Bain called for a limited number of majors tied to the needs of the local economy (such as business and information technology.)"[61] You needn't be a corporate skeptic like me—much less a lawyer worried about conflicts of interest—to question the wisdom of pinning your institution's future to the needs of a protean business world, and of becoming the handmaidens of entities that have, to say the least, not always acted responsibly for the greater good. Remember the first Internet boom and crash around the turn of the millennium? Remember the pre-2008 days when going to work on Wall Street was not only a sure thing financially but at least vaguely socially respectable? If the local economy suddenly shifts, what internal compasses will those students be left with to respond to the changes? Yet I have no doubt that the so-called forward thinking driving those business partnerships is born of a great, unquestioned, and troubling assumption in American life: corporate partnership is always a positive good. Universities are about

59. Selingo, *College (Un)bound*, xii.

60. Ibid., xii–xiii.

61. Ibid., xiii.

helping students build independent minds, selves, even souls. When we say "rich lives," we're not talking about money—but money is the only language corporations recognize. Like technology, the inherent qualities of corporate partnership inherently undermine the nature of what is—necessarily—our countercultural work, focused on cultivating the unguessable, unquantifiable, inward, and defiantly unprofitable texture of the individual. And technology is one of the forces that can smooth away that texture to make the individual little more than a good consumer, hooked on the added "value" of the complexity-easing, fun toy provided to you at your college orientation with a lot of empty rhetoric about how it enhances your educational experience. Your interaction with real people in a learning-centered physical space enhances your educational experience. No Twitter feed or obsolete-on-birth Jornada can change that.

When we look at the way technology has inserted itself as a "solution" to human complexities in education, we can see, again, the way that engineering-think (again, when you have a hammer, the world looks like a nail) means misinterpreting and warping the nature of the very thing you're trying to "fix" and impoverishing the users you claim to serve. One example of this is MOOCs, or "Massively Open Online Courses"—a fad of the last couple of years, now apparently (and thankfully) in decline. In what is obviously my partial, prejudiced, and ignorant definition—to paraphrase Jane Austen[62]—MOOCs are basically packages of videotaped lectures and online quizzes sold by elite universities and their corporate partners to smaller universities under a smiling mask of "student empowerment." Usually, students enrolled in a MOOC watch filmed lectures by a professor from another, more elite university, take tests, and conduct discussion forums online—sometimes while they are still enrolled at their actual college, the faculty of which might well be displaced from their own classrooms by the MOOC. Sure, online courses can give access to non-college students who want to learn from professors too, which is great. But their presence in universities at least ostensibly built on real professors is fueled by a tautology: technology must be the best solution because it is the most efficient (and profitable) which makes it the best because it is technology. But poke this bubble (or the cloud?) with one fact and it pops: real education is fundamentally antithetical to such uses of technology, because it thrives on just the sort of human nuance, complexity, and relationships in particular places and times that technology would erase as "inefficient" because they don't reduce to numbers. As Hannah Arendt and others after her have accurately discerned,

---

62. From the title of Austen's satirical manuscript "The History of England from the reign of Henry the 4th to the death of Charles the 1st, by a partial, prejudiced, & ignorant Historian" (1791), written when she was fifteen.

"efficiency" so often means sanding down the edges of human particularity until everyone reaches an ideal of perfection as determined by a central totalitarian—or corporate—entity which has wedged itself into a human relationship for its own benefit. I think of Arendt when Anat Agarwal, president of for-profit MOOC company edX, "described the standard professor as basically just 'pontificating' and 'spouting content'" (even in front of the very professors and administrators to whom he was trying to sell the course—doesn't that violate the basic law of public relations?). Or when Sebastian Thrun congratulates himself in "Matrix" terms for abandoning the practices of traditional education: "There's a red pill and a blue pill, and you can take the blue pill and go back to your classroom and lecture your twenty students. But I have taken the red pill."[63]

The MOOC boom is now being called to account for the educational fad—even fraud—that it is. On April 29, 2013, the philosophy faculty of San Jose State University published an open letter to Harvard professor Michael Sandel, the creator and star of the "JusticeX" MOOC (an online version of his deservedly famous political theory course "Justice.") San Jose State had been "asked to pilot" JusticeX as part of a new contract with edX (a company associated with MIT and Harvard.) They refused to do so, explaining,

> There is no pedagogical problem in our department that JusticeX solves, nor do we have a shortage of faculty capable of teaching our equivalent course. We believe that long-term financial considerations motivate the call for massively open online courses (MOOCS) at public universities such as ours. Unfortunately, the move to MOOCs comes at great peril to our university. We regard such courses as a serious compromise of quality of education and, ironically for a social justice course, a case of social injustice.[64]

One by one, they name the costs of shifting to MOOCs. Students lose mentorship and interaction with a live specialist in the field and with fellow learners. Some professors (especially adjuncts) may be fired, replaced with another university's talking heads on a screen. A passively watched video of a distant classroom flattens diversity of perspectives and of relationships to the place where students actually are. Professors can no longer design their own courses to fit their own students' needs. And education based on interaction with a real person becomes the domain of the privileged, just as the expensive preschool features hours of cognitively enriching play while

63. Bromwich, "The High-Tech Mess," 50.

64. Text available at http://www.chronicle.com/article/the-document-an-open-letter/138937.

the bargain preschool parks kids in front of a TV set. "Public universities will no longer provide the same quality of education," they write, "and will not remain on par with well-funded private ones. Teaching justice through an educational model that is spearheading the creation of two social classes in academia thus amounts to a cruel joke."[65]

Of course, as philosophy professors, they discern what's really at stake. "We believe the purchasing of online and blended courses is not driven by concerns about pedagogy," they write, "but by an effort to restructure the US university system in general, and our own California State University system in particular. If the concern were pedagogically motivated, we would expect faculty to be consulted and to monitor quality control. On the other hand, when change is financially driven and involves a compromise of quality it is done quickly, without consulting faculty or curriculum committees, and behind closed doors. This is essentially what happened with SJSU's contract with edX," which seems to have been presented to the faculty more or less as a *fait accompli*.[66]

Fundamentally, higher education has to keep insisting on the value of the web of human relationships—student, professor, and ideas—that only we can provide in the way we do, and we have to resist corporate efforts to insert themselves in between, particularly with technology as the Trojan horse. If assessments, measurements, scores, and the like are so all-encompassing and reliable as the way to measure what students are doing, and if Technology in the Classroom is so all-fired good for them and for us, how can I account for the unquantifiable thing I see among even the best-measured, highest-scoring students I teach—a longing for meaning, a sense that the affluent, technologically smoothed society they're living in is cheating them out of some rich texture of experience on this Earth? If technology is such an unmitigated good for human beings, why hasn't it eradicated rather than (as Hannah Arendt claimed) exacerbated war, oppression, and their fundamental cause—the notion that with technology all obstacles to whatever one desires, including other people, can be engineered away? For instance, I believe another of the "disruptors" we've discussed—the "regrouping of American communities"—is linked to and even exacerbated by technology: even as American public life fragments into armed opinion camps and individual living rooms lit by TV sets, cognitively rich educational and even life experiences (digital and not) are becoming the domain of children and families with money. Affluent schools at all levels are able to provide carefully designed activities and contact with teachers—the hands-on variety of

65. Ibid.
66. Ibid.

pedagogies and experiences, including contact with caring adults, that has been shown to improve not only children's social skills but the literal structures of their brains, and that poorer schools literally can't afford. And these differences in preparation are visible all the way up the academic chain— including in our classrooms. To borrow a notion from that wild American "disruptor" and abolitionist John Brown, we as a society and as individuals are sowing the wind to reap the whirlwind if we can't get real about the way our tools are remaking our selves and our lives.

So here I am again, back at my old-school, highly unprofitable belief: college is ultimately not about money, and it needs to help students see that life is about more than money too. This goal is obscured by a lot of other confusion (including some highly profitable confusion) about what education in general is and is for. My own answer, again: college is about becoming a self with something constructive to say. That independent, flexible, curious self is going to be able to adapt and get along wherever it is. And to get the most out of your education, you have got to keep money, and the values and language structured by it, out of places where it doesn't belong. Money may just be the thing that enters and confuses the real purpose of higher ed as it enters and confuses politics—cutting *we the people* out of both. That's why we've got to cast money out—or at least back into its proper role, in our minds and institutional structures—to clear our own thinking about what we, and they, are really working for. The critical thinking practices woven into a good college education prepares you for navigating these systems, and what they do to our world, and what they do to you.

It's one of my fondest hopes that college helps people do this, prompting a trickle-down, trickle-up, trickle-out-and-all-over effect that makes all aspects of our society more dignified and more worthy of full, ethical human flourishing. Becoming a self with something to say also means being able to hold yourself to account, to call bullshit on yourself in addition to those around you, to push yourself to be just a little bit better of a person than you are right now. It's a tall order, and it's complicated by the reality that college-educated people are still functioning in a world where sub-literate best sellers, political cliché, and celebrities' Instagram feeds are offered to us as food for adult minds. This means we need to ask, as students and teachers and administrators: how are we building selves that can not just survive but reshape this world? In farmer and writer Shannon Hayes's book *Radical Homemakers* (2010), a woman describes being with her friend as she dies—loving, attentive, standing up sturdily to the grief, and simply being there.[67] I've been there myself. When I read this

67. Hayes, *Radical Homemakers*, 152–153.

book years ago, a question flickered through my brain: *as a teacher, am I helping to make people who can do* this? Philosopher Theodor Adorno (1903–1960) famously wrote, "The premier demand upon all education is that Auschwitz not happen again . . . . Every debate about the ideals of education is trivial and inconsequential compared to this single ideal: never again Auschwitz."[68] I see the truth in that, and elaborate on it to myself: Am I helping students assert their own human value against the technological and economic forces bent on reducing them to unthinking consumers or easily replaceable workers? Am I helping students to become people who honor that which is beyond themselves and their own present needs—who can get lost in wonder at a book, another creature, a scientific theory, a work of art, and so many other signs of the big web of life beyond oneself? If "never again Auschwitz" is the goal of any education worth the name— and I think it is—how *are* we preparing students to identify and resist the threats to compassion, freedom, dignity, and responsibility in their own lives and in the world? What will prevent us from committing a crime as great as Auschwitz against our fellow humans and nonhumans on our frail Earth, as the global warming emergency deepens, if not for the imperishable conscience we carry, cherish, and sustain within ourselves?

So I teach courses that explicitly ask first-year students: "What is your education for? What are you doing here?" I talk with students who find their way to my office, in conversations that have been known to last for an hour, sometimes two. I try not to be afraid to let a silence fall. I meet with advanced creative writing students once every two weeks to read drafts of their senior projects, nudging them to think of audiences beyond Luther and of themselves as writers, not just students. Outside on a gorgeous fall day, we try to find the perfect onomatopoeic word for the sound of leaves in the wind or the feeling of a fuzzy caterpillar's hundred legs crawling over your skin. In my syllabi, there is one section labeled "course rules" and another called "your rights." In my seminar on William Blake, students and I learn to make prints with relief etching—copper, wax, acid, and press— just as he did two hundred years ago. We go to undergraduate research conferences and to the Iowa Writers Workshop, three hours south of us, and I glow with pride as my students stand in a circle, chatting with Gary Shteyngart, while I'm on the other side of the room. We try to say to each other, in a variety of ways, *This is your one wild and precious life. This is your chance. What will you do next?*

At the end of one semester, saying goodbye to a passionate and committed group of creative writers, I spoke from the heart. You'll find there are

68. Adorno, "Education After Auschwitz," 191.

basically two tracks most people get through school, I said. One is doing the minimum to get by, and the other is doing more than the minimum, but always, and only, with an eye to what's "correct," driven by pleasing someone else. What you want to do is hit the third track, the third rail—that's where the electricity is, that's what drives the train forward.[69] That's the path you want to follow—discover what's going to make your education matter to you, stumble across that live wire of interest and energy in your spirit and your life, and ride that rail all the way into your future as far as it takes you. Figure out what's at stake for you in pursuing your education, and keep plugging your-self into that. Of course, the electrical metaphors (as this group reminded me, laughing) are potentially unfortunate. But their eyes shone. They knew what I was getting at. They saw the truth of what my father, soon to retire from his forty-year surgical career, had said to me the week before: "Ours is not a society where 'being rich' is a sufficient goal in life anymore. It's just out of reach for most honest people. The ordinary people like you and me are going to have to find some inner motivation for life, some way to take delight in what they see around them and what they do every day."

"Yes," I said, "that is what I try to teach my students." And I do. If I can believe I have helped to prepare resilient, curious selves for the world—and for the way, in Pema Chodron's words, it will throw them out of the nest, again and again—then I will have been a true educator, and done a good life's work to touch the world, and other lives beyond my own, in ways I can't yet see.

69. See Weldon, "The Third Rail."

6

Practice a self-reliant, hands-on life, which means asking what you really need and want in the place you really are.

> "Call a thing immoral or ugly, soul-destroying or a degradation of man, a peril to the peace of the world or to the well-being of future generations; as long as you have not shown it to be 'uneconomic,' you have not really questioned its right to exist, grow, and prosper."

> —E. F. SCHUMACHER, *SMALL IS BEAUTIFUL: ECONOMICS AS IF PEOPLE MATTERED* (1973)[1]

> "You don't think your way into a new kind of living. You live your way into a new kind of thinking."

> —HENRI J. M. NOUWEN

GIVEN THAT MONEY HAS been perhaps the single most persistent challenge in my life, I might seem like an odd person to be growing $64 tomatoes. Perhaps I exaggerate—I've never counted up my actual cost per tomato. But writer William Alexander did, and that gave him the title of his 2006 book *The $64 Tomato: How One Man Nearly Lost His Sanity, Spent a Fortune, and Endured an Existential Crisis in the Quest for the Perfect Garden*. In a series of calculations factoring in (and amortizing over twenty years the cost of some of) the construction and hardware and supplies and plants and excluding his own labor for his backyard garden, Alexander arrives at a cost of $64 per tomato and a new respect for professional farmers. "Every time I'm done

---

1. Schumacher, *Small is Beautiful*, 44.

picking sugar snap peas or rise from my stoop, aching, from picking green beans," he writes, "I marvel that I can buy this stuff in the green market for a dollar a pound. How can anyone possibly grow green beans for a dollar a pound? I can't even pick them for a dollar a pound, it takes so long. It's a miracle that any farmer stays in business, but God bless them."[2]

I throw out the $64 tomato—sorry, unfortunate choice of words—to get a common objection to backyard gardening and "sustainable" home DIY (do-it-yourself) projects on the table: isn't it cheaper to just buy it at the farmer's market? Or buy it at the store? Even as the writer of a blog called the Cheapskate Intellectual, I've always hesitated to do a breakdown on my cost per home-raised food item, because although I know the cost wouldn't be $64 each, it would probably be higher than I could justify in economically rational terms, almost certainly higher than the lovely organic vegetables at my local farmer's market and food co-op. Yet I still keep nosing into this question, because it's the next part that's really worth answering: "Is it worth all that trouble?"

Keep your eyes on those two terms—*worth* and *trouble*—because they swirl around within a current DIY renaissance, agitating our desires, fears, and hopes like a set of homemade, hand-felted fabric-softening dryer balls. Books and blogs, including mine, on urban homesteading, sustainable living, simple living, cooking/cleaning/canning, and similar terms number in the hundreds by now, with more every day.[3] I'm not going to be adding to that abundance of riches by turning this chapter into DIY how-to alone, but I will discuss my own DIY home practices to illustrate a larger continuing journey toward my own version of self-reliance and awareness, why I think it's important, and how you might try your hand at it too. My reasons for DIY are less about monetary value (although they do save me money, especially long-term and in terms of health) than about continually reminding myself and others what *value* on our ecologically interconnected planet means, and has to mean. Since *economy* comes from the Greek *oikonomia*—literally, "running of the *oikos*," or house—it benefits each of us to remember that the national "economy" we are used to seeing worshiped as an abstract, distant god is still a collection of individual households and their individual decisions.[4] My DIY practices keep me grounded (literally)—connected to and mindful of actions and consequences, rooted in a mini-ecosystem called *home* that is irreversibly connected to other systems, everywhere.

2. Alexander, "Excerpt: 'The $64 Tomato.'"

3. And, of course, there's *The Onion's* inimitable satire (February 21, 2001): "Grueling Household Tasks Of 19th Century Enjoyed By Suburban Woman" (http://www.theonion.com/articles/grueling-household-tasks-of-19th-century-enjoyed-b,1519/).

4. Thanks to Philip Freeman for this information.

Good gardening is about noticing—when that weed is about to go to seed, whether there are caterpillars on the cherry tree leaves, when the broccoli or tomatoes or eggplant is really ripe or needs to sit for one more day, when the birdbath needs to be emptied and refilled to flush out mosquito larvae. Caring for and living within that system is a matter of good habits that form the less tangible "ecosystem" of the self as well. It's good for a person to feel connected to and responsible to the world around her. For the same reason I go to yoga class and work to fit in writing time no matter how busy the school week is, I garden and hang out my clothes on the line and compost my scraps. Practice is a powerful thing. What some call *trouble* in this context I call a *reminder*—an action that lets me literally re-mind myself by refreshing and refocusing my attention. When I walk or get on my bike instead of into my car (and in my small town in the summer, I can often go at least two weeks without driving at all), I reroot myself in the reality that there is no "away," that "convenience" is purchased at a lot of (often invisible) costs to the environment, and that when I choose this action I vote against a mass of corporate and political decisions that would take away my right to make choices at all, if they could.

If you read a book like *Never Done* (1982), Susan Strasser's fascinating history of American housework, or if you think about the twentieth century, you'll remember the strange effect of domestic technologies justified (as we justify our iPhones and laptops) by *convenience*—washing machines and dishwashers and other "labor-saving devices" liberated women from what truly was backbreaking drudgery but sent us into a tailspin of anomie and confusion prompted by what suddenly became a whole new question of selfhood, identity, and what was a "worthwhile" way to spend all that newly opened-up time. Betty Friedan's *The Feminine Mystique* (1963) famously identified "the problem without a name" as housewives took their children to school, loaded their brand-new dishwashers and clothes dryers, mopped their kitchen floors, looked around their quiet houses, and wondered, "Is this all there is?" As seen in Shannon Hayes' groundbreaking book *Radical Homemakers* (2010), this effect of "homemaking" can make home DIY a difficult sell, especially in feminist terms. "It was no small wonder that Betty Friedan's book sparked the revolution that sent American women into the workforce in droves," Hayes writes, "seeking opportunities to challenge themselves, fulfill their creative potential, and have a meaningful impact on society."[5] When "housework" becomes equated with limitation, even a form of slavery, for women—and domestic work was, and is, seen as women's responsibility—unhooking housework from gender and

5. Hayes, *Radical Homemakers*, 31.

proclaiming that women should not be the only ones responsible for it are necessary and welcome acts.

However, the movement of women into the workforce—without any corresponding effort by men to pick up the slack in parenting and home-making—re-implicated them in a web of economic injustice and marketing exploitation. Marketers had once tried to massage the housewife's anomie into consumer desire: researchers interviewed by Friedan in the late 1950s and early 1960s stated with amazing candor that "the store will sell [the housewife] more if it will understand that the real need she is trying to fill by shopping is not anything she can buy there."[6] They stepped into that gap of desire by selling women more of the same—more household goods and per-sonal care products, to reinforce what more and more women experienced as a bright, superficial shell of "housewife" identity without ever touch-ing their underlying need for meaning. Yet once women moved into the workforce, business "seized an even greater opportunity, whereby a cheaper labor force could be recruited and even more products could be sold to fill the empty spaces that were now left at home."[7] Those "empty spaces" were often filled not only by highly processed "convenience" foods but by workers (often other women) from socially disadvantaged groups, since, as historian Glenna Matthews writes, "if [domestic] work is despised, it will be performed by someone whose sex, class, or race—perhaps all three—consign her to an inferior status. If such work is despised, we will be much more likely to allow corporate America to manipulate the nature of homes and of housework."[8] As *Radical Homemakers* argues, hiring help becomes a problem when it reinforces notions of the home as a sphere of effort *not worthy* of sustained attention or time. Many of the "radical homemakers"—men *and* women—Hayes interviews have stepped away from professional careers in order to step off what they came to experience as a hamster-wheel cycle of "getting and spending" (Wordsworth again) that ultimately left their families disconnected and their bodies and minds scattered, with no sense of an ordered domestic world in which to recuperate and be together. Hayes quotes RH-er Rebecca James, "who grew up in a series of suburban neighborhoods and now lives with her family on three acres of land in the rural Northeast," as saying, "I think that we're losing and risking emotional connectivity in the pursuit of stuff constantly. It's a sickness, and so many of us don't even realize how much we're doing it, how ubiquitous it has be-come . . . our actual needs are so much larger emotionally and so much

6. Ibid., 30.

7. Ibid., 31.

8. Ibid., 45.

smaller [materially] than we have come to describe them in American society."[9] There is no one model of "radical homemaking" or "do-it-yourself," as Hayes's book and many others indicate—although "changing your home from a locus of consumption into a locus of production" is a basic tenet—but what they all have in common is the desire to foreground your own household's needs and values, as you have defined them, against social, material, and corporate imperatives that you choose to question or to reject.

We can't forget: the nature of a corporation is to manipulate public opinion in order to increase profit and value for its shareholders. That's its nature. But despite the marketing strategies attempting to conceal this fact, global capitalism's prerogatives increasingly clash with our own, and with the reality of life on an ecologically interconnected and imperiled planet. As seen in Naomi Oreskes' and Eric Conway's *Merchants of Doubt* (2010), the same "scientific evidence" fueling global warming denial (and continued corporate profits) is provided and disseminated by the same public relations firms that helped Phillip Morris and other big tobacco companies carry out their "smoking is good for you" campaigns in the mid-twentieth century. Yet if we look at the behavior—rather than the public rhetoric—of companies facing climate change, we can see some interesting acknowledgements of reality: "in recent years," Naomi Klein writes, "quite a number of major multinational corporations have begun to speak openly about how climate change might impact their businesses, and insurance companies closely track and discuss the increased frequency of major disasters."[10] Big business also understands that when ordinary people wake up to the reality of global warming and to the role of our own buying choices in it, we will a) be really freaked out and angry and b) adjust those buying choices accordingly, which means c) a lot of businesses will lose a lot of money. Therefore, it's in their financial interests to keep us doubting the science and happily shopping-'n'-driving just as long as they can, with a little greenwashing here and there. Yet as I've said earlier, the marketing-fueled desires on which their mythologies float—your pursuit of your desires and conveniences has no cost; we live in a world of limitless abundance for everyone; there will always be "more" of whatever you want when you want it, right there on the shelf at the store, with no effort or sacrifice from you—are no longer affordable, for our planet or for us.

If you look around you, you can see this kind of corporate consumerism in the form of a million big-box stores and chain restaurants creeping over our land and towns, flattening us into dependent consumers and

9. Hayes, *Radical Homemakers,* 118.
10. Klein, *This Changes Everything,* 49.

erasing the distinctive details of particular places. Yet in recent years movements like Slow Food and the Ark of Taste, along with memoirs by farmers
and chefs like Kristen Kimball (*The Dirty Life*) and Dan Barber (*The Third
Plate: Field Notes on the Future of Food*), assert what I want to call the humanity of food—the fact that food, like people, expresses its particular rootedness
in and birth from a place in a certain combination of qualities you can only
find there. (This is the winemaking notion of *terroir*, applicable, I'd argue,
to other kinds of food, too.) Small farmers and artisan producers are fighting back against the corporate steamroller, and, crucially, they are assisted
by consumers themselves. As Paul Kingsnorth writes, "These corporations
aren't afraid of governments and laws—they can buy their way around those.
They're afraid of consumers, and what happens when we use our power . . . .
What I'm after is the diversity and character which is created when people are
given the freedom and the power to express themselves without interference
from deskbound, rulebound profit-watchers in some distant business park.
What I'm after is the chimera which the ever-expanding consumer economy
promises us constantly, but rarely seems to deliver: choice."[11]

This is why it's so important to push at those two terms, *value* and
trouble, alongside Morton's *ecological thought* (from my early chapters) and
the overall concept of *attention*. What makes "radical homemaking" as it is
practiced in many homes (including mine) different from the stifling cage
of midcentury "housewife" conformity—imposed on many women without
their consent—is that RH (for shorthand convenience) is based on constant
self-evaluation and choice, all aimed at resistance to corporate exploiters,
marketers, and manipulators in the service of greater goods whose truth
you, yourself, see and believe in, and it involves the meaningful participation of all members of the household. You treat your consumer dollars as a
powerful vote that you make every day by what you buy or what you don't.
This means you work to short-circuit your own habitual default choices
with active ones, considering the impact of your choice on yourself, your
thinking, and the ecological web in which you're included. For instance,
I don't have backyard chickens, although some of my friends do, because
chickens, in my life, would be the one-thing-too-much to do and manage
every day. So I buy eggs at the farmer's market or co-op. Where I spend
money is always in adjustment, and I try to do it not only to get good value
but to shift conversations about what value is and who's been getting to decide that, as opposed to who should.

Running home ecosystems can take you into some interesting places.
Let me show you my worm bin—or, the slightly more socially acceptable

11. Kingsnorth, *Real England*, 41.

term, "vermicomposting system." Like the rest of my rural Southern family, I have a pretty specific starting point with worms, based on memories of jamming tubes of ivermectin paste between a struggling horse's back teeth. At some level of my thinking, worms may always be animal, parasitical, their interactions with humans vaguely squeamish unless a hook and fishing line are involved. Yet the first time I thrust a shovel into my black Iowa river-bottom backyard soil and turned, and marveled at how honeycombed with wormholes it was—and watched the rosy earthworms, some as big as baby snakes, wriggling out of sight—I realized worms build the soil that builds my food. Not for nothing, perhaps, is one of the many brain-busting mysteries of physics called by this homely word—wormholes. Who knew that there were even different species of worms, that the yard worms are different from these small ones that can live in their house bin in the dark, turning food scraps into soil? Not me.

After reading about vermicomposting and talking to some friends who'd done it, I decided to get some worms of my own. First I went to see a local gardening legend and mentor of mine, David, who maintains a multistory vermicomposting bin (sold as the Worm Factory 360) in his basement. He lifted the lid and scooped out three big wriggling handfuls of little red earthworms mixed with coffee grounds and vegetable scraps. The smell was earthy and sweet. "That's how fast the worms work," he advised. "I just fed them, and boy, that stuff didn't smell this good when I put it in there." He dropped them into the plastic tub I'd brought along and within five seconds they were gone, burrowed into the mass of scraps I'd prepared for them. I discovered quickly that the plastic tub was not the way to go (no drainage and too little space), so I got a Worm Factory myself, which has served me well ever since. A series of stacking plastic trays with perforated bottoms set over a drainage basin, the Worm Factory lets worms migrate upward into fresh layers of compostable scraps (when one tray fills, you stack another on top of it and fill that one, too) while the finished compost builds up in the lower layers and moisture drains out from the bottom. Periodically, you can empty the lower trays of finished compost into your garden and turn the spigot on the drainage basin to release the dark brown "worm tea" into a container, then dilute it with water to apply to your plants. (Potted citrus trees love it; so do the pale, dispirited end-of-season annuals you can pick up for cheap at your garden store.) The worms go about their business in the dark in a corner of my basement next to the chest freezer. Fruit-fly issues are addressed with simple homemade traps made from an inch or two of cider vinegar in the bottom of a jar and a paper cone to lure them in, but not out. I can't smell the worm bin until I descend into the basement and stand over it, and even then, it's not a bad smell. Overall, the worm bin has been a big help; able to eat literally everything but meat, dairy, citrus, or onions (including vacuum cleaner–canister contents, newspaper, coffee grounds, fruit cores, vegetable peels, old bread, and dryer lint), the worms, along with my backyard compost pile and recycling practices, have reduced my household waste dramatically. In a typical month, the standard 13-gallon trash can in my kitchen takes at least two weeks to fill.

Despite the "gross!" reflexes they inspire, worms take you into the heart of the processes that turn your body, and the earth, with the seasons, and make both of them grow. Food becomes soil becomes more food becomes more soil, and we are nudged to rethink what we may too easily label "dirty," including compost, food waste, soil, and worms. Reality is bound to cycles of the land and the body to which so much in modern consumer culture, with its insistence on tidy cliches and store-bought solutions and a reality created and mediated by things with screens, is deeply traitorous, and deeply false. Acknowledging the messy grandeur of biological reality—death, birth, dirt, blood, entropy, growth, at once rooted in and reaching beyond human life— can yield in us an attitude of what I can only call a kind of cosmic unflappability. Look how much happier and healthier we become, as people and families and communities, when we lose our hysterical insistence on tidying and on intellectually sanitizing the sources of our food, in particular, out of sight, letting ourselves and our children believe that grapes and ground beef alike magically appear in the aisles of our local SuperTarget, untainted by labor violations or animal cruelty. Look how our lives improve when we let go of the need to make our houses look like magazine centerfolds; clean and pretty doesn't have to mean scorched by groundwater-polluting, fragrance-added chemicals or cluttered with tchotckes made by children in Bangladesh. (So often, "clean," especially in terms of food, has come to mean "made somewhere else, by someone else.") Look what happens when we accept that the meat on our plate came from an animal that died and that our actions and choices in killing and consuming it can make its death and life dignified or degrading, or when we choose not to eat meat. Look at everything that changes when we make peace with the fact that reality is cyclical, entropic, messy, and beautiful beyond any definition of beauty that our modern screen "reality" can offer. Look at how our vision of the physical world and the realities it embodies can become—well—incarnational. Here is the physical, sensory world. And here we touch the edge of all the intangible things that it can mean. You really can touch that edge, and travel as far along it as you want. As Episcopal priest and author Barbara Brown Taylor writes in *An Altar in the World*, "What is saving my life now is becoming more fully human, trusting that there is no way to God apart from real life in the real world."[12]

Let me show you my clothesline. When it's a warm, sunny day and a breeze is blowing, hanging laundry on my outdoor line rather than tossing it in an electric-run clothes dryer is an obvious move. With a few minutes of "work" (run the retractable line across the yard, hook it to the corner of the garage, bring a basket of wet laundry—washed in eco-safe detergent and cold water, to save water-table contamination and water-heating fuel costs—up from the basement, and clip it piece by piece to the line), I've saved burning money and fossil fuel by burning calories instead (which feels really good when you sit at a desk as much as I do.) The pleasures of this small task are considerable: the simple repetitiveness of clipping humble wooden clothes-pins to cloth, the satisfaction of sheets billowing in the sun, the savor of those line-dried pillowcases against my face at night before I go to sleep.

A hands-on life isn't about giving up all convenience, it's about sec-ond-guessing yourself to make sure you aren't participating, out of habit, in things you'd rather not. Convenience would say I should put the clothes in the dryer even on a sunny day, but what would I save by doing that? If I threw those clothes in the dryer, I'd be spending not just money but—again—fossil fuels, the irreplaceable bones of dinosaurs. Would I really have done anything more pleasurable or useful with those three minutes than standing outside in the sun and wind? Do I really want to wind myself one notch tighter in the web of peak oil because I decline to spend three minutes clipping clothes to a line—even aside from the fact that clothes smell better, keep their shapes, and wear longer if they aren't tumble-dried?

When defeated in one line of argument, "convenience" takes a Protean shape to slip in line for another attack: appearances. Some neighborhoods don't allow clotheslines; even when tucked behind someone else's house, they look "messy." So, of course, is a Appalachian mountaintop-removal mine. But these appearance-based attacks can unveil the hypocrisy of aesthetics based on pleasure, convenience, and the out-of-sight cushion of fossil fuel that holds them up. A couple years ago, two of our small town's gardening group members—following a neighbor's anonymous complaint—were no-tified that they might be in violation of a city ordinance against gardening in the boulevard, the strip of grass between sidewalk and curb in front of most houses. Yet our members' gardens—neat and attractive in both cases—did not actually create visibility problems for those in cars and driveways (a legitimate concern), as the city police chief and the city manager confirmed. Luckily, we avoided problems of the kind that have plagued other gardeners

12. Taylor, *An Altar in the World*, xvii.

like the woman in Tulsa whose attractive front-yard garden was bulldozed for being "too tall" or the woman in Michigan who drew fire from her neighbors over a pretty, attractive front yard that in most gardeners' terms was just edible landscaping.[13]

To be clear: nobody should have to live next to a yard overgrown, untended, or filled with trash; having had neighbors neglect dead squirrels deep in long grass and kiddie pools filled with mosquito-breeding rainwater, I know that laissez-faire doesn't work for yards in a community. What you do in your yard affects your neighbors' property values, health, and enjoyment. But we shouldn't leap to the notion that if it's anything but a close-clipped slate of chemically greened grass, it's overgrown. Objections to gardens make you ask, "What is this really about?" Why do so many people object so viscerally to the sight of gardens in a front yard (or even a back yard) even when those gardens present no sight line-blocking or other hazard? Why do so many people consider even the best-tended and most aesthetically pleasing garden "messy," worthy only to be in the backyard, if anywhere? What accounts for the strange hostility with which some people *do* still approach food gardens? Why do we build golf courses in the desert? And why, when we as Americans need to practice household self-sufficiency and sustainability more than ever, are so many of us still hamstrung by aesthetic preferences we can literally no longer afford?

The answer, I think, lies in the fact that so much of our aesthetic standards, especially when it comes to that great class-aspirant possession, our homes, are based on distance and yearning—specifically a yearning *up,* in terms of an interlocking web of race and social class. Once you get past a certain baseline of tidiness and sanitary cleanliness that's good for everybody (see *dead squirrels and mosquitoes,* above), you start to run into the fact that standards of taste often recur back to who's in and who's out, who's us and who's not, who must be held at a distance and who stands at that distance, longing to get in. (It's not for nothing that the archetypical image of wealth and prosperity in American culture is a mansion on a hill, from Cotton Mather's "shining city" to the Kern/Hammerstein standard "The Folks Who Live on the Hill" to Neil Young and Bruce Springsteen.) An aesthetic ideal gets more desirable as it gets harder for the greater number of people to achieve. Perhaps it's logical, then, that so many of our aesthetics of personal grooming, decorating, and landscaping are still based on wealthy white folks, who are positioned even today as the ultimate aspirational class: bodies toned by lots of sports, straight hair, expensive clothes

13. See http://grist.org/cities/tulsa-authorities-bulldoze-edible-garden-for-being-too-tall/ and https://www.wired.com/2011/07/michigan-woman-may-get-93-days-in-jail-for-planting-a-garden/.

worn casually, and housing and landscape seeming to exist only in response to pleasure, never to need—a *weltanschauung* based on restraint and the bedrock of privilege and wealth that makes possible such (apparent) effortlessness. (Food gardens must be out of sight, but golf courses—ecological nightmare temples to pleasure—are always prominently displayed.) As a curly-haired gardener, I can testify there's a strain of prejudice that links the keep-your-garden-out-of-sight mind-set with the straighten-your-hair kind: gardens and curly hair alike are ethnic, wild, uncontrolled, signs of troublesome bodies and their troublesome natures that will never be quite subdued, and never quite fit in with "our" way of doing things. And as anyone who's been paying attention to the last fifty years or so has noticed, climbing up into wealth is a game that's now so difficult it's nearly impossible.[14] But that doesn't mean we'll stop trying.

This all has its roots (pardon the pun) in an idea of gentlemanliness I recognize from the rakish Romantic poet Lord Byron and the even older Italian ideal of *sprezzatura*—doing everything with ease, remaining always faintly removed from the fray, never appearing to work too hard for anything. Yet a look at English history shows that even uber-gentlefolk weren't afraid to adjust their cultural aesthetics when the need arose. Even more than Americans, the British countered the food rationing of World War II with victory gardens, farm-volunteer programs, and efforts to use every available scrap of ground to raise food, including the moat in the Tower of London. As Bill McKibben writes in his book *Eaarth*: "In the course of the war years, Britain managed to increase food production 91 percent. Small gardens—allotments, the English call them—sprang up everywhere. For example, the wife of the keeper of coins and medals at the British Museum planted rows of beans, peas, onions, and lettuces at the museum's entrance. Almost seven thousand 'pig clubs' sprung up throughout the country, with swine being kept in, among other places, 'the (drained) swimming pool of the Ladies Carlton Club in Pall Mall.'"[15] Even this toniest of destinations set aside codes of "taste" to get personally involved in the war effort, acknowledging no illusory distance between "over there" and "at home." Fundamentally, as we've seen, human misunderstanding of ecology involves similar illusions of distance—"I am not a part of this." An understanding of "landscaping" as something merely ornamental, featuring big-box–store annuals clustered politely around a tablecloth of lawn, is outmoded and, again, unaffordable. This water- and pesticide-heavy aesthetic of "gardening," modeled on the golf course, is a kind of damage that keeps on giving.

14. See Thomas Piketty, *Capital in the Twenty-First Century*.
15. McKibben, *Eaarth*, 166.

It makes your interaction with your yard, or your garden, a hands-off one: mow, spray, cut, forget.

The good news is that the spray-it-and-forget-it aesthetic is under attack, not only from the reality of water shortages (even in California and Las Vegas, where they love their defiantly artificial worlds) and the threats pesticides pose to bees (without whom we've got no food supply) but from ordinary people discovering the pleasures of gardening. One July day I was cutting my front yard with my manual reel mower when I felt someone watching me. Two little boys on bicycles were pulled over to the curb, staring round-eyed at the spinning blades. "You want to see how it works?" I asked. Half an hour later, the boys (and their parents) were still pushing the mower back and forth, eating strawberries, exploring my bean teepee, and asking questions. Children often love to garden if given the chance. A seven-year-old neighbor helped me plant blue and white potatoes in the raised bed between my house and his, monitored them daily, then, with great and well-deserved pride, helped me grabble them—oh, wonderful potato-specific verb!—out of the dirt to share with his mom. My eleven-year-old niece feeds, waters, and maintains her backyard chicken flock entirely on her own.

Every summer our urban-gardeners club ("urban" being used loosely in our little town) hosts what we call our "Wok-Out:" a range of members from age two to seventy-five bring produce from their summer gardens to cook in a giant wok set over a charcoal grill, and everyone eats as much as they can hold. This year's meal was typical: into the wok went two kinds of kale, three kinds of eggplants, three kinds of beans and peas, four kinds of peppers, garlic, onions, carrots, chard, broccoli, squash, and a few others I'm forgetting, tossed in olive oil and a mix of simple seasonings—rice wine, soy sauce, sesame oil, and umi plum vinegar. There was rice, wild harvested mushrooms, cucumber-and-tomato salad, and 's'mores on the side. People devoured the food, then sat around chatting in the sun or touring our host's garden (always a side benefit of the wok-out.) A little girl streaked down the hill, shouting "This way to the secret magic cave!" Several of us confessed to thinking the same thing: This event is always so fun, and it's so simple. Wouldn't the world be a great place if *everybody* could eat like this? Maybe, if more people had gardens, more people could. It's our gardening group's hope (enacted through community mentorship programs for new gardeners) that more people will decide to grow something of their own, even if it's just one herb in a pot. Once you eat food that comes from your own soil—miraculously rich and flavorful, a different order of vegetable than what comes from even a very good store—you might never not be a gardener again.

Adjusting our thinking about convenience and aesthetics as DIYers, and our larger attitudes about consumer decisions and financial values, is made more difficult not just by our neighbors' stares but by what's going on in our own brains. You might remember from Chapter One that our neuroanatomy, particularly in young adulthood/late adolescence, can create in us a "present bias," making it harder for us to pay attention to anything beyond our current emotion or pleasure or need. This "present bias" is heightened by a consumer culture constantly shrieking *buy, watch, consume* this *to become* this *type of person*, reducing people to things and identities to trappings of things. Creating consumers is about creating or heightening anxieties, then offering purchasable commodities as "solutions" to those anxieties. Thus before they know it, twentysomethings in particular can get stuck in a perfect storm of consumerism, debt, and anxiety created by what after all could be called socially and even neurologically normal goals: creating social connections in community, building an identity in others' eyes and your own, and generating stimuli and experiences that construct the brain's bank of memory—and thus, perhaps, the self—from the inside. Perhaps that new handbag or pair of shoes or book or item of outdoor gear or dream vacation adventure is, for the younger brain, literally harder to resist, especially when no other experience of the world exists yet to set against it. Just as it's easier to fume against those on one side of an issue if you don't actually know anyone affected by it in ways you aren't, it's easy to grasp at the available straw of consumer goods to cement that always-in-progress thing, your own identity, and dispel that most uncomfortable emotion—fear—when you've got no other way to turn down the volume of that "need" shrieking in your ear.

As I write, I'm smiling a bittersweet smile: in my twenties and early thirties, I went through exactly this. I got good grades in college, where I thrived in a double English and Journalism major and a newly formed Honors Program, edited the literary magazine, took as many creative writing classes as I could, and learned I loved writing, for real. An internship at an advertising firm became a job there, from which I made the transition to graduate school in literature. Yet although my performance in graduate school was outwardly as "successful" as my undergraduate career had been, I couldn't fully admit how deeply panicked and out of my depth I felt. (Now I know this feeling is perfectly normal, and damn near universal.) I'd always read and written pretty much what I wanted and been able to get away with it, seldom working as systematically as I should. Despite my high grades, rapport with students, happiness in the program, and conviction this was the right place for me in the world, I still felt like an imposter, bitten deep with the hidden fear so many academics feel: *they're going to find me out and send me home.* I worked hard. I read constantly. I published scholarly articles and short stories while teaching undergraduates and taking courses and qualifying exams and going to conferences. I made friends and threw parties. But it never felt like enough.

So I went after the external trappings of professional academic identity with everything I had—specifically, every credit card. By the time I graduated with my PhD and secured my first tenure-track job, I was carrying $50,000 in consumer debt. Some was justifiable: I'd had to finance a new car and job-search suits and plane tickets to MLA, the professional conference where I interviewed for jobs. But easily half of it was clothes and meals and concert tickets. Most of all, it was books, from the three different used bookstores and excellent on-campus new bookstore I haunted. If I read about it or met the author at a reading or conference and could justify its purchase to myself—I could write about this! I could teach this! It will help me with my dissertation!—I usually bought it. In addition to the neat little piles of new acquisitions on my apartment coffee table, I kept the library books I'd also checked out. Unsurprisingly, overextension in every direction meant unproductivity in any direction, and too often that those books got read hastily or not at all. I worked multiple jobs and earned a stipend and kept myself afloat, but the bubble of credit card expenditures also lifted me artificially high. I alternated between exuberance and comfort and choking panic when I looked at my books. So much hope and possibility. So much obligation I feared I'd never live up to. So much enthusiasm, so many sparks of new information and ideas. So much fear. All of it was fueled by promises and hard work and following through and discovering but also by a series of little lies to myself that steadily deepened: *I'll get a job and pay all this back. It'll be okay. I'm only twenty-five/-six/-seven/-eight. I have a lot of time.*

I tell this story now to emphasize how common versions of it are, how quickly what seem like defensible consumer choices can turn on us, and how we use money to prop up artificial visions of the people we want to be. I spent years fighting to pay down that debt (which was paid off in full around the time I got tenure) and get these old habits under control. Every year I get better at evaluating purchases and possessions by the truth of my own instincts and emotions: *do I really like and want this in my life as my life is right now? Will I still want this in a week? Do I feel a sense of real pleasure and possibility when I look at this, or do I feel that kind of dutiful 'I should do something with this?'* ('Should,' I've learned, tells me that something's probably not going to happen.) In the past two years alone, I've given away, from my office and from home, at least twelve boxes of books, although more, of course, have come in; as large as it still is, my library has grown into a self-balancing ecosystem with its own estuarial ebb and flow, like the place where a river meets the sea. When I saw how many of the giveaways were new scholarly texts bought in fits of conference or dissertation optimism and barely (or never) opened, I thought about the anxious girl who bought them, and I forgave her. *It's okay. You have enough now, and will continue to have enough.* And that's what it's really all about: let your frontal lobe talk to the rest of your brain about reality, the person you actually are and the life and career you actually have and want. Let yourself settle down and look at what is, and leave space for the good things still to come.[16]

Of course, you can't talk about individual choices for Radical Home-making and DIY without talking about the communities that enable or dis-able them. You can find people practicing self-directed, sustainable living everywhere; for instance, Kelly Coyne and Erik Knutzen, authors of the popular books *The Urban Homestead: Your Guide to Self-Sufficient Living in the Heart of the City* (2008), *Making It: Radical Home Ec for a Post-Consum-er World* (2011), and the blog *Root Simple*, live in Los Angeles. But a DIY journey is easier if it's supported by the resources, choices, and attitudes of a community. I know and regret that everyone's journey is not. But I'm happy to say that my journey is.

In 2005, I moved to Decorah, Iowa, a town of 8,000 people located just south of the Minnesota line and one county west of the Mississippi River. Known for its scenic rivers and towering limestone bluffs and Norwegian-immigrant past, anchored by my school, Luther College, which had been established as a seminary in 1861, Decorah is also more walkable, bikeable, and affordable than any other place I'd ever lived. At first I couldn't believe that the Norman Rockwell-ish things I saw every day were real: kids pedaled along sidewalks in packs, thriving small businesses lined a busy main street, volunteers trundled around in golf carts on summer evenings to water the petunia baskets dangling from each streetlight, spontaneous four-part har-monies erupted from surrounding tables whenever someone sang "Happy Birthday" in a restaurant. (This is deeply Lutheran, I've learned.) There is a twice-weekly farmer's market and a food co-op and little new residential development to be seen—instead, blocks of Victorian homes on streets lined with mature oak, maple, and walnut trees are maintained and updated over time by successive generations of owners, never really having to be reclaimed because they have never been abandoned for new subdivisions in the first

---

16. I've never forgotten a bit of advice Julie Morgenstern received from some fel-low professional organizers that her home "was beautifully organized but *full*. If some-one wanted to send me a huge bouquet, they argued, I'd have no place to put it." My own organizing cycles have taught me this is true: holding onto old stuff can block the flow of new stuff, including new ideas, opportunities, and experiences, into your life. See Morgenstern, "A Style Is Born," 118.

place. The independent bank that anchors Decorah's economy is owned and run by two generations of the family that founded it. When the bank and the school board were working jointly to develop a parking lot—endangering the huge, lovely ash tree that stands there—neighbors and I met with the bank co-vice-president (a grandson of its founder) to ask him to spare the tree. The tree is not only still there but thriving; the bank had it professionally pruned and supported, then had more trees planted on the slope around it. That bank was also a major donor to the eleven-mile bike trail that now circles the town, and it installed new solar panels on its new building's roof. The other co-vice president (the tree-saver's brother) can often be seen out behind the bank on summer weekend afternoons, mowing the grass. On summer evenings, there are community dances with a string band in a century-old schoolhouse outside of town, with windows open to the night and an outhouse in the yard; everyone from teenagers to six-year-olds to couples in their seventies whirls by, waltzing and polka-ing and doing the schottische. There's a craft brewery that beer nerds tell me is a pretty big deal. By one count, there are thirty-nine producers of organic produce, meat, and dairy products in our area. Luther College, where I teach, was one of the first signatories of the American College and University Presidents' Climate Commitment and now maintains a wind turbine, college gardens, and a solar array. All of this is maintained matter-of-factly, with pride and care and little of the hipster preciousness that can mark such downtown revival elsewhere; community life thrives here because it never went away. "We don't really get the boom cycles of the rest of the country, with housing or anything else," explained a local clothing shop owner to me, "but we also don't get the busts." Of course, no community is perfect. But Decorah has offered me more than I ever thought a small rural Iowa town could.

In the years I was getting my own life straight financially and professionally, Decorah gave me a place from which to watch systems unraveling elsewhere, and to think of how to put them right. My time here—2005 to the present—has coincided almost perfectly with the banking crisis, the collapse of the housing bubble, the rise of smartphones and the infiltration of the Internet into every area of our lives, and the crisis of global warming and anxiety about food and energy systems it's prompted. These are also the years that have seen skyrocketing attention to local food, do-it-yourself ways of life, and—a crucial word—resilient communities. Towns and cities that can't supply at least the majority of their own food, water, and energy needs and that lack the sense of civic cohesion that can keep neighbors working together more or less peacefully in emergencies will struggle in the years to come. As many are discovering at their cost, walkable neighborhoods and downtown cores that have become deserted in decades of suburban flight are expensive to reconstruct, in situ or in simulacrum somewhere else. Hurricane Katrina in 2005 and Hurricane Sandy in 2012 brought the world's attention to the plight of coastal cities overwhelmed by rising waters, but inland cities aren't immune, and may have special problems of their own. Phoenix and Las Vegas, car-dependent, sprawling cities made livable by dramatically overdrawn Southwest rivers and air conditioners to mediate the heat that miles of asphalt hold even in the cool desert nights, may go dark in a climate-insecure future, experiencing, as many modern cities will, what urban planners are calling "infrastructure failure interdependencies."[17] And according to William deBuys, author of *A Great Aridness: Climate Change and the Future of the American Southwest* (2011), such cities will have little if any human capital, neighborly cooperation and civic infrastructure, to soften the blows: deBuys calls Phoenix "a city threatened by its particular brand of local politics and economic domination, shaped by more than the usual quotient of prejudice, greed, class insularity, and devotion to raw power."[18] As I wrote a draft of this chapter at 10 PM Central Standard Time on July 1, 2013, the West Coast was experiencing a heat wave with temperatures reaching as high as 125°F. The temperature in Phoenix, where it was nearing sundown, was 109°F. (In Decorah, it was 71°F.) The writer Leslie Marmon Silko, a resident of Tucson, puts this Arizona desert heat in perspective: "Newcomers to Tucson's summer heat are amazed to find their car's rear view mirror lying on the front seat because the glue melts. Car windshields become solar furnaces capable of melting plastic objects left on the car dashboard, including cell phones, sunglasses, cameras, DVDs, and credit cards."[19] And California is now struggling under drought and land subsidence, a settling and sinking of the earth caused by depletion of underground water tables, both of which are fueling fierce competition among farmers, residents, and cities for what resources remain.[20]

Surely more Americans will know the peculiar pain experienced by the people of the Maldives and other Pacific islands as rising seas flood their homelands—the pain of becoming climate refugees, climate exiles. And it might come as a shock to those not tuned in to the environmental-books-and-blogs frequencies to which I'm half-unwillingly addicted. You can be an intelligent person and a diligent watcher of the network news—which breathlessly report "extreme weather" with little or no connection to

17. DeBuys, "Phoenix in the Climate Crosshairs."

18. Ibid.

19. Silko, *The Turquoise Ledge*, 88.

20. See "Water Wars," an episode of the news program *Reveal*: https://www.reveal-news.org/episodes/water-wars/.

"climate change"—and still not know what fracking is, or what 400 parts per million means, or how many animals go extinct each week, or close to how many edges human beings, as a species, are skating, right now. You can be a good person who cares, and you can still not know—not only because your media input is faulty, or incomplete, but because a part of you knows it is just too scary to confront what's going on.

I look at what I have just typed and think, *good grief, what are you doing, holding forth about all this dire stuff? What on earth will people do with this information? No wonder it's hard to talk to anyone about this because it is depressing as hell. What will you say if they ask you, "How do you keep going, knowing all of this?"*

I will take a breath and say: I have to admit reality, including rage, incredulity, and despair. Humans have altered our planet beyond the recognition of our great-great grandparents in many ways, and ignoring that is ignoring reality. Yet I also wake up each day into a reality in which I can move and act and try to do the right thing. I have hope, because, among other reasons, I have a garden. I have tomatoes and eggplants and jars of a type of dried black bean that the Cherokee Nation originally brought out of my homeland and theirs on the Trail of Tears. I have strawberries and raspberries and collards and kale and lettuce and potatoes and beets and okra and sunflowers, for myself and the birds. I have lilies and peonies and my grandmother's lamb's-ear from Alabama, which has seeded itself joyfully all over the yard. I have two plum trees (subject of Ross Gay's great poem "Burial") and a peach tree and a little cherry tree. I can put things in the ground and make them grow. I can sustain myself, at least in some small way. And there is hope in that.

Small personal actions, some say, won't save us. But to know the crisis facing us and to register no response in your own life is to go slowly mad, from the internal pressure of your own denial if nothing else. To bewail the crisis and to offer no solutions and to take no steps is to drive others mad along with you. As outlined in Bill McKibben's *Oil and Honey: The Education of an Unlikely Activist* (2013), divestment from fossil-fuel investments is one of the ways we can still act, within our capitalist system, to press against the drivers of global warming, but ours is a future in which every person will also have to choose positive change in her own life and relationships and communities, every day. Decorah isn't paradise—no place is. But one thing I keep relearning here is that you have to work together with neighbors to build community, even when it's hard, and that maintaining and strengthening an existing community (in terms of its social and physical infrastructures) is less expensive and more sustainable than trying to create (or recreate) one from scratch. This place is small enough to feel approachable, able for me to involve myself in. And one person's actions can show others that change is possible, as change was modeled and continues to be modeled for me. I repeat: I have hope, because I have a garden. Like Keats, I try to balance in the negative-capability gap between foolish optimism and despair and a grounded, practical hope. And because I have seen the changes in my own thought, and life, and capacity to act and to believe that have trickled upward from it, and because others—namely, my students—are looking to me, I dare to keep working, and to keep hoping.

Over time, my little house and yard have become a laboratory for my own version of a hands-on life. As chronicled on the blog I started keeping in 2011, The Cheapskate Intellectual, I started by scratching out a vegetable garden in the back corner of the yard in 2006; this expanded into perennial, herb, and vegetable beds and trees that now surround the house. A retractable clothesline in a little round case stretches from a fencepost on one side of the yard to a hook in the eaves of the garage on the other side. Two rain barrels in back and one in front collect water from the gutters. In the basement I have my vermicomposting bin, a chest freezer, and a cabinet full of homemade preserves. There's a larger compost pile behind the garage. For years my lawn mower was a twenty-inch manual Scott's Classic reel mower with rotating blades that scissored the grass off as I pushed it; now it's a Black & Decker rechargeable electric battery-powered mower, no gas required. I recycle, rinse, and reuse Ziploc bags when I can, and keep my heater and air conditioner off for as long as I can stand it. I don't have cable TV. I held out until May 2017 with my pay-as-you-go flip phone. Sometimes I think, wryly, that my domestic setup is frozen back in the Carter administration, but, really, why not just put on a sweater when you get a little cold? Sure, I have wireless internet and a DVD player, (hooked to the old TV a friend gave me when he moved) but I also have a houseful of books and trusty old wooden chairs painted yellow and orange in the back yard, where I can sit and watch lightning bugs float above my lilies on a summer evening.

Mostly I feel comfortable with and able to maintain what I do, and I try to use it to save money and to redirect my attention to the fallacy of distance: "that thing, or those people, over there have nothing to do with me" is a way of seeing the world that has real consequences. Think of political decision-making at its worst. Think of war, in which drones and bombers devastate the lives of people thousands of feet below. Think of the mountaintops shoved off into streams to reveal the coal that gives us light when, in our houses, we flip on a switch, oblivious of the cushion of other beings on which we ride through every day. In contrast, a view of the world based in a hands-on view of life—which a garden is a near-unsurpassable way to practice—keeps you grounded and connected in reality, community, responsibility. It's hard for a gardener to be otherwise. In his memoir *House of Stone* (2012), the late journalist Anthony Shadid walks past the site of an almond orchard that has been razed to rows of stumps by Israeli bombs. Then, in the back yard of his great-grandfather's house in Lebanon, Shadid plants jasmine vine and olive trees, which can live to be hundreds of years old. The gardener in me shivers sympathetically at the first and cheers at the second, at its promise of ordinary lives being rebuilt amid political chaos, at people sustaining themselves in a place they call home. There's a kinship among people who grow things to feed themselves and plow their own refuse, energy, and care back into the earth, everywhere, that will sustain us as global climate change, and its consequences, accelerate. It's the human kinship, too, if we'll only acknowledge it.

I learned this truth firsthand when epic floods hit Iowa in June 2008, the same year the world was learning about the 350 parts-per-million threshold. Circled by a strong levee, Decorah was technically safe, but in hours the Upper Iowa River rose to a Mississippi-wide torrent that filled the entire river valley, battered the underside of the College Drive bridge, and crept into basements on Winneshiek Avenue. A nursing home close to the river had to be evacuated, straining the hospital to capacity. All day long, people went up to the high overlook at Phelps Park and stared down at the raging brown water in which a whole tree, every so often, went tossing by.

Answering a call for volunteers, I spent all day bent double in a downpour, gloves gritty, holding open the mouth of a feed sack as someone shoveled sand into it, then taking turns with the shovel, twisting the bag's neck shut, tying it with twine, and heaving it into a heap behind us. Teenage boys in pickups and Kawasaki Mules and Bobcats ferried the finished sandbags away. I remembered the quiet victory of that kind of work in summers of stacking square bales of hay onto a flatbed trailer on my parents' farm in Alabama—the salty searing heat, burning arms and necks—then riding on the stack back to the barn. As we were sandbagging against the flood, my parents' fields were baking under 98-degree heat and four months of drought. "Wish you could send us some of that rain," said my mother on the phone. "We won't make a hay crop this year."

The Upper Iowa River was about fifteen feet too high on that early June Sunday; it would reach seventeen feet overnight, rising almost to the top of the dike that wraps around Decorah like a protective arm. Two giant Case tractors roared at the end of the dike, pumping water from around a flooded house. Fire trucks skewed across the road. As I bagged sand, an elderly man walked toward me on the sidewalk, his jaw trembling, on the verge of tears. We didn't meet each other's eyes. Which house is his, I wondered. Which basement, full of what treasures saved or beyond redemption. Which garden full of prize tomatoes or peonies nodding their drowned heads. Because that was the week for peonies. bright pink or white against the gray sky and the green grass. And the water.

By the next morning, the river had risen almost to the top of the dike. Several of us had already been to stand on it and look down at the brown water lapping the green grass three and a half feet below our toes. The owner of the local radio station, a friend, who was live-reporting all over town, drove by and told me my neighborhood was evacuating. If that levee broke, that river would be in my yard instantly, too fast for me to leave. So I secured my basement drains as best I could and started packing.

While I packed, I listened to that radio station, which took a call on air amid the scramble. A man quietly gave his name and announced that his father's funeral would have to be postponed "because of the high waters." My grandmother had died three weeks earlier, and I pitied this man: how would it be to have your father's funeral literally washed aside, to grieve him and fear the loss of your home, to not be quite sure what to do first? How it would have felt if my family had had to postpone my grandmother's funeral to sandbag their house or load up their precious things and leave? How it would have been to be a Sandy or Katrina victim, thinking of your loved ones floating in their aboveground tombs?

What did I snatch to throw in the car? Out of all my books, only a few, including some signed by my friend Elizabeth Spencer and former teacher Barry Hannah. Files containing my insurance policy, birth certificate, will, and passport. My journal and novel manuscript. My laptop. My great-grandmother's rings (as well as the note in my grandmother's shaky hand-writing that came with them.) The oldest photograph album in my stash. Fruit. Wine for the friends who hosted me. Clothes, toothbrush, makeup, phone. Three snarling cats in carriers to board at the vet. Pillows and blan-kets for someone else's floor.

What did I leave behind? It chills me to think of it now. Heaps of books and twenty-one years' worth of journals on the top floor. The hand-hewn bread bowl and hand-shaped brick from a 175-year-old house in Alabama that burned, and my picture of that house itself. My grandmother's china and my great-grandmothers' wineglasses and table linens, serene in their cabinet. Original art by John Henry Toney of Seale, Alabama. A handmade cedar gun cabinet that my parents converted into a bookcase for me. Ticket stubs and autographs from rock shows I went to in grad school: My Morning Jacket, Jonathan Richman, Johnny Marr, Gillian Welch, the Pixies. And roots that I'd sunk in this ground: tomatoes and peppers and eggplants and lettuce furled in crisp cockades so thick I ate salad every day. Stargazer lilies that have mul-tiplied and mixed with the wild orange lilies that were there already. In this house were my life in the South, the place I still call home, and my life here, which is now my home too. I left this house. Except for what I could carry away of the past and the present on my back and in my head. Like Aeneas out of burning Troy with his old father across his shoulders and his little boy by the hand. I left it there to drown.

Like Lot's wife, you turn back to look at your home. Every object shrieks, "Take me! Take me!"

How do you live with the fear they won't be there when you come back?

You don't look too long at the slick brown water pounding the bridge. You don't think about all three bridges closed because the water's almost level with the road. You set out into the bright morning, Led Zeppelin and Memphis Minnie taking turns on "When the Levee Breaks" in your head—grimly compelling and very loud—and think, *surely it'll all hold up. The rain will stop.* You try to ignore helicopters overhead; too much like the Ninth Ward, too grim and fierce. Too much like the real floods on the news. Pigs on a barn roof in North Carolina. People in New Orleans struggling through holes chopped in their attic roofs, waving, and weeping. You never thought it would happen to you. That you would be—even in this small way—a climate refugee.

But I was lucky. A neighbor offered me refuge high above the river, where we assembled a dinner of roast chicken and vegetables and steak fajitas and a tart of apples from a yard in Highlandville. The next day I was back to teaching my summer course, back in my blessedly unharmed house, cutting my shaggy grass, conferring with my neighbors. *When are you putting your stuff back in the basement? Aren't we supposed to get more rain Thursday?* We'd wait till after the weekend, we all decided.

Even after I'd returned to my routine and the river had receded, the flood lingered in my mind with the unreal, nagging persistence of a dream. *I remember it so clearly, but did it really happen?* I was back in my house, baking bread for the friends who hosted me, whose basement was full of water, who helped me carry some of my things upstairs. Was it real? It was. Am I safe? I am, for now. What did the water leave behind? Chugging pumps, flooded homes, dried borderlines of twigs and mud, a drowned community garden. Bare spots where the current blasted swallows' nests off the bridge. Soon, though, the swallows had rebuilt those colonies from which they fly in clouds on summer evenings, swarming around the bridge as you walk across. It isn't only river mud swallows build nests from. They can make a special substance inside themselves, a glue to attach their nests anywhere.

The week after the flood, I took my creative writing class to the Vesterheim Norwegian-American Heritage Museum in our town to write poems that pair the objects inside with the world outside. In the vaulted center hall of the museum, next to the twenty-five-foot sailboat TradeWinds, is the ships' log of Harald Hamran, who sailed from Norway to New York in that boat with his brother Hans in 1933. He was about thirty-seven, three years older than I was then, a bachelor and a born adventurer. *Such a nature as mine finds no peace, no satisfaction in a soft, comfortable life or watching the clock,* he writes. *It does not seem like real life to me. Far better to take chances with storm and difficulties even if life itself must be staked.* Shifting between English and Norwegian, in witty but spotty grammar, he records his fears—*In weather like this one realize what a little nutshell the "Tradewind" really are*—and strengthens his own resolve—*Good humor must be had at all costs.* His face in the picture is stubbly, laconic, but his outlook is fundamentally optimistic, even joyous. *We have biscuits and bacon and raw vegetables—and life is in spite of all, wonderful.* Watching a sunset, he exclaims, *God—its glorious to live!* Drawing within sight of the cliffs of Dover: *Beautiful sun—beautiful world!*

What have I learned from this voyager? From these days with the threat of water, the threat of lifting and floating away from my home, from the hours of frantic work alongside strangers and friends to save the home that's ours? I have preserved pictures and words of the distant and dead, because something about them is still alive for me. But my life is more portable than I think. If I had to start again, I probably could. A life without challenge is not a life. A person untested is not a person, yet. The cushion of comfort on which we float every day—water, power, safe homes, health—is so precious, and so precarious. As Americans, we can trust that comfort, so regularly punctured, or absent, in other parts of the world. Until it happens to us. And then we never really take it for granted again. As a farm girl, I've always welcomed rain, anywhere, with the instinctive thought: *oh good, the pastures are so dry.* Now rain makes me a little nervous. It probably will for a while.

In a time and a country where "community" is more endangered than ever, I know that community is here, and I know that I am a part of it now. "Something like this changes your relationships to people," says my mother, who refugeed out of New Orleans with my grandmother and me to escape Hurricane Carmen in 1974, when I was a week old. The tiny outlying communities (Highlandville, Spillville, Ft. Atkinson) are no longer just abstractions to me, nor is "community" itself. Our Upper Iowa River had reached its highest-ever crest, a so-called "hundred year" flood in its rarity and seriousness. Our community is preparing for the reality that hundred-year floods will become fifty-year floods, maybe even twenty-five, as climate change accelerates; we have seen other serious floods in the last five years. Yet as I shoveled sand with strangers and worried about their flooded basements,

I took some comfort in feeling that I was not alone. Water washes some things away. But it strengthens roots. Sends them deeper.

Deep roots, connections to communities and family and friends in specific places, will help us survive what comes, and it's within our power to build them. Those who live there will know best where to start. Surely it is worth a try.

One afternoon a few Septembers ago, with the smell of fall caught and blowing around in the trees, I went out to the Seed Savers Exchange near Decorah to visit the heirloom apple orchard. The Seed Savers Exchange is a local treasure with an international reach, preserving the living biodiversity of seeds deemed too "slow" or otherwise unsuited for corporate agriculture but beloved by small farmers and backyard gardeners. And the sky is a particular shade of blue in an apple orchard in September that you don't get to see anywhere else.

That fall, there was something new in the orchard: Gloucestershire Old Spots pigs, penned in movable fence under the apple trees to eat windfalls. We never had pigs on our farm in Alabama when I was a child, and like the rest of the country we've got a wild hog problem now, but I've always been fascinated by pigs, even as there's something faintly unnerving about their intelligence. (George Orwell, who knew his way around a small holding and had a vegetable garden, chickens, and a goat named Muriel, made pigs the ringleaders in *Animal Farm* for a reason.) They'll tear up your leg or your dog if you catch them wild, out hunting; they'll root out your quail or turkey nests. If you were a Methodist child like me, you may be haunted by images of the Gadarene swine into which Jesus cast demons, squealing and racing over a cliff into the sea. If you're a classicist, you may recall the special place of piglets as sacrifices to Demeter, goddess of the harvest, during the all-women religious festival of Thesmophoria in ancient Athens. Yet looking at these pigs in their fall-afternoon bliss, nosing and sampling windfall apples, flicking their floppy ears and grunting just to hear themselves talk, I thought, *something about this feels right*, indicative of a deep, sustaining web of people and other beings in a place. These pigs have long been the domestic companions of people, living in pens near the house, eating human leftovers, cleaning up windfall apples in orchards (legend says their famous spots are bruise-marks from falling apples) and—however you feel about this—ending their lives as food for the people who have cared for them. Maybe this relationship is one way to say *culture*.

Anthropologist Gregory Bateson told a story about being at New College, Oxford, and hearing them talk about replacing the huge oak timbers: "there's some more oaks out back," he recalls the men saying, "a couple hundred years old, planted just for this," and then, he says, "I thought, 'that's the way to run a culture.'"[21] If you think about culture the way I do, as a life-sustaining human presence in a world to which it is responsible, made and grown in layers over time by layers of touch—that's my working definition of culture, human touch matured by time—you ask yourself, how can technology alone ever approach this sort of warm, lively, and sustaining intimacy? How can we ever build a real and enduring culture without honoring living things and learning from their relationships? Bateson wrote a lot about this. And when you look at pigs in an orchard, you see it in action.

While pigs, like dogs, are resourceful enough to go feral, they also live close to people, feeding off by-products of small-farm life: whey, cider pressings, vegetable scraps, and—yes—windfall apples. When I make my basic ricotta cheese and end up with a bowl full of whey, I always wish for a pig to feed it to, like we used to toss old watermelon rinds and cornshucks over the fence for the horses and cattle. Taking compost down to the worm bin is a subtle delight—look how what was grown from this soil and eaten in this house now feeds other creatures in this house and goes back to this soil!—and it makes me wish for more animals to thrive on what I can't use. Pigs, unfortunately, are not allowed in town.

But I can still enjoy these Old Spots under their heirloom apple trees in Iowa, and understand more deeply the webs of household and agricultural and historical interconnection in which I still live because of them. Old Spots are the oldest breed in England, chosen pig of the Royal Family's table; although nobody really knows how old this breed may be, it's very, very old. Remembered on a warm fall afternoon, this story heightens my quiet happiness in being here where human and animal history meet, and braid together. That's the way to run a culture. And to more fully inhabit your very own hands-on life.

21. See the documentary *An Ecology of Mind*, directed by Nora Bateson.

Bibliography

Abadi-Nagy, Zoltan. "Walker Percy: The Art of Fiction No. 97." *Paris Review* 103 (Summer 1987). https://www.theparisreview.org/interviews/2643/walker-percy-the-art-of-fiction-no-97-walker-percy.

Abbey, Edward. (1977) *The Journey Home: Some Words in Defense of the American West*. New York: Plume, 1991.

Addams, Jane. (1893) "The Subjective Necessity for Social Settlements." In (1893) *Philanthropy and Social Progress*, edited by Henry C. Adams. New York: Thomas Y. Cromwell. Republished as chapter six of Jane Addams, *Twenty Years at Hull House*, New York: Macmillan, 1910. http://www.infed.org/archives/e-texts/addams.htm.

Adorno, Theodor W. "Education After Auschwitz." In *Critical Models: Interventions and Catchwords*, edited by Theodor W. Adorno and Henry W. Pickford, 191–204. New York: Columbia University Press, 2005.

Alexander, William. "Excerpt: 'The $64 Tomato.'" NPR.org, May 1, 2006. http://www.npr.org/templates/story/story.php?storyId=5360768.

Alighieri, Dante. *Inferno*. Translated by John Ciardi. New York: Signet Classics, 2001.

Anderson, Debra. *Split Estate*. DVD. Santa Fe, NM: Red Rock Pictures, 2009.

Arendt, Hannah. (1963) *Eichmann in Jerusalem: A Report on the Banality of Evil*. New York: Penguin, 2006.

———. "Hannah Arendt: From An Interview." *New York Review of Books,* October 26, 1978. http://www.nybooks.com/articles/1978/10/26/hannah-arendt-from-an-interview/.

———. (1958) *The Human Condition*. Chicago: University of Chicago Press, 1998.

———. *The Life of the Mind: Thinking*. New York: Harcourt, 1981.

———. (1951) *The Origins of Totalitarianism*. New York: Harcourt, 1985.

———. (1971). "Thinking and Moral Considerations." In Hannah Arendt, *Responsibility and Judgment*, edited and introduced by Jerome Kohn, 159–189. New York: Schocken, 2003.

Auden, W. H. "Lame Shadows." *New York Review of Books,* September 3, 1970. http://www.nybooks.com/articles/1970/09/03/lame-shadows/ and http://www.nybooks.com/articles/2013/10/24/lame-shadows/.

Barber, Dan. *The Third Plate: Field Notes on the Future of Food*. New York: Penguin, 2014.

Barnard, Anne, and Karam Shoumali. "Image of Drowned Syrian, Aylan Kurdi, 3, Brings Migrant Crisis Into Focus." *New York Times*, September 3, 2015. https://www.nytimes.com/2015/09/04/world/europe/syria-boy-drowning.html?_r=0.

Bassett, Laura. "Chuck Winder, Idaho Lawmaker, Suggests Women Use Rape As Excuse For Abortions." *The Huffington Post,* March 20, 2012. http://www.huffingtonpost.com/2012/03/20/chuck-winder-rape-abortions_n_1366994.html.

————. "Tom Smith, GOP Senate Candidate: Pregnancy From Rape Similar To 'Having A Baby Out Of Wedlock.'" *The Huffington Post,* August 27, 2012. http://www.huffingtonpost.com/2012/08/27/tom-smith-rape_n_1834234.html.

Bateson, Nora, dir. *An Ecology of Mind: A Daughter's Portrait of Gregory Bateson.* Oley, PA: Bullfrog Films, 2011. http://www.anecologyofmind.com/index.html.

Bennett, Jane. *The Enchantment of Modern Life: Attachments, Crossings, and Ethics.* Princeton: Princeton University Press, 2001.

Berger, John. *Ways of Seeing.* New York: Penguin, 1977.

Bergman, Megan Mayhew. "The Long and Pretty Good-bye." *Paris Review* blog, December 16, 2016. https://www.theparisreview.org/blog/2016/12/16/the-long-and-pretty-goodbye/.

Berry, Wendell. "Faustian Economics." *Harper's,* May 2008, 35–42.

Bilger, Burkhard. "Auto Correct." *The New Yorker,* November 25, 2013, 96–109.

Bilton, Nick. "Alex From Target: The Other Side of Fame," *New York Times,* Nov. 12, 2014. https://www.nytimes.com/2014/11/13/style/alex-from-target-the-other-side-of-fame.html?_r=0.

————. "Steve Jobs Was A Low-Tech Parent," *New York Times,* Sept. 10, 2014. https://www.nytimes.com/2014/09/11/fashion/steve-jobs-apple-was-a-low-tech-parent.html.

Blair, Elizabeth. "The Strange Story of the Man Behind 'Strange Fruit.'" NPR.org, September 5, 2012. http://www.npr.org/2012/09/05/158933012/the-strange-story-of-the-man-behind-strange-fruit.

Blake, William. *The Marriage of Heaven and Hell* (1790). In *Blake's Poetry and Designs,* edited by Mary Lynn Johnson and John E. Grant, 66–82. New York: W. W. Norton, 2008.

Blum, Susan D. *I Love Learning, I Hate School: An Anthropology of College.* Ithaca, NY: Cornell University Press, 2016.

Bok, Derek. *Higher Education in America.* Princeton: Princeton University Press, 2013.

The Book of Common Prayer and Administration of the Sacraments and Other Rites and Ceremonies of the Church, Together with the Psalter or Psalms of David, According to the Use of the Episcopal Church. New York: Church Publishing, 1979.

boyd, danah. *It's Complicated: The Social Lives of Networked Teens.* New Haven: Yale University Press, 2014.

Bromell, Nick. "The Liberal Imagination of Frederick Douglass." *The American Scholar,* Spring 2008, 34–45.

Bromwich, David. "The Hi-Tech Mess of Higher Education." *New York Review of Books,* August 14, 2014. http://www.nybooks.com/articles/2014/08/14/hi-tech-mess-higher-education/.

Browning, Robert. (1887) "With Bernard de Mandeville." *The Works of Robert Browning,* Vol. X, 157–167. London: Smith, Elder & Co., 1912.

Bruni, Frank. *Where You Go Is Not Who You'll Be: An Antidote to the College Admissions Mania.* New York: Grand Central, 2015.

Byrne, Richard. "A Nod to Ned Ludd." *The Baffler,* 2013. http://www.thebaffler.com/salvos/a-nod-to-ned-ludd.

Cagle, Susie. "The Case Against Sharing: On Access, Scarcity, and Trust." *Medium,* May 27, 2014. https://medium.com/the-nib/the-case-against-sharing-9ea5ba3d216d.

———. "Through the Watching Glass: On Privacy, Etiquette, and the Ever-Expanding Glasshole." *Medium,* March 4, 2014. https://medium.com/the-nib/through-the-watching-glass-59e09d27432a.

Čapek, Karel. "The Gardener's November." In *The Gardener's Year,* introduced by Verlyn Klinkenborg, 99–104. New York: Modern Library, 2002.

———. *The Gardener's Year.* Introduced by Verlyn Klinkenborg. New York: Modern Library, 2002.

———. "Holiday." In *The Gardener's Year,* introduced by Verlyn Klinkenborg, 41–43. New York: Modern Library, 2002.

———. "How A Man Becomes A Gardener." In *The Gardener's Year,* introduced by Verlyn Klinkenborg, 6–8. New York: Modern Library, 2002.

———. *R.U.R. (Rossum's Universal Robots)* (1921). Introduced by Ivan Klima, translated by Claudia Novack. New York: Penguin, 2004.

———. "Save Yourself If You Can." In *Believe in People: The Essential Karel Čapek,* selected and translated by Sarka Tobmnanova-Kuhnova, 255–258. London: Faber and Faber, 2010.

———. "The Soil." In *The Gardener's Year,* introduced by Verlyn Klinkenborg, 87–89. New York: Modern Library, 2002.

Carr, Nicholas. *The Glass Cage: Automation and Us.* New York: W. W. Norton, 2015.

———. "Is Google Making Us Stupid?" *The Atlantic,* July/August 2008. http://www.theatlantic.com/magazine/archive/2008/07/is-google-making-us-stupid/306868/.

———. *The Shallows: What The Internet Is Doing To Our Brains.* New York: W. W. Norton & Co., 2010.

Carson, Rachel. (1962) *Silent Spring.* New York: Mariner, 2002.

Chodron, Pema. *Getting Unstuck: Breaking Your Habitual Patterns and Encountering Naked Reality.* Audiobook. Louisville, CO: Sounds True, 2005.

———. *Living Beautifully With Uncertainty and Change.* Boston: Shambhala, 2002.

———. *When Things Fall Apart: Heart Advice for Difficult Times.* Boston: Shambhala, 1997.

Chung, Sonya. "What We Teach When We Teach Writers: On the Quantifiable and the Uncertain." *The Millions,* Oct. 29, 2010. http://www.themillions.com/2010/10/what-we-teach-when-we-teach-writers-on-the-quantifiable-and-the-uncertain.html.

Clark, Dorie. "Actually, You Should Check Email in the Morning." *Harvard Business Review,* March 7, 2016. https://hbr.org/2016/03/actually-you-should-check-email-first-thing-in-the-morning.

Colette. (1922, 1929) *My Mother's House & Sido.* New York: Modern Library, 1995.

Crawford, Matthew. "The Case for Working With Your Hands." *New York Times,* May 21, 2009. http://www.nytimes.com/2009/05/24/magazine/24labor-t.html.

———. *Shop Class as Soulcraft: An Inquiry into the Value of Work.* New York: Penguin, 2009.

———. *The World Beyond Your Head: On Becoming an Individual in an Age of Distraction.* New York: Farrar Straus Giroux, 2015.

Crews, Harry. "Introduction." In *Classic Crews: A Harry Crews Reader,* 9–16. New York: Poseidon, 1993.

Curtis, Kimberly. *Our Sense of the Real: Aesthetic Experience and Arendtian Politics.* Ithaca: Cornell University Press, 1999.

Curzan, Anne. "Why I'm Asking You Not To Use Laptops." *Chronicle of Higher Education,* August 25, 2014. http://chronicle.com/blogs/linguafranca/2014/08/25/why-im-asking-you-not-to-use-laptops/.

Crowther, Hal. *Gather at the River: Notes from the Post-Millenial South.* Baton Rouge: LSU Press, 2005.

Darwin, Charles. (1859) *On the Origin of Species,* edited by William Bynum. New York: Penguin Classics, 2009.

Darwin, Francis, ed. *Charles Darwin: His Life Told in an Autobiographical Chapter, and in a Selected Series of his Published Letters* [abridged edition]. London: John Murray: 1892. http://darwin-online.org.uk/content/frameset?pageseq=41&itemID=F1461&viewtype=side.

Davis, Wade. *Light at the Edge of the World: A Journey Through the Realm of Vanishing Cultures.* Madeira Park, British Columbia: Douglas & McIntyre, 2007.

——.*The Wayfinders: Why Ancient Wisdom Matters in the Modern World.* Toronto: House of Anansi, 2009.

Dean, Michelle. "The Listless Boredom of The Bling Ring." *The Nation,* June 25, 2013. https://www.thenation.com/article/listless-boredom-bling-ring/.

DeBuys, William. "Phoenix in the Climate Crosshairs: We Are Long Past Coal Mine Canaries." *Tom Dispatch,* March 14, 2013. http://www.tomdispatch.com/blog/175661/william_debuys_exodus_from_phoenix.

Delbanco, Andrew. *College: What It Was, Is, and Should Be.* Princeton: Princeton University Press, 2013.

Deresiewicz, William. "The Disadvantages of an Elite Education." *The American Scholar,* June 1, 2008. https://theamericanscholar.org/the-disadvantages-of-an-elite-education.

——. *Excellent Sheep: The Miseducation of the American Elite and the Way to a Meaningful Life.* New York: Free, 2014.

Diamond, Jared. *Collapse: How Societies Choose to Fail or Succeed.* New York: Viking, 2005.

Draaisma, Douwe. *Why Life Speeds Up As You Get Older: How Memory Shapes Our Past.* Cambridge: Cambridge University Press, 2004.

Duhigg, Charles. "How Companies Learn Your Secrets." *New York Times,* February 16, 2012. http://www.nytimes.com/2012/02/19/magazine/shopping-habits.html.

Edsel, Robert. *Saving Italy.* New York: W. W. Norton, 2013.

Eggers, Dave. *The Circle.* New York: Knopf, 2013.

Ehrenreich, Barbara. *Nickel and Dimed: On (Not) Getting By In America.* New York: Henry Holt, 2002.

Eligon, John and Michael Schwirtz. "Senate Candidate Provokes Ire With 'Legitimate Rape' Comment." *The New York Times* Aug. 19, 2012. http://www.nytimes.com/2012/08/20/us/politics/todd-akin-provokes-ire-with-legitimate-rape-comment.html.

Eliot, George. (1871–2) *Middlemarch.* Edited by Rosemary Ashton. New York: Penguin, 1994.

Fanon, Frantz. (1961) *The Wretched of the Earth.* New York: Grove, 2004.

Ferguson, Charles, dir. *Inside Job.* DVD. Los Angeles: Sony Pictures Classics, 2010.

Flannery, Tim. "They're Taking Over!" *New York Review of Books*, Sept. 26, 2013. http://www.nybooks.com/articles/2013/09/26/jellyfish-theyre-taking-over/.

Ford, Martin. *Rise of the Robots: Technology and the Threat of a Jobless Future*. New York: Basic, 2015.

Forster, E. M. (1910) *Howards End*. New York: Bantam Classics, 1985.

Fountain, Henry. "For Already Vulnerable Penguins, Study Finds Climate Change Is Another Danger." *New York Times*, January 29, 2014. https://www.nytimes.com/2014/01/30/science/earth/climate-change-taking-toll-on-penguins-study-finds.html.

Francis (Pope). Address to Second World Meeting of the Popular Movements. July 10, 2015. http://americamagazine.org/issue/pope-francis-address-second-world-meeting-popular-movements.

Frazier, Ian. "High-Rise Greens." *The New Yorker*, January 9, 2017, 52–59.

Freedman, Samuel G. "Immigrants Find Solace After Storm of Arrests." *New York Times* July 12, 2008. http://www.nytimes.com/2008/07/12/us/12religion.html.

Freeman, Philip. *Searching for Sappho: The Lost Songs and World of the First Woman Poet*. New York: W. W. Norton, 2016.

Gardner, Sarah. "How to Support Yourself After the Robot Revolution." *Marketplace*, December 7, 2016. http://www.marketplace.org/2016/12/07/economy/silicon-valley-thinks-about-buying-lumpenproletariat.

Gay, Roxane. "The Rumpus Interview with Terry Tempest Williams." *The Rumpus*, July 4, 2013. http://therumpus.net/2013/07/the-rumpus-interview-with-terry-tempest-williams/.

Gibson, James William. *A Reenchanted World: The Quest for a New Kinship. with Nature* New York: Metropolitan, 2009.

Greene, Graham. (1943) *The Ministry of Fear*. London: William Heinemann, 1956.

Griffiths, Jay. "Artifice vs. Pastoral." *Orion* 28.2 (March/April 2009) 20–27.

————. *A Country Called Childhood: Children and the Exuberant World*. Berkeley: Counterpoint, 2014.

Grossman, Cathy Lynn. "Christians Lose Ground in New Portrait of U.S. Religion." *Religion News Service*, May 12, 2015. http://religionnews.com/2015/05/12/christians-lose-ground-nones-soar-new-portrait-u-s-religion/.

Grossman, Elizabeth. "High-Tech Wasteland." *Orion*, July/August 2004. http://www.orionmagazine.org/index.php/articles/article/142/.

Hankins, Gabriel. "Henry James on Twitter." *The New Everyday: A Media Commons Project*, April 20, 2011. http://mediacommons.futureofthebook.org/tne/pieces/henry-james-twitter-0.

Hansen, James, et. al. "Target Atmospheric CO2: Where Should Humanity Aim?" *The Open Atmospheric Science Journal* (2008), vol. 2, 217–231. DOI: 10.2174/1874282300802010217. https://arxiv.org/abs/0804.1126 and https://350.org/about/science.

Harris, Paul. "Monsanto Sued Small Farmers to Protect Seed Patents, Report Says." *The Guardian*, February 12, 2013. https://www.theguardian.com/environment/2013/feb/12/monsanto-sues-farmers-seed-patents.

Hawken, Paul. *Blessed Unrest: How the Largest Social Movement in History is Restoring Grace, Justice, and Beauty to the World*. New York: Penguin, 2007.

Hayes, Shannon. *Radical Homemakers: Reclaiming Domesticity from a Consumer Culture*. Richmondville, NY: Left to Write, 2010.

Hedges, Chris, and Joe Sacco. *Days of Destruction, Days of Revolt.* New York: Nation, 2012.

Heller, Nathan. "Bay Watched." *The New Yorker,* October 14, 2013, 68–79.

————. "California Screaming." *The New Yorker,* July 7 & 14, 2014, 46–53.

Hensher, Philip. *The Missing Ink: The Lost Art of Handwriting.* New York: Faber and Faber/Farrar Straus Giroux, 2012.

Hochschild, Adam. *King Leopold's Ghost: A Story of Greed, Terror, and Heroism in Colonial Africa.* New York: Mariner, 1998.

Holbrook Pearson, Melissa. *The Place You Love Is Gone: Progress Hits Home.* New York: W. W. Norton, 2007.

Holmes, Oliver Wendell. "Homesick in Heaven." *The Complete Poetical Works of Oliver Wendell Holmes, Illustrated.* New York: Grosset & Dunlap, 1890.

Hochschild, Adam. *King Leopold's Ghost: A Story of Greed, Terror, and Heroism in Colonial Africa.* New York: Mariner, 1998.

Honan, Mat. "I, Glasshole: My Year With Google Glass." *Wired,* December 30, 2013. https://www.wired.com/2013/12/glasshole.

Hughes, Karen. "Communication Lessons from Election." *Politico,* November 9, 2012. http://www.politico.com/story/2012/11/communication-lessons-from-election-083632.

Irankunda, Pacifique. "Playing at Violence." *The American Scholar,* Summer 2013. https://theamericanscholar.org/playing-at-violence/.

Iyengar, B. K. S. "Foreword." In Michael Stone, *Yoga for a World Out of Balance: Teachings on Ethics and Social Action* (Shambhala, 2009), xi–xii.

Jacobs, Tom. "Even Just The Presence of a Smartphone Lowers the Quality of In-Person Conversations." *Pacific Standard,* July 14, 2014. https://psmag.com/even-just-the-presence-of-a-smartphone-lowers-the-quality-of-in-person-conversations.

Jamieson, Dale. *Reason in a Dark Time: Why the Struggle Against Climate Change Failed —And What It Means for Our Future.* New York: Oxford University Press, 2014.

Jay, Meg. *The Defining Decade: Why Your Twenties Matter and How to Make the Most of Them Now.* New York: Twelve, 2012.

Jeide, Anna. "@ Luther College: Pay Attention." *Luther College Chips* (February 13, 2014), 9.

Johnson, Trebbe. "Gaze Even Here," *Orion* 31:6 (November/December 2012) 66–71.

Joyce, James. (1922) *Ulysses.* New York: Vintage, 1986.

Kaag, John. "Books' Fragile Bodies." *Chronicle of Higher Education,* December 11, 2016. http://www.chronicle.com/article/Books-Fragile-Bodies/238601

Kadison, Richard D. and Theresa Foy DiGeronimo. *College of the Overwhelmed: The Campus Mental Health Crisis and What To Do About It.* Hoboken, NJ: Jossey-Bass, 2004.

Katz, Steven B. "The Ethic of Expediency: Classical Rhetoric, Technology, and the Holocaust." *College English* 54.3 (March 1992) 255–275.

Keats, John. *Complete Poems,* ed. Jack Stillinger. Cambridge: Harvard University Press, 1982.

————. *Letters of John Keats: A Selection,* ed. Robert Gittings. Oxford: Oxford University Press, 1970.

————. "This living hand." In *Complete Poems,* edited by Jack Stillinger, 384. Cambridge: Harvard University Press, 1982.

————. "To Autumn." In *Complete Poems*, edited by Jack Stillinger, 360–61. Cambridge: Harvard University Press, 1982.

————. "Sleep and Poetry." In *Complete Poems*, edited by Jack Stillinger, 37. Cambridge: Harvard University Press, 1982.

————. "When I have fears." In *Complete Poems*, edited by Jack Stillinger, 166. Cambridge: Harvard University Press, 1982.

King, Stephen. (1977) *The Shining*. New York: Pocket, 2002.

Kingsnorth, Paul. *Real England: The Battle Against the Bland*. London: Portobello, 2008.

Klein, Naomi. *This Changes Everything: Capitalism Vs. the Climate*. New York: Simon & Schuster, 2014.

Kluttz, Bonnie. "Reading Debate Continues to Rage: Groups Demand Balance." *The Daily Tar Heel* (Thursday, July 17, 2003) 1.

Kolbert, Elizabeth. *The Sixth Extinction: An Unnatural History*. New York: Henry Holt & Co., 2014.

Kolowich, Steve. "How Many College Students Are Going Hungry?" *Chronicle of Higher Education*, November 3, 2015. http://chronicle.com/article/How-Many-College-Students-Are/234033?cid=trend_right_h.

Konnikova, Maria. "What's Lost as Handwriting Fades." *New York Times,* June 2, 2014. https://www.nytimes.com/2014/06/03/science/whats-lost-as-handwriting-fades.html.

Lanier, Jaron. *Who Owns the Future?* New York: Simon & Schuster, 2013.

————. *You Are Not A Gadget*. New York: Vintage, 2011.

Leopold, Aldo. "The Round River." In *A Sand County Almanac, With Other Essays on Conservation from* Round River, 175–187. New York: Oxford University Press, 1966.

Lipstadt, Deborah E. *The Eichmann Trial*. New York: Schocken, 2011.

López, Ian Haney. *Dog Whistle Politics: How Coded Racial Appeals Have Reinvented Racism and Wrecked the Middle Class*. New York: Oxford University Press, 2014.

Losh, Elizabeth. *The War On Learning: Gaining Ground in the Digital University*. Cambridge: MIT Press, 2014.

————. "Who Was The Experimenter in the Twitter Experiment?" *The New Everyday: A Media Commons Project*, March 29, 2011. http://mediacommons.futureofthebook.org/tne/pieces/who-was-experimenter-twitter-experiment#footnote1_u8d1mnf.

Ludwig, Art. "Principles of Ecological Design: Integrating Technology, Economics, and Ecology." http://oasisdesign.net/design/principles.htm.

Lutz, Deborah. *The Brontë Cabinet: Three Lives in Nine Objects*. New York: W. W. Norton & Co., 2015.

Lythcott-Haims, Julie. *How to Raise An Adult: Break Free of the Overparenting Trap and Prepare Your Kids for Success*. New York: Henry Holt, 2015.

Mahoney, Rosemary. "The Hardest Art." In *Selfish, Shallow, and Self-Absorbed: Sixteen Writers on the Decision Not To Have Kids,* edited by Meghan Daum, 227–244. New York: Picador, 2015.

Markell, Patchen. "Tragic Recognition: Action and Identity in *Antigone* and Aristotle." *Political Theory* 31.1, February 2003, 6–38. DOI: 10.1177/0090591702239437.

Martin, Craig. *Masking Hegemony*. Oakville, CT: Equinox, 2010.

Masson, Stephanie Reese. "The Death of Cursive Writing." *Chronicle of Higher Education Vitae* Blog, December 1, 2016. https://chroniclevitae.com/news/1625-the-death-of-cursive-writing.

McCalman, Iain. *The Reef: A Passionate History: The Great Barrier Reef from Captain Cook to Climate Change.* Scientific American/Farrar, Straus and Giroux, 2014.

McDonough, Katie. "Texas Abortion Bill Sponsor Doesn't Know What a Rape Kit Is." *Salon,* June 24, 2013. http://www.salon.com/2013/06/24/texas_abortion_bill_sponsor_doesnt_know_what_a_rape_kit_is/.

McKibben, Bill. *Eaarth: Making a Life on a Tough New Planet.* New York: St. Martin's Griffin, 2010.

Mead, Rebecca. "The Scourge of Relatability." *The New Yorker* online, August 1, 2014. http://www.newyorker.com/culture/cultural-comment/scourge-relatability.

————. "The Troll Slayer." *The New Yorker,* September 1, 2014, 30–36.

Melville, Herman. (1851) *Moby-Dick.* Edited by Harrison Hayford and Hershel Parker. New York: W. W. Norton & Co., 1967.

"Men Adrift: Badly educated men in rich countries have not adapted well to trade, technology, or feminism." *The Economist,* May 30, 2015. http://www.economist.com/news/essays/21649050-badly-educated-men-rich-countries-have-not-adapted-well-trade-technology-or-feminism.

Mendelsund, Peter. *What We See When We Read.* New York: Vintage, 2014.

Michaels, Rob. "Harry Crews: Pen-Packin' Old Boy." In *Getting Naked With Harry Crews: Interviews,* edited by Erik Bledsoe, 247–254. Gainesville: University Press of Florida, 1999.

Miller, Laura. "Fresh Hell: What's behind the boom in dystopian fiction for young readers?" *The New Yorker,* June 14, 2010: 132–136.

Monke, Lowell. "Is It Time To Unplug Our Schools?" *Orion,* September/October 2007. Online: http://www.orionmagazine.org/index.php/articles/article/334/

Morgenstern, Julie. "A Style Is Born." *O Magazine,* October 2004, 115–122.

————. *Never Check Email in the Morning.* New York: Touchstone, 2005.

Morozov, Evgeny. *To Save Everything, Click Here: The Folly of Technological Solutionism.* New York: Public Affairs, 2013.

Morton, Timothy. *The Ecological Thought.* Cambridge: Harvard University Press, 2012.

Nesi, Eduardo. *Story of My People.* Translated by Anthony Shugaar. New York: Other, 2014.

Oliver, Mary. "The Summer Day." In *Contemporary American Poetry* (8th ed.), edited by A. Poulin, Jr. and Michael Waters, 386. New York: Houghton Mifflin, 2006.

————. "Where Does The Dance Begin, Where Does It End?" In *Contemporary American Poetry* (8th ed.), edited by A. Poulin, Jr. and Michael Waters, 381. New York: Houghton Mifflin, 2006.

Orwell, George. "In Front Of Your Nose." In *Essays,* selected and introduced by John Carey, 1040–1044. New York: Everyman's Library/Alfred A. Knopf, 2002.

————. (1949) *Nineteen Eighty-Four.* New York: Harcourt Brace, 2003

————."Politics and the English Language." In *Essays,* selected and introduced by John Carey, 954–967. New York: Everyman's Library/Alfred A. Knopf, 2002.

Oxfam America. "An Economy for the 99 Percent." January 15, 2017. https://www.oxfamamerica.org/explore/research-publications/an-economy-for-the-99-percent/.

Paley, Grace. "September." In *Begin Again: Collected Poems*, 70. New York: Macmillan, 2014.

Palmer, Parker. *Healing the Heart of Democracy: The Courage to Create A Politics Worthy of the Human Spirit.* San Francisco: Jossey-Bass, 2011.

———. "We Need To Find A Third Way." *On Being*, May 27, 2015. http://www.onbeing. org/blog/we-need-to-find-a-third-way/.

Parry, Marc. "Conference Humiliation: They're Tweeting Behind Your Back." *Chronicle of Higher Education,* November 17, 2009. http://www.chronicle.com/article/Conference-Humiliation-/49185?cid=rclink.

Penman, Maggie. "#AirbnbWhileBlack: How Hidden Bias Shapes the Sharing Economy." NPR.org, April 26, 2016. http://www.npr.org/2016/04/26/475623339/-airbnbwhileblack-how-hidden-bias-shapes-the-sharing-economy.

Percy, Walker. (1961) *The Moviegoer.* New York: Vintage International, 1998.

Piketty, Thomas. *Capital in the Twenty-First Century.* Cambridge: Harvard/Belknap, 2014.

Plato. *Republic,* translated by Robin Waterfield, 242–246. New York: Oxford World's Classics, 1994.

Potter, Claire. "Bye Bye Birdies: Sending the Kids Away to College." *Chronicle of Higher Education,* July 28, 2014. http://www.chronicle.com/blognetwork/tenuredradical/2014/07/bye-bye-birdies-sending-the-kids-away-to-college.

Preston, Julia. "After Iowa Raid, Immigrants Fuel Labor Inquiries." *New York Times,* July 27, 2008. http://www.nytimes.com/2008/07/27/us/27immig.html.

———. "Iowa Rally Protests Raid and Conditions at Plant." *New York Times,* July 28, 2008. http://www.nytimes.com/2008/07/28/us/28immig.html.

Primack, Richard B. *Walden Warming: Climate Change Comes to Thoreau's Woods.* Chicago: University of Chicago Press, 2014.

Reding, Nick. *Methland: The Death and Life of An American Small Town.* New York: Bloomsbury USA, 2009.

Richtel, Matt. "A Silicon Valley School That Doesn't Compute." *New York Times,* Oct. 22, 2011. http://www.nytimes.com/2011/10/23/technology/at-waldorf-school-in-silicon-valley-technology-can-wait.html.

Rilke, Rainer Maria. "The First Elegy." In *The Selected Poetry of Rainer Maria Rilke,* edited and translated by Stephen Mitchell, 151–55. New York: Vintage, 1989.

Roberts, Renae, dir. *Rooted Lands (Tierras Arraigadas).* DVD. Cerrillos, NM: R3 Productions, 2012.

Robin, Corey. "The Trials of Hannah Arendt." *The Nation,* May 12, 2015. https://www.thenation.com/article/trials-hannah-arendt/.

Rockmore, Dan. "The Case for Banning Laptops in the Classroom." *The New Yorker* blog, June 6, 2014. http://www.newyorker.com/online/blogs/elements/2014/06/the-case-for-banning-laptops-in-the-classroom.html.

Ronson, Jon. *So You've Been Publicly Shamed.* New York: Riverhead, 2015.

Rosin, Hanna. "The End of Men." *The Atlantic,* July/August 2010. https://www.theatlantic.com/magazine/archive/2010/07/the-end-of-men/308135/.

———. "The Overprotected Kid." *The Atlantic,* March 2014. http://www.theatlantic.com/features/archive/2014/03/hey-parents-leave-those-kids-alone/358631/.

Sax, David. *The Revenge of Analog: Real Things and Why They Matter.* New York: PublicAffairs, 2016.

Scarry, Elaine. *Dreaming by the Book.* New York: Farrar Straus Giroux, 1999.

————. *Thinking in an Emergency.* New York: W. W. Norton, 2011.

Schlesinger, Stephen. "Ghosts of Guatemala's Past." *New York Times,* June 3, 2011. http://www.nytimes.com/2011/06/04/opinion/04schlesinger.html.

Schumacher, E. F. (1973) *Small is Beautiful: Economics as if People Mattered.* New York: HarperPerennial, 2010.

Searcey, Dionne, Eduardo Porter, and Robert Gebeloff. "Health Care Opens Stable Career Path, Taken Mainly by Women." *New York Times,* February 22, 2015. https://www.nytimes.com/2015/02/23/business/economy/health-care-opens-middle-class-path-taken-mainly-by-women.html.

Selingo, Jeffrey. *College (Un)bound: The Future of Higher Education and What It Means for Students.* Boston: Houghton Mifflin Harcourt, 2013.

Seneca, Lucius Annaeus. "On the Shortness of Life." In *Seneca: Dialogues and Essays,* translated by John Davie, introduced and edited by Tobias Reinhardt, 140–162. Oxford: Oxford World's Classics, 2007.

Senior, Jennifer. *All Joy And No Fun: The Paradox of Modern Parenthood.* New York: HarperCollins, 2014.

Sewall, Richard B. *The Life of Emily Dickinson.* Cambridge: Harvard University Press, 1980.

Shadid, Anthony. *House of Stone: A Memoir of Home, Family, and a Lost Middle East.* New York: Houghton Mifflin Harcourt, 2012.

Shakespeare, William. (1604–5.) *Hamlet Prince of Denmark.* In *William Shakespeare: The Complete Works,* edited by Alfred Harbage, 930–976. New York: Viking, 1977.

Shklovsky, Victor. "Art as Technique." In *Russian Formalist Criticism: Four Essays,* translated by Lee T. Lemon and Marion J. Reis, 3–24. Lincoln: University of Nebraska Press, 2012.

Shtenygart, Gary. "O.K., Glass." *The New Yorker,* August 5, 2013, 32–37.

Sklar, Julia. "Meet The World's First Completely Soft Robot." *MIT Technology Review,* December 8, 2016. https://www.technologyreview.com/s/603046/meet-the-worlds-first-completely-soft-robot/.

Silko, Leslie Marmon. *The Turquoise Ledge: A Memoir.* New York: Penguin, 2010.

Silverman, Jacob. *Terms of Service: Social Media and the Price of Constant Connection.* New York: HarperCollins, 2015.

Sinclair, Iain. "Bulls & Bears & Mithraic Misalignments: Weather in the City." In *Lights Out for the Territory: Nine Excursions in the Secret History of London,* 89–131. London: Granta, 1997.

Skenazy, Lenore. *Free-Range Kids: Giving Our Children the Freedom We Had Without Going Nuts with Worry.* New Jersey: Jossey-Bass, 2009.

Skitolsky, Lissa. "Tracing Theory on the Body of the 'Walking Dead': Der Muselmann and the Course of Holocaust Studies." *Shofar: An Interdisciplinary Journal of Jewish Studies* 30.2 (2012) 74–90. http://scholarlycommons.susqu.edu/phil_fac_pubs/5/.

Smail, Daniel L. *On Deep History and the Brain.* Berkeley: University of California Press, 2008.

Smith, Zadie. "Generation Why?" *New York Review of Books,* Nov. 25, 2010. http://www.nybooks.com/articles/2010/11/25/generation-why/.

Sobel, David, "Feed the Hunger." *Orion* 31:6 (November/December 2012) 72–74.

Solnit, Rebecca. "Diary." *London Review of Books,* Feb. 7, 2013. http://www.lrb.co.uk/v35/no3/rebecca-solnit/diary.

————. "Welcome to the (Don't Be) Evil Empire: Google Eats the World." *Tom Dispatch*, June 25, 2013. http://www.tomdispatch.com/post/175717/tomgram%3A_rebecca_solnit,_how_to_act_like_a_billionaire.

Spencer, Elizabeth. *The Voice at the Back Door*. New York: McGraw Hill, 1956.

Sullivan, Andrew. "I Used to Be A Human Being." *New York*, September 18, 2016. http://nymag.com/selectall/2016/09/andrew-sullivan-technology-almost-killed-me.html.

Surowiecki, James. "Companies with Benefits." *The New Yorker*, August 4, 2014, 23.

Tacy, Chris. "Don't Be A Fucking Douchebag Part Three," June 11, 2013. http://christacy.blogspot.com/2013/06/dont-be-fucking-douchebag-part-three.html.

Taylor, Astra. *The People's Platform: Taking Back Power and Culture in the Digital Age*. New York: Metropolitan, 2014.

Taylor, Charles. *A Secular Age*. Cambridge: Harvard University Press, 2007.

Taylor, Barbara Brown. *An Altar in the World*. New York: HarperOne, 2009.

Taylor, Charles. *Sources of the Self: The Making of the Modern Identity*. Cambridge: Harvard University Press, 1989.

Thompson, Derek. "A World Without Work." *The Atlantic*, August 2015. http://www.theatlantic.com/magazine/archive/2015/07/world-without-work/395294/.

Thoreau, Henry David. (1854). *Walden*. In *Walden and Other Writings*, edited by Brooks Atkinson, 1–312. New York: The Modern Library/Random House, 1992.

Tolstoy, Leo. (1873–1877). *Anna Karenin*. Translated by Rosemary Edmonds. New York: Penguin, 1978.

Trilling, Lionel. (1950) *The Liberal Imagination: Essays on Literature and Society*. New York: NYRB Classics, 2008.

Trubek, Anne. *The History and Uncertain Future of Handwriting*. London: Bloomsbury, 2016.

Turkle, Sherry. *Alone Together: Why We Expect More From Technology and Less From Each Other*. New York: Perseus, 2011.

Vaidhyanathan, Siva. *The Googlization of Everything (And Why We Should Worry)*. Berkeley: University of California Press, 2011.

Webb, Amy. "We Post Nothing About Our Daughter Online." *Slate*, Sept. 4, 2013. http://www.slate.com/articles/technology/data_mine_1/2013/09/facebook_privacy_and_kids_don_t_post_photos_of_your_kids_online.html.

Weil, Simone. "The Iliad, or the Poem of Force." In Simone Weil and Rachel Bespaloff, *War and the Iliad*, translated by Mary McCarthy, 3–37. New York: NYRB Classics, 2005.

Weldon, Amy. "Claiming Your Right to Say No." *Chronicle of Higher Education* "Vitae" blog, January 5, 2017. https://chroniclevitae.com/news/1657-claiming-your-right-to-say-no.

————. "Darwin's Beetle: On Geeking Out." *Ideas and Creations* Luther College faculty blog, October 23, 2013. https://www.luther.edu/ideas-creations-blog/?story_id=503962.

————. "Diana Athill: The Sufficient Self." *Bloom*, July 1, 2013. http://bloom-site.com/2013/07/01/diana-athill-the-sufficient-self/.

————. "In Her Own Words: Diana Athill." *Bloom*, July 3, 2013. https://bloom-site.com/2013/07/03/in-her-own-words-diana-athill/.

————. "Keats-Shelley House: Rome, Italy." *The Common*. https://www.thecommononline.org/keats-shelley-house-rome-italy/.

―――. "A Miniature Handbook for New Woman Activists" in *Fracture: Essays, Poems, and Stories on Fracking in America*, 38–48. North Liberty, IA: Ice Cube, 2016.

―――. "The Spinning Self: On Pottery and the Rest of My Life." *Bloom*, December 19, 2014. https://bloom-site.com/2014/12/19/the-spinning-self-on-pottery-and-the-rest-of-my-life/.

―――. "The Third Rail: or, Why are you here?" *Ideas and Creations*, September 16, 2014. https://www.luther.edu/ideas-creations-blog/?story_id=572057.

Widdicombe, Lizzie. "The Higher Life." *The New Yorker*, July 6 & 13, 2015, 40–47.

Wilson, Bee. *The Hive: The Story of the Honeybee and Us*. New York: St. Martin's Griffin, 2004.

Wordsworth, William. "Lines Written A Few Miles Above Tintern Abbey." *The Oxford Authors: William Wordsworth*, edited by Stephen Gill, 131–135. Oxford: Oxford University Press, 1984.

―――. *The Prelude: 1799, 1805, 1850*. Edited by Jonathan Wordsworth, M. H. Abrams, and Stephen Gill. New York: W. W. Norton and Co., 1979.

―――. "The world is too much with us." *The Oxford Authors: William Wordsworth*, 270.

World Economic Forum. *Insight Report: Global Risks 2012*, Seventh Edition. Geneva: World Economic Forum, 2012. https://www.weforum.org/reports/global-risks-2012-seventh-edition.

Young, Dean. "I See A Lily On Thy Brow." In *Bender: New and Selected Poems*, 111. Port Townsend, Washington: Copper Canyon, 2012.

Young-Bruehl, Elisabeth, *Why Arendt Matters*. New Haven: Yale University Press, 2006.

"Young Egyptians Spread Their Message," *New York Times*, Feb. 8, 2011. http://www.nytimes.com/slideshow/2011/02/08/world/middleeast/20110209_DREAM.html.

Zepel, Tara. "Revisiting the Twitter Experiment (In Context.)" *The New Everyday: A Media Commons Project*, April 6, 2011. http://mediacommons.futureofthebook.org/tne/pieces/revisiting-twitter-experiment-context-0.